SUMMER TWILIGHT

SUMMER TWILIGHT

BOOK 1

BRIDGET SMITH

May your mind stay curious,
your shot true,
and your heart brave.

NEW DEGREE PRESS

SUMMER TWILIGHT

Book 1

ISBN   978-1-63676-517-4   *Paperback*

           978-1-63676-047-6   *Kindle Ebook*

           978-1-63676-048-3   *Ebook*

To all my former students: Never forget you can do anything you set your mind to. I believe in you, now and forever. Be brave, take risks, and grab every opportunity there is. I'm cheering you on the entire way.

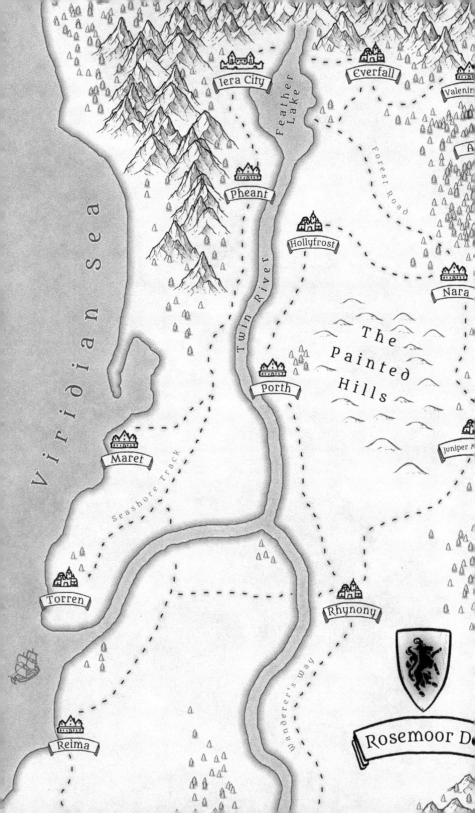

CONTENTS

———

AUTHOR'S NOTE

———

When I was in sixth grade, my entire world fell apart. My parents divorced, my dog passed away—and that was on top of the raging hormones and social pressure that define middle school. Desperately trying to cope with the myriad disasters in my life, I turned to writing. In a few months, I had churned out a two-hundred-page dramatic odyssey entitled *The Story of the Unicorns*, which, as one might imagine, featured unicorns heavily.

Writing has always helped me process the big moments in my life, and this story is no exception. When I was seventeen, I broke my ankle, and then was afflicted by a rare chronic pain condition. Multiple doctors looked me in the eye and told me I would never walk again. It felt like my world was ending. It is no coincidence that at the same time, the characters in this book walked into my head. But to me, fantasy isn't only about unicorns and magic; it's a way to process the real challenges we all face every day.

Today it feels like the world, once again, is ending—but this time it's the whole world, not just mine. The endless news cycle seems trapped in a whirlpool of doom and gloom. As I write this, a pandemic is sweeping the globe.

But even here, amid a global threat unlike anything else in modern history, the differences between people have emerged. The pandemic has disproportionately affected people of color and our most vulnerable populations. Grocery workers, Uber drivers, and teachers have found themselves thrust onto the frontline; medical personnel face overwhelming trauma and limited resources in an escalating crisis.

In a world like this, it feels like our differences are what define us. The labels we carry—some by choice, others by force—determine not only how others see us but how we see ourselves. We identify by our genders and sexual orientation, our politics and wealth, our location and profession. Left behind are the beautiful intersections of humanity which crisscross society. We all experience depression and anxiety; triumph and joy; struggle and achievement. But it's all too easy to forget that amidst our labels and differences.

Just like every other person who has ever lived, or ever will live, I have faced and overcome challenges in my life. I clawed my way out of a wheelchair with the unending patience and support of physical therapists and friends. But, shortly thereafter, I was knocked out once more by crippling anxiety—something I struggle with to this day. Anxiety and insecurity for me have been the most difficult personal obstacles to defeat. They permeate every element of my existence, redefining the way I see the world and myself.

And once again, I've returned to differences. In the throes of an anxiety attack or at the depths of my insecurities, I don't feel connected to the world. I focus on my flaws and the things that make me different. It's an impossible way to live. Differences themselves—labels themselves—are not inherently bad; they're bad if we let them define us. With conscious strength, we can overcome these definitions and labels, and grow into the people we are at our heart; the people we *can* be.

This book has grown from my belief that we are bigger and better than the differences which currently define us. We all suffer and struggle. We all triumph and overcome. I believe we all have the strength to choose who we want to be, and to leave these differences and labels behind. We can choose to see one another as we *want* to be seen, as our authentic selves, rather than whatever the world has prescribed to us.

In *Summer Twilight*, my characters are not superhuman. They are not flawless or perfect, wise beyond measure, or powerful beyond belief. They are real humans, just like you and me, who happen to live in a magical, fantastical world. Alex and Caidy are, above all else, deeply and imperfectly human—humans who must learn to struggle with and adapt to the way society sees them, just like you and me.

Alex and Caidy deal with anxiety and fear, insecurity and loneliness, confusion and embarrassing moments. They face the challenges of young adulthood and internalized Imposter Syndrome (though perhaps in less psychological terms). For me, they have served as an anchor as I've navigated my way through my early twenties and a lodestone for redefining myself on my terms—not anyone else's.

Fantasy novels are a wonderful escape from the overwhelming reality we live in, and *Summer Twilight* is no exception. If, like me, you've been searching for a place to forget your problems, a narrative meditation set in an idyllic countryside, look no further. In this story you will find a wonderfully layered adventure to lose yourself in—a place to set aside your own burdens and travel far, far away on a fantastical journey. Ready to step into a magical world? Turn the page.

Bridget Smith
December 2020

THE WHISPERS
OF THE WINDS

———

An excerpt from the revered text by Archmage Nuhalvarn Timewalker, held in the library of Rhiamor College.

The world was born when the Winds of Magic burst forth from the Mystical Plane. Tendrils of energy warped and stretched the Dark and Treacherous Universe, banishing the Ancients and sparking new life. Coursing magic carved rivers through mountains, drove lava from volcanoes, and raised islands from oceans.

The World glittered with magic in every corner. It dusted high peaks and clung to oceanic trenches; it sparkled in the sand and danced on the breezes. Strange and fantastic creations spanned the World—from fairy lights spinning through the night to the great Rainbow Mountains, flashing with every known color.

From the Magical Winds, Beings strode forth to protect the New World. These Magical Beings tended and shaped it carefully. Some brought new life while others brought a natural end.

As the centuries slipped by, the New World aged and became Not-So-New, and the Beings retreated to the divine—stewards rather than citizens. The Beings protected the peoples of the Not-So-New World.

Some of them, the Most Powerful Beings of the Not-So-New World, became known as Gods by the mortals they guarded, joining a Divine Pantheon. These High Gods cared for their people, performing miracles, spreading faith, and sprinkling magic far and wide.

The Magical Beings who were Not-So-Powerful became Lesser Gods. While the High Gods of the Pantheon were widely worshipped and called upon—indeed, they spent as much of their time answering prayers as doing much else, the Lesser Gods truly knew the people. In all their many forms, the Lesser Gods walked among the mortals of the Not-So-New World, offering blessings and guidance.

The Lord of the Seven Tribes of the Glittering Sands had never, and would never, meet the Viridian Wavewalker, but both held the World together. Each and every Lesser God shepherded their own small flock through the twisting currents of time, and together they guided the world. Exceptional mortals might ascend to join the ranks of Lesser Gods as the need arose. This is, of course, how the Golden Maiden and the Master of Tasseled Hats came to be. Most mortals, however, never became Lesser Gods.

As the years slid to millennia, the Divine Realms flourished. Gods bickered, of course, for Gods and mortals are spun of the same cloth, woven by the Winds so many millennia ago. Their squabbles spilt over to the Mortal Plane, sparking war and strife among the peoples. It ebbed and flowed in a peaceful rhythm, violence fading to harmony, and rising in tides to conflict once more. Great empires conquered and collapsed under the watchful guidance of the Higher and Lesser Gods.

And as the Not-So-New World grew, so too did the Winds.

Suddenly and without warning, the Winds of Magic—the little-understood power underlying everything in the Known and Unknown Universe—shifted. Instead of a gentle breeze cradling all that is and ever will be, the World trembled, buffeted to and fro by gales unlike anything ever seen before.

As the gusts grew stronger, something vital snapped. Abruptly, the steady connection between the Beings and their people was shattered. The Most Powerful and Not-So-Powerful Beings were swept from their Pantheon, tumbling through the Universe like so many dried leaves on the breeze.

When the Gods were ripped from the Mortal and Divine Realms, the Not-So-New World was sundered. Torn heart from soul, the World screamed.

And so began the tumult of the Imperial Age, born in the midst of this violent sundering. Civilizations crumbled under the weight of the pain as the earth shook and the clouds thundered. The stories told of the End of Days, trembling from the wrath thrashing the world. Desperate Prophecies danced on the edges of the disasters, bringing a faint glimmer of hope back to the mortals, that one day the great Cataclysm would end.

In the aftermath, the Not-So-New World was no longer so innocent or so pure but rather older and wiser. With that maturity came a gentle peace, which wrapped the Not-So-New World tightly in a protective cocoon and began healing the deep wounds that had torn the earth in two. Slowly, civilization reemerged. Kingdoms rose, battled, and fell. The Abandoned Peoples persevered, in conflict and harmony, as they always had—and always would.

In the midst of this peaceful aftermath, mortals began to forget the Magical Beings who had loved them; Gods became the stuff of legend rather than mundane existence. In some, perhaps more superstitious places, the myths ran wild, taking on a life of their own.

Although the Beings spun through the Universe, they were curiously not completely at the mercy of the Winds. Their Temple Orders, their followers, and their worshippers remained a tenuous tether—a lifeline to their World amid the eternal eddies of time. Through this faint, vital connection, the Winds of Magic continued to nurture the Not-So-New World, gifting seeds of power to those Abandoned Peoples who had proven themselves worthy.

But then, Desperate Prophecies, forgotten since the beginning of the Imperial Age, started to take shape in the Not-So-New World. Skeptics and scholars alike watched in stunned disbelief as ancient words spoke new and alarming truths, and the feeble bonds to the Winds of Magic appeared to fade to the infinite emptiness of the Dark and Treacherous Universe.

As I write this, the Beings are at risk of being lost forever.

Soon, when even the crustiest magicians are gripped by a sense of overwhelming fear, a Search unlike any the Not-So-New World has seen before will begin. Magicians will scour the earth, hunting for fragments of visions, and searching for a Savior who has not yet been woven into the complex tapestry of time.

But, as often seems to happen, an odd series of coincidences will shift the very fabric of the Known and Unknown Universe. An unerringly mortal chain of events, including an accidental ritual and a not-so-accidental drowning, will lead to the prophesied moment. The Savior will emerge, quietly, into the aching melancholy of the Not-So-New World.

And, as has been predicted by the very folds of time and space, the Savior will herald a new Age. The remnants of the Cataclysm will fade from memory, and light will once more bathe the Not-So-New World. Under the gentle love of the Savior, volcanic glass will melt to granite and the Winds of Magic will shift once more, caught in a sweet undertow of soft ease.

PROLOGUE

20th Day of the Harvest Moon

I sprint down the endless stone corridor, blinded by darkness and fear, nearly colliding with a heavy door. My fingers scrabble uselessly at the handle, shaking so badly I can barely grip it. Hissing as the cold metal burns my skin, I let out a shriek of frustration when the door refuses to give.

This can't be the end—Gods, this door has to open.

I brace both feet and pull again, screaming with effort and gasping for air. With an agonizing slowness, the door creaks open. Squeezing myself through the gap, I feel the rough stone scrape my stomach and back as adrenaline keeps driving me forward. When the door thuds shut behind me, I stumble, nearly falling to my knees.

Don't stop. You have to warn them.

Driven by an unseen force, I leap to my feet and take off again down another endless stone hall. Reverberations from the door chase me—ice clinging to the rocks around me releasing splinters and sharp shards to rain down. I cover my head with my arms, yelping as a sliver of slices along one shoulder, cutting to the bone.

Deep red drops splatter the ground, staining my habit. I press on with fresh tears spilling to blur the world. An overpowering sense of dread fills the cold stone hall, seeping into my bones and making my movements slow and sluggish. I fight against the exhaustion and fear, all my strength focused on moving forward, but my steps slow. The stone and ice close in…

No! Get to the Eladyr. You have to save them.

The words echo inside my head, and suddenly I am free once more, sprinting headlong into a massive cavern buried deeply within the ice. Twisted, fragmented light forces its way through the glaciers above and I skid to a halt, fighting for air while bracing my hands on my knees.

When I look up, my world shatters.

Too late.

Four people—four of the most powerful mages in the World—are crumpled on the ground. Bone and limb twist together, mangled and contorted, and mouths stretch in agony. Blood drips from broken bodies, staining the stone and seeping slowly toward the flame of the Eladyr cradled in a deep recess at the center of the room. Before I can do more than take a step, the magical flame vanishes, snuffed out as though it had never been.

Pain shoots through my chest, and my heart feels like it has burst. Blinded by pain, I feel myself hit something hard as I lose control of my limbs, my fingers twitching and my body convulsing on the ground.

Nothing matters anymore; all is lost.

A thousand memories flash through my mind, tangled together in a nauseating mural. A deep sense of loss overwhelms even the pain racking my body and I curl into a small ball, trembling.

I failed.

The weight of the whole world presses me into the hard stone.

It would be so easy to give up, to let myself be crushed...

You are not done.

Straining, I force myself to my knees.

There's still time. Get to the Eladyr.

As I stagger to my feet, time freezes. The ice that just moments before glittered on the walls and ceiling is dull and lifeless. A deathly silence fills the room, thick and heavy.

I slowly take one step forward and then another until I am face-to-face with my reflection, trapped in one of the mirrored walls. Tears freeze to my cheeks as I reach up, touching the twisted, corrupted image looking back at me, unfamiliar and terrifying.

It can't be.

Get out.

I stumble backward, searching for a door that doesn't exist anymore.

I have to warn someone, anyone. I have to tell them what's coming.

My foot slips and I fall once more, this time tumbling endlessly, screams ripping painfully from my chest. The world warps, dragging me down. I roll toward the flameless Eladyr, stopping at the very edge of the deep, darkened recess.

The bodies surround me. Their faces are painted in despair—eyes stretched, mouths contorted, skin already pale with the cold. Blood spatters the floor beneath them. I raise my hand and then watch with a growing sense of foreboding as a drop of scarlet rolls down my fingertip, crystallizing before it falls to the ground.

An inhuman howl tears through the room, seeming to come from the very air itself.

The ice clinging to the walls shatters, turning into freezing daggers tumbling toward me. I bury my head under my arms feeling ice pelt my body, slicing skin from bone. An ear-splitting tremor ripples through the air.

They're gone, gone, gone...

You failed.

CHAPTER 1

———

3rd Day of the Harvest Moon

Alex shook himself awake in the cool, predawn twilight. Lying on his back, staring up at stars strewn across the darkness, he stretched expansively, yawning and trying to rub the sleep from his eyes.

Today is the day. He knew he'd reach Iera, the capital of Rosemoor, by first light. If he'd pushed a little harder, he could have gotten there yesterday, but he wanted to be fresh and braced for the encounter to come. He felt wide awake, even though he'd tossed and turned through most of the night on the hard-packed earth.

Distracted thoughts had spent the night doing their best to ward off sleep. Would his parents be at the castle or home with his younger sister? Would the guards recognize him? *Probably not*, he thought ruefully. *It's been a hard few years.*

Nervously, he ran his fingers through his hair, feeling the welcome cool of night on his scalp. *May as well get on with it.* With a heavy sigh, mostly for dramatic effect—though his only audience was his horse, who looked at him with one tired eye—he rolled to his feet.

He packed quickly, storing his bedroll with practiced ease and saddling his mount. Enough moonlight still shone so he could see what he was doing—though at this point muscle memory had taken over his motions. *I've been on the road too long*, he decided as he tightened the girth around his horse's belly.

"I promise you all the hay and apples you can stand, my girl," he murmured, running his fingers through the mare's knotted mane. "No more long trips for a while. If I don't screw it up, we should be here for a few years, at least."

The pair had been riding for the last few, hot weeks of summer, from the Whispering Planes in southern Danen up past Glassfall Lake, following the Twin River to the north and racing to beat the Imperial missive that would warn the province of his arrival. A constant pull, a magnetic drag on his discipline, had grown stronger the further he rode. He'd come to realize that, for the first time in a long time, he was excited to return.

"I can't believe we'll be home. Well, I'll be home. You've never been somewhere that gets this cold," he continued, checking the straps on his bedroll behind the saddle. "The stables stay fairly warm, though. I *think*."

His mare snorted and turned her head away, and Alex chuckled to himself. Humming a tuneless song under his breath, he finished packing up his campsite with the efficiency of one who is just as comfortable sleeping under the sky as in a bed. It was also a convenient way to ignore the tingle of nerves in his fingertips and stomach.

I have nothing to be nervous about, he tried to reassure himself. *I'll just get my orders signed and then fade into the back alleys.* The small voice in the back of his head pointed out there were, in fact, many things to be nervous about—from seeing *her* again to withstanding the infamous temper of the Lord of Rosemoor. But he chose to ignore his nerves, instead imagining the first steaming flagon of honeycomb tea he'd enjoy as a reward for his journey. *It's been years since I've gotten real honeycomb tea.*

Hauling himself into the saddle, Alex groaned as he forced his legs to straddle the mount. Everything ached, from his eyebrows to his toes, and fierce bruises felt like a permanent new addition to his thighs. *I'd forgotten how uncomfortable it is to ride for two weeks straight,* he thought ruefully. Once he settled, excitement fizzed through his veins once more. He'd see Caidy again…

As her name echoed through his mind, guilt grew hot in his stomach, tangled with the nerves. "She's going to be furious," he muttered, turning his mare and trotting back toward the main road. "She'll never let me live it down."

In all fairness, he guessed that disappearing in the middle of the night to travel halfway across the Empire probably wasn't conducive to a healthy, long-term relationship. *Easier for me,* he thought. *If she's angry, I don't have to lie to her.* Caidy's fury was nearly as famous—in noble circles—as her father's.

Long journeys, Alex knew too well, had a way of melting days and weeks together until the end seemed forever out of reach. In some ways, he'd been waiting to come home for the past several *years*, not merely the weeks he'd been riding. It seemed like something from a drunken hallucination, then, when his horse crested a hill, and the moon-drenched valley he had grown up in was unfurled before his eyes.

"Finally," he murmured, rubbing a hand along his horse's warm neck and feeling himself smile, genuinely, for the first time since his ride began.

Rolling hills covered in lush farmland and neatly kept homes stretched across the basin filled with common folk leading easy, comfortable lives. A lazy river turned through the valley, tumbling into rapids as it flowed west toward the Viridian Sea. Light woodland covered most of the eastern side of the dale, stretching up the mountains.

Across the valley, a city surrounded by high stone walls blanketed the lakeshore, glittering with torchlight. *Iera.* Even from here he could make out the great plaza atop City Hill, which gave a panoramic view of the entire valley. Iera was one of the largest cities in Rosemoor, and the capital of the province. A paved road curved from the city proper up the mountainside, leading to a castle perched amid the great peaks lining the northern end of the valley. Everything was gilded with moonlight, lending a haunting sheen to the world.

A wintry wind caused his horse to stamp nervously, tossing its head and snorting. Summer was fading, and the chill of autumn was in the air that morning. Alex checked the clasp on his cloak—a circular piece of metal split in two with a single line—as the wind caught the underside of the wool, cutting into his chafed skin.

Wrapping the cloak tightly around his shoulders, he leaned into his stirrups, letting the weight of his heels stretch the back of his calves, and urged his horse down the steep mountainside. He instinctively leaned back to remove weight from the shoulders of his weary mount as they picked their way through the rocks and into the valley.

To him—and to most—Rosemoor Dell, the northwesternmost province of the Mezrani Empire, was idyllic in nearly every sense of the word. Nestled between the peaks and plateaus of the Somber Mountains and the white-capped waves of the Viridian Sea, the province was mostly removed from the politics of the Empire and boasted prosperous farmland. It was a life steeped in village festivals and market days, in which honest folk worked hard and the nobility didn't concern themselves with much outside their manors. Days here were simple and filled with a gentle satisfaction.

He had grown up here, had whiled away a childhood filled with stars and mountain twilight, a life of rolling down hillsides and scampering through city streets. It seemed a world apart from the one he knew now. If he closed his eyes, the air still tasted like fresh buns stuffed with cinnamon and honey with plenty of laughter and smiles to go around. There had been mountains to climb, hidden corridors of the castle to explore, and plenty of adventures to be had on the Twin River in a makeshift raft. *Those were the days.*

As he wandered through his memories, a part of Alex's mind remained calmly alert, watching a flock of starlings spring into the morning air and listening closely for the tired mumblings of civilization. Farmers would be awake soon, and merchants would start trundling their caravans to Iera's markets. The cool, predawn wind continued to tug at the blue wool of his cloak, whipping off his hood as his horse slid and scrambled down the rocky trail. Soon, the path flattened into the valley and a stone bridge arched over a tributary, leading into a patchwork of lightly wooded farmland.

A guardhouse stood by the bridge, and the provincial guard inside waved Alex onward without any hassle. *That doesn't instill confidence*, he thought, frowning. Guardhouses like these were designed as checkpoints to ensure nothing strange or dangerous was making its way too close to Iera. *The last thing I need is lazy guards letting a criminal—or, Gods forbid, a Freelark Dandelion—into the city.*

He caught a glimpse of chairs drawn up to a table inside the guardhouse, tankards and some sort of game scattered across the surface. He clicked his tongue impatiently against his teeth, absently digging his heels into his horse's warm sides and rewrapping the reins around gloved hands.

They clattered across the bridge, his horse adopting a smooth, rocking canter. Nearing the outskirts of the city, Alex's nerves returned. It felt very strange, he realized, to be coming home because Rosemoor didn't completely feel like home anymore. He'd done quite a good job forcing that out of his mind during the journey, pushing himself and his mount to a breaking point rather than thinking about the past. Now, drawing unavoidably closer to Iera and the world he'd left behind, it was impossible to ignore.

There was no forgetting the night he'd been taken from his bed, spirited across the Empire to arid deserts unlike anything he'd ever known, or the hot earth burning his feet in the hard, endless expanse of sand and stone. During those first years of his training, thoughts of home—of Caidy—had pulled him through. He had dreamt of coming back to her, leaving the hard, distrustful world of the Blades behind, trading it all for a life at her side.

When had that changed? He couldn't point to any one moment in his recent memory when he had turned his back on Rosemoor, on Caidy, and dedicated himself to the service. And yet, now mere moments from his home—from her—the longing he'd felt had faded. He missed her, but there was more to life now. He had responsibilities to people and ideas greater than himself.

Alex reached the fortified gates of the city just as the first shafts of sunlight dappled the fields and farmers began to emerge from tidy homes nearby. Slowing to a trot, his horse passed unimpeded through the gate, dirt turning to cobblestones underfoot.

It was still early, so very few people were outside. Those who were moved with lethargy, rubbing sleepy eyes and ambling slowly through the streets. *Good*, he thought. *Less of a chance I'll be waylaid.* Traffic outside the city would pick up as farmers brought their wagons to the market for the day. It was faster to wind through the twisted city streets than fight through the mire of oxen, horses, produce, and people outside.

Despite the quiet inside the city walls, he guided his horse through back alleys—the less well-to-do areas of Iera—avoiding the city center and busier streets. They passed a pig snuffling through a pile of damp leaves and three chickens pecking at the bare dirt of a small, fenced yard. From inside houses, the domestic sounds of children waking up, babies crying, and parents cooking breakfast floated toward them on the breeze.

Riding past a market square, the tantalizing smell of fresh meat pasties and honeycomb tea wafted past them. Alex drew his mount to a halt, letting the smell wash over him. The horse stamped its hoof to express its displeasure at stopping. "Easy, my friend, we'll be there soon enough," he murmured.

Unexpectedly, he felt his breath catch in his throat as he looked around, and he leaned forward, burying his face in the rough mane of his horse. Everything washed over him at once: sharp pangs of loneliness, deep unsettled fears, and an overwhelming sense that he didn't belong. He felt foreign and unfamiliar in a city he had once roamed as a child, holding court on the sidewalks and clambering on rooftops. It was a strange and terrifying feeling to be returning as a stranger to his hometown.

"I hate it," he whispered into his horse's neck. "Everything feels wrong."

The world around him—the warm honeycomb tea and fresh meat pies he used to enjoy on the edge of a fountain and the quiet burble of families starting the morning—was all discordant. He found himself desperately, painfully, wishing he had never left.

Alex allowed himself one more moment. He forced himself to take several deep breaths before wrapping his arms tightly around his mount's neck until he felt his heartbeat slow. Objectively, he had always known it would be different. *Why was different so hard?*

Straightening and rubbing his eyes with gloved fingers, he longed to dismount and wait until the market opened. A hot meal would help everything feel better. It always did. *But then,* he argued with himself, *rumor of a Blade could reach Lord Mattias before I can. That won't do.* Regretfully, he discarded the notion of stopping. He had almost reached the end of his trek across the Empire. If he dismounted now, he wouldn't have the grit to pull himself back into the saddle.

He rolled his shoulders twice and then squared them. Drawing himself in and forcing his emotions away, he urged the horse forward once more. A moment of weakness was natural, he told himself, but now it was time for action, and action required disciplined control. He could no longer afford even the perception of vulnerability. *A Blade knows all, sees all, and tells few.* He wrapped himself in the aura of mystery his new station provided.

By the time horse and rider emerged at the western edge of the city, the first few wagons were jostling through the gates with goods to sell, and children were appearing in doorways, clinging to their mothers' skirts. It was still early enough that most people moved slowly with heads down, though several sets of children wound their way between horses' legs and wagon wheels, bored from their trip to the city and excited for the candies and toys, which would soon be for sale. Struggling through the tide of animals and carts, Alex exited through the western gate, toward the castle on the hill.

They passed the major crossroads where many of the merchants and farmers were fighting their way toward the market stalls. The road to the castle itself was much emptier, a winding series of switchbacks built into and around the hill. It was carved into the gentlest part of the slope, and the rest of the hillside either melted into the surrounding mountains or dropped away into rough, rocky ledges.

Eyeing the defenses as he passed, he noted only one gatehouse in a wooden stockade between the castle and the city, manned by three sleepy guards who had their crossbows unstrung on a table. At the two sharpest switchbacks there were defenses higher up the path—cauldrons for pitch, and traps filled with boulders intended to block travel. He also noted the tightly oiled packets, which were just visible, wedged into the stone beneath the corners. As he rode by, he leaned out of his saddle slightly and then nodded. He could see a faint opalescent sheen coating the parcels and knew they held magefire jelly.

The jelly was a trap from before the Cleansing, a sticky, viscous substance that was highly combustible. He suspected these parcels were tied to magical command keys, which could be snapped to collapse part of the road. That was the idea, anyway. It was just as possible, if not more likely, that the keys had been lost, or that the parcels were old defenses that no one had bothered to remove.

It was an odd vestige of paranoia in the sheltered province. Rosemoor had not faced assault since the Cleansing, a few generations ago. However, despite the impressive variety of defenses, the only set of patrolling guards Alex rode by seemed disinterested and distracted, ready for the shift change—likely in a few hours. He ground his teeth in frustration. *What use are traps if no one mans them?*

A messenger, clothed in a gold-striped tunic and leggings, jogged past him and down the hill, carrying a satchel meant for someone in the city. Seeing as she was on foot, it obviously wasn't urgent.

Alex turned away from her as she passed, keeping his face in shadow, and then twisted to watch her disappear down the road toward the knot of wagons at the base of the hill. His horse tossed its head impatiently before snorting in satisfaction when they continued on their way. "Do you have something else to do today?" Alex quipped, a little amused.

When they reached the gate at the top of the hill, Alex paused for a moment, leaning back in the saddle and looking up at the castle. It was an old fortress, the tall stone walls built into the side of the mountain and slotted with arrow slits. The battlements overlooked one of the most beautiful vistas in the entire Empire. Towers scraped the sky behind the wall, and he counted three sets of guards.

He felt a scratchiness in the back of his throat and a heat behind his eyes as he looked up at Iera Castle. It had been home for many years, and the worn stones were as familiar as the scent of honeycomb tea sold in the city.

Taking a deep breath, he steeled his nerves for what was to come. There was no way out now.

CHAPTER 2

3rd Day of the Harvest Moon
Nudging his horse forward, Alex approached the castle gate. It was imposing with tall oak and iron doors and a smaller sally gate that was propped open. The bands of iron were tempered into thick, sturdy reinforcements, and he could see space above for pitch or archers.

A guard he didn't recognize came forward, wide awake despite the early hour. Alex noted absently that, despite his attentiveness, the guard was rather portly and didn't look capable of stopping a servant, much less some sort of invading force. Filing the information away for later, he nodded to the guard.

"Well good morning to you, sir! May I ask your name?" The guard gave him a jovial smile.

"Alexander Laurent." Alex returned the smile brightly, shrugging his hood onto his shoulders. *No going back now. In two hours, half of Iera will know I've returned.*

The guard did a poor job concealing surprise when he heard his name. "Laurent, did you say? Of House Laurent?"

Alex ran a gloved hand through his hair, ruffling some of the strands straight up. "No longer of the House; I'm here on official business." Shifting in the saddle, Alex moved slightly so the early sunlight glinted off the pin on his shoulder.

At the sight of the pin, the guardsman straightened. "Of course, sir. Give me just a moment." He scurried back to the guardhouse.

Probably gone to tell half the castle, Alex sighed to himself. His scalp tingled from the cold morning air, and his eyes swept the open courtyard twice. When the guard returned a few minutes later, he remarked, "I've been gone for years but it seems like not much has changed."

"Yes, sir. Some repairs here and there but life is largely the same. I returned from a tour in Torren about a year back, and the slow pace life takes here is just what I needed." The guardsman paused. "Are you here for an audience with the Lord and Lady?" He scratched at his shoulder, reaching under the joint of his splint armor.

"Yes. Is it a busy time?"

"Not more than normal, sir. There's the usual crowd of merchants and nobles talking the ears off anyone who'll listen, but my Lord and my Lady are available."

The corner of Alex's mouth twitched in a wry smile. "Some things are the same, no matter where you are." In Rosemoor, it had never been difficult to gain audience with the Roussels. Lord Mattias prided himself on being a man of the people, and most mornings either the Lord or Lady held a public audience to meet with subjects.

"Right you are, sir. Will you require an escort?" The guard raised his hand to signal a servant walking nearby, but Alex interjected before he could open his mouth.

"No, thank you." Deciding to soften the conversation, seeing the tension outlined in the guard's body, he tugged one of his gloves off with his teeth and flipped the guard a coin from the purse at his belt. "I appreciate your help. Be sure to grab a drink after you're finished here for the day." He smiled brightly as he wiggled his fingers back into the glove, and the guard nodded his thanks.

"Very well then, sir. Best of luck," The guard stood aside, allowing him to pass into the courtyard.

That could have gone worse, Alex decided.

The main gate opened into a large courtyard paved in cobblestones with an attractive fountain shooting streams of crystal-clear water to the skies and surrounded by a carefully overgrown garden. A few shrines were tucked into the shade of the winding vines and flowering bushes, representing some of the many deities worshipped across the Empire.

To the left lay barracks and training courts, and slightly further back sat the military stables. Alex observed that, despite the cool of the morning, no guards were out training. Indeed, no light shone from within the barracks either, despite the dawn bell having rung. It was a stark difference from Danen, the province where he had completed his training. There, life was ruled by violence and power, and guards were drilled every day to protect the goods their masters bought, sold, and stole.

To the right, an elegant temple stood, dedicated to Caldir, the Patron God of Rosemoor. He held power over the harvest and prosperity and was dutifully worshipped by the superstitious farmers across the province. Alex didn't put much stock in the Gods. He had little interest in attempting to prove himself to a disembodied being. That was a job for the Temple Orders and their mages. His job was to keep it safe enough that folk could lounge about and contemplate the Gods rather than fighting to defend their way of life.

He guided his horse to the guest stables tucked between the castle and the temple, dismounting as a stable hand approached. As his feet hit the ground, pain lanced up his thighs, and he fought off a wince.

When the moment had passed and he was able to straighten, he handed the reins to the stable boy. "Make sure she gets an extra apple or two. Alright?" he instructed.

The boy nodded eagerly, and Alex dug for another coin for a tip. Once his horse was taken care of, he turned on the heel of his boot and limped gingerly toward the castle kitchens, tucking his gloves into a pouch on his belt and favoring his cramping legs. *Better walk this off before court,* he thought ruefully.

Despite the pain, walking—instead of riding—was an incredible feeling. His legs ached, his feet were numb, and the world felt like it rocked back and forth. But he didn't care. It was liberating. His shoulders felt lighter than they had in weeks, and the pounding headache behind his right temple eased. The crisp air brought a touch of vigor to his stride, and his gait loosened ever so slightly.

He circled behind the main entrance, looping past the training yards to confirm his earlier suspicions. No one was about. The straw archery targets hung limply from wooden posts, and the dirt underfoot appeared undisturbed. A tattered training schedule was pinned to an announcement board, and he walked closer to look at it. *They can't have had morning exercises since before the winter snows,* he thought, touching the shredded edges of parchment and examining the faded ink.

He backtracked, ducking through another garden to emerge into the vegetable patch. Then he crossed quickly to enter the main kitchens. Alex was drawn by habit more than anything else as he'd spent many hours haunting the kitchens of the castle. *It's as good a place as any to let the rumors swirl a little longer,* he decided. *Plus, I might be able to swipe some breakfast.* He conveniently ignored the fact that eating breakfast might undermine his mysteriousness. The head cook's food was too good.

As he walked through the gardens, he passed two servants, both absorbed in a deep discussion. One of the servants, an older woman he knew used to work for the tailors, frowned at him, like a memory she couldn't quite place. He smiled politely as he passed the pair and approached the kitchens.

It was a path he had trod hundreds of times before, though now it all looked smaller and vaguely unfamiliar, like walking in a dream. He shook himself slightly, ruffled his hair again, and then pressed his hand against the worn kitchen door, feeling the smooth knot of wood under his palm. The itchy lump returned to the back of his throat.

The kitchen had always been one of his favorite places, smelling of basil and garlic and roasting meat. He'd spent many mornings squirreled away in a corner of the pantry, eating pastries stuffed with honey and nuts. The head cook, Bartholomew, resembled a string bean and had taken a liking to Alex years ago when he realized the boy would eat anything—burnt or unburnt. The familiar scent made his mouth water, and his stomach shifted uncomfortably.

The cook's habits, it seemed, had not changed. When Alex eased into the kitchen, Bart was braiding bread dough. The door creaked open—it needed oiling—and the cook glanced up, his hands continuing to braid from years of habit and muscle memory. Bart was bespectacled and often had flour or sauce splashed on his nose and forearms. He blinked twice at Alex and his brow furrowed before his eyes widened in recognition, causing his glasses to slip down his nose toward the bread dough.

"Young Master Laurent? Is that you?" The cook smudged his nose with flour as he fixed his glasses. "You've grown."

All thought of decorum and mystery forgotten, Alex grinned widely and crossed the space between the door and work table in two long strides, gripping the cook in a tight hug. "It's good to see you, Bart."

The cook abandoned his bread and returned the hug warmly, his fingers leaving smudges of flour on Alex's cloak. Four years ago he had been much taller than Alex; however, now he was only half a head shorter than the cook. He knew he looked different. Years of hard training and work did that to a person.

Alex removed the clip holding his cloak in place and tossed it across the back of a chair nearby. "Can I help with that?" he offered, gesturing to the half-braided bread.

"You look like you haven't had a proper meal in days," Bart said, ignoring his question. "Here, this is from last night." The cook scraped some thick stew into a bowl, and thumped it on the table in front of him. When he hesitated, Bart frowned. "Sit. Eat."

He sat. Many of the castle's inhabitants were a bit skittish around the cook. But Alex had always liked Bart's no-nonsense manner, and his food was delicious. He nibbled carefully on a chunk of mystery meat in the bowl before abandoning his trepidation and wolfing down gulps of onion, potato, venison, corn, and several other delicious, unidentifiable morsels. Even cold and slightly congealed, it was the best meal he'd had in several days.

When he began to eat, Bart returned to the bread dough, his hands moving deftly. "So," the cook began carefully after a few minutes of silence had passed and he had finished braiding two loaves. "Where in the Three Hells did you go?"

Alex swallowed his entire mouthful of onion and meat with some difficulty, feeling the lump slide slowly down his throat as he took a swig from the water skin at his hip. Instinctively, he wanted to recoil from the question. In Danen, Blades were more often greeted with a punch to the throat than with open arms. *Rosemoor is different*, he reminded himself. *Blades aren't a threat here. To most, anyway.*

Making his first attempt at striking the delicate balance between mystery and competence, he sat back on the bench, rolling up his sleeves as he answered the question. "I left to serve the Empire," he said, choosing his words carefully. "I've spent the past several years training to keep the Empire safe." It was the truth—as far as truth went, anyway.

Bart glanced over his shoulder, looking over his spectacles. "Did you now? Didn't see your name on the military enlistment scrolls." The cook sprinkled more flour over the dough in a puff of white.

"There are a lot of different ways to serve the Empire, you know," Alex replied wisely, examining his fingernails. *Disinterest is off-putting*, his old mentor, Starling, used to say.

The cook did not appear off-put. "Yes, my lad. I'm asking you which way you chose."

Considering the question, Alex let the silence hang between them to build effect. "I put in for the Blades," he replied calmly after a moment had passed.

The rhythm Bart had developed in braiding wavered for a second as his fingers shook slightly. Alex noticed the tremor but kept his face impassive and his posture relaxed. He leaned back against the bench and stretched his legs out, crossing his ankles and interlacing his fingers on top of his stomach. It was the effect he had hoped for. *Once you've got them nervous or surprised, keep them off balance. You're young. You need your reputation to proceed you into a room.*

"The Blades, eh? That's what your pin is for?" Bart thrust an elbow at the small silver brooch on Alex's shoulder, which had held his traveling cloak—a circle with a single line splitting the center.

Alex nodded, rubbing the pin reflexively with his thumb. "Yeah. Anyway, after spending a few years out and about, I've been assigned to Rosemoor. I just arrived this morning." He sat up and returned to the stew, watching Bartholomew from under his eyelashes.

The cook looked decidedly uncomfortable as he took the third braided loaf away for baking. When he turned back, however, his face was smooth and the warm twinkle had returned to his brown eyes. "Well, I missed you, my boy. I'd wager some other folks will be glad you're back too." He winked.

Alex raised an eyebrow, feigning surprise. "Oh really?"

Bart let out a booming belly laugh, deep for a man of his stature. "Oh, I've no doubt about it." He paused. "She was never quite the same after you left, you know. We all thought you'd just had a falling out, but then when you didn't return, well…" The cook trailed off.

Alex kept his face inscrutable, focusing his energies and emotions on the final gulp of stew in his bowl rather than the snake nest of nerves, which had just sprung to life in his belly. "I'm sure she's betrothed by now," he said after a moment, when he was sure he could control his tone.

"Courting, aye, but word among the servants is that she's refusing to marry. The Lord an' Lady are in fits about it."

"Huh." Alex scraped the bowl with his spoon, carefully avoiding the slightest change in his expression and disciplining his thoughts away from that path. *There's no future between us anymore*, he told himself sternly. *Besides, this is one of the most important days of my life. If I get this meeting wrong, I'll be ten paces behind for months.* He had one chance at a second first impression, and he had to hit the nail on the head.

He whiled away a few hours in the kitchen until he knew the royal family would be awake and dining, letting news of his arrival slowly seep through the castle.

Chopping carrots and scallions, he passed the time chatting with Bart and wiping down knives as the old cook finished with them. It was mindless, easy work, which allowed him to start to process and file his observations from the ride, sorting through the important and mundane to understand what he was walking into. *Observation is your advantage in any situation.*

Perhaps it was his inclination to curiosity and unpredictability, but something was deeply unsatisfying about the way Rosemoor seemed to be caught in time. So much had changed over the past four years. He'd swum through the famous salt tunnels of Tanunt, chased rebels through the Whispering Plains of Danen, and dined with the most powerful noble houses in the Empire. It had been ages since he had last seen these people, trotted through these gardens, and wandered the halls of Castle Iera.

And yet, mere days could have passed. Bart rambled about daily life: Lord Mattias still squabbled with House Valance and House Myreall; Lady Julianna wavered between lilies and roses for the new bouquets for the great hall; the kitchens were in a frenzy trying to prepare for the Harvest Festival; the market had a new exotic tea dealer, whom the ladies of the court adored.

How can they be so content with the mundane? he wondered.

When the ninth bell of the morning rang, he excused himself from the kitchen. Nearly all of the servants were there now, making pastries, cleaning dishes, bustling in and out carrying various breakfast orders, and creating wonderful smells Alex knew would stick in his head all day. He knew they also carried news of his presence with them, to the guards and advisors of the royal family. Hopefully, word would have reached Lord Mattias by now. It would make introductions easier.

Slipping back into the courtyard, he beat his cloak to release the flour that had settled on it and then wrapped it around his shoulders. Looping back around to the front of the castle, he passed a small knot of women clustered together in a garden—young noblewomen, if he'd had to guess, though none he recognized immediately. *The next crop of courtiers, off to find husbands*, he decided.

They were delicate and pale, wrapped in brightly colored skirts and giggling. Their flirtations seemed rather impractical, but he gave them a smile and wink anyway. The giggles bubbled louder and then were abruptly smothered as they shushed one another. Rolling his eyes, he lengthened his stride and took the steps to the main doors two at a time, his cloak billowing about his legs. Every step still sent jolting pain through his body, yet somehow he felt more awake than he had in weeks. And his stomach had finally stopped growling for food.

The atrium was large and airy. Twin staircases curved up and away to other floors, and stones of various shades of gray lay underfoot. There were no carpets this close to the doors since they would just be ruined by rain, mud, and frequent use. Vases of flowers decorated many of the surfaces, and several groups of people—from servants to merchants—stood chatting and waiting before the double doors directly across from where Alex stood.

These doors led to the great hall, where Lord Mattias and Lady Julianna would be settling in for breakfast, or so he hoped. *It's now or never,* he thought. *Get in, get out, get on with it.*

Disregarding the various people milling about, he confidently strode to the large doors. Pausing, he glanced around once and caught the eye of a servant, who watched him in horror. Unable to resist, he winked cheekily at the servant and then pushed open both doors before sauntering inside.

CHAPTER 3

3rd Day of the Harvest Moon

It had all felt like a beautiful, gauzy dream. They had danced, surrounded by fireflies and stars, her skirts swirling gracefully like something from a fairytale as soft strands of harp music echoed across the terrace. The evening had flown by, a cascade of bright colors, sparkling lights, and blackberry wine.

Despite the haziness of the dawn, moments from the night before stood out: walking gracefully to her seat on Geoffrey's arm, Theresa's face ugly with jealousy; tiny, delicate, candied flowers drizzled in honey; her head spinning from wine and delight as Geoffrey tugged her outside; collapsing on a bench, out of breath, her hair struggling out of its pearl-inlaid pins as he lifted her chin to engulf her in a kiss that had lasted what seemed like hours...

Caidy groaned and rubbed exhaustion from her eyes. The muddled memories clouding her vision made her ears pound. It was too early to have this many thoughts crowding her head. With a muffled moan, she rolled over, tangling herself in her sheets, kicking a packet of rosemary to the ground, and burying her face in a pillow. A sharp pain jabbed her scalp and she wrestled a pin from her curls, yelping as several hairs came away with it.

A particularly vicious jolt twisted behind her left eye and she abandoned the idea of sleep. She wasn't going to let anything ruin the floating feeling that buzzed throughout her entire body, making her fingers tingle and tracing goosebumps down her arms. She unceremoniously tossed her blankets aside, straightening the shift she had fallen asleep in, and hopped off her bed onto the cold flagstones.

Unfortunately, her foot tangled in the dress she had left in a crumpled pile a few hours previously, and she stumbled, slamming her elbow into the carved bedpost with a painful *thwack*. At the same time, the door opened with a soft scraping noise and Margot, her maid, backed into the room, holding a tray. A squeak of surprise escaped Margot as Caidy said several very unladylike words and rubbed her elbow.

"Are you alright?" Margot was there, gently gripping her upper arm and helping her stand. She was energized, despite the ungodly hangover settling behind her eyes.

"I am *wonderful*," she declared, deciding if she said it enough, it would become true.

With a heavy, patient sigh, Margot shepherded her to the sitting room, where the maid had set out a morning snack—a bowl of oats and fruit drizzled with honey and cinnamon and a steaming mug of tea. Caidy tried to read a manuscript detailing the expansion of the Mezrani Empire as she ate, but the words swam together, and she couldn't focus.

Giving up on the scroll, she glanced around the room, with its sunlit window seat, tidy table, and many assorted scrolls, paintings, and books, all neatly arranged on shelves.

The evening played over and over in her head. She relived every touch, every breathless, stolen kiss, and every adoring look. As her oats and tea grew cold, she gave up on eating and wandered through the bedroom.

Margot had already made her bed, piling a mound of blankets and pillows on the soft mattress. A vanity and dresser took up most of one wall with the stool she perched on while the maid did her hair and painted her face each day. Caidy paused, sniffing a new fragrance the maid had set out for later. She detected notes of lavender and sage. Deciding her day would be wholly useless if she didn't settle her mind, she entered her workroom, absently tracing her fingers over the rough walls and through the thin curtains before gathering parchment and some supplies from a table.

She draped herself on pillows scattered across the floor and began to sketch with charcoal, tracing flowing, swirling lines as her mind drifted. Art always had a way of helping her settle a thousand thoughts and relax. The dance had been wonderful, but in the light of morning, it was marred by Geoffrey's suggestion of marriage. Before last night, she had not taken his courtship seriously. An alliance between her family and his would strengthen the throne, but he was so *predictable*.

His steady keel through life infuriated her. His days reminded her of recipes—a sprinkle of this, a pinch of that, with always the same result. He seemed content to glaze over the exciting details of life in favor of consistency and comfort. He was an attentive noble and a kind person but grindingly boring. He shrugged with disinterest when she suggested adventures and rolled his eyes with her parents when Caidy lost herself in daydreams. She'd long since given up on the allure of romance, accepting the order and constancy that invaded her life. Deep down, she knew it was in the best interest of her people.

Spinning in dreams, the world that drained from her fingers into the charcoal was intoxicating and maddening, full of divine power and magic with brave heroes and adoring villagers. It was a world of dynamic opposites: abhorrent horrors, noble sacrifice, endless sorrow and overwhelming jubilation all rolled together. It was a gilded, pastel world, she knew, but it was *so* much more delicious than the harsh lines of reality.

When Margot came to fetch her, Caidy had straightened her thoughts and poured the tangle of emotions into her charcoal. The maid handed her a mug of something that smelled like spearmint and lemon, and with three hard swallows the remaining cobwebs and honeyed thoughts that slowed her brain were gone. She blinked furiously several times as her head began to pound in earnest and swore under her breath. "That was *awful*," she said to Margot, slowly pushing herself off the floor and accepting the maid's offered hand.

"I wouldn't know, milady." Margot's eyes twinkled and Caidy rolled her own. A sharp, twisting pain centered behind her eyes as she did so. "Finishing the tea should help with your head," the maid said wisely.

She did as she was told, swallowing the bitter, steaming concoction as quickly as she could and burning her tongue in the process. "Hag's teeth," she muttered as she bit her aching tongue, but the drink did help and the pounding in her head eased. "How much wine did I drink?"

The maid pursed her lips as she guided Caidy to a silken poof in front of the mirror, pressing lightly on Caidy's shoulders to settle her in place. "I couldn't possibly say," Margot responded dryly.

"That doesn't sound good at all." Caidy scratched her nose as Margot fussed over the tangled mess of hair that had once been shining, delicate curls. "Be honest with me." She caught her maid's eye in the mirror.

Margot smiled. "It wasn't nothing, milady. Master Geoffrey really had too much to drink. You just couldn't back down from the competition. You two disappeared for a while and came back all giggles and blushes, but that boy has no idea what he's doing so—" she cut herself off, and Caidy felt her cheeks flame. A moment passed and then both women collapsed into stitches of laughter.

When the maid stepped back several moments later, Caidy had been transformed. Her tangled mess of curls artfully cascaded over her shoulder, and the shadows under her eyes had melted away. She looked fresh and bright, as though she had slept through the night and spent a leisurely morning relaxing. "Thank you," she said politely as Margot held out an undergown for her to step into.

Finishing dressing, Caidy swept from her suite, eager to start her day. "Good morning, my Lady," her longtime bodyguard, Merric Adley, nodded at her as she emerged from Margot's clutches. A tall man with muscle that came from hard fighting and discipline, Merric had kept her safe as long as she could remember. He led a small contingent of the Rose Guard, the elite personal bodyguards of the ruling family of Rosemoor.

"It *is*. Isn't it?" Caidy lifted her arms and spun around, skirts whirling. "I love the morning after a good party. Everything still feels slightly magical."

"Of course, my Lady." Merric fell into step behind her.

On a whim, she decided to take the long way to the great hall. She was in no hurry to sit in an uncomfortable wooden chair, make small talk with courtiers, or listen to a lecture from her father. The day was simply too fresh and beautiful.

Yanking open one of the doors, which led to the castle walls, she tilted her face up toward the sky. She closed her eyes, letting the warm summer sun soak into her skin. A cool breeze tinged the air with the first quiet breaths of autumn.

Opening her eyes, she strode along the wall. "I wonder if the Player's Guild finished sourcing the new costumes for Iya's performance," she said, musing out loud. "The shipments were due in from Torren yesterday." The Harvest Festival, three short weeks away, had presented a never-ending list of details for her to arrange.

"You think I made the right choice with the chrysanthemums. Right?" She glanced over her shoulder at Merric.

"I've always liked chrysanthemums," the older man agreed amiably.

"Me too." Caidy paused, looking out over the front gates.

The sun was just starting to claw its way into the sky, shafts of light dappling the valley that stretched below her. A deep sense of pride settled in her chest. All of this was *hers*. In the city she knew merchants headed to market, Temple Mages led prayers to Caldir, Iya, and the plethora of other Gods who dotted the pantheon. Fleets of fishing boats already scoured Feather Lake and the Twin River, hunting for the day's fresh catch.

"Do you think we'll be invaded?" she asked as her mind began to wander, glancing at Merric again.

The guard snorted. "I'd consider it unlikely, my lady. Nothing, of course, is impossible. But I'm not particularly worried."

Sighing, Caidy braced her hands on the stone and leaned forward, looking down the hill. "I was reading about the invasion, when the Mezrani conquered Rosemoor. Is it true they used flags to send messages on the battlefield?" In her mind's eye, war raged in the idyllic, bountiful valley below, smoke billowing toward the sky in long, dark columns.

"Aye, my Lady. Still do, as far as I know. That's a practice our Provincial Guard has adopted, since many of them are veterans of the Imperial Army." He stepped next to her, following her gaze out over the valley. "I'm not hoping for a fresh battle anytime soon, my Lady. We've enough trouble with the Danen border."

The clash of swords and yells of soldiers faded from her ears. "You're right. I suppose it's a terrible thing to wish for." She continued her trek along the wall.

"War is glorious until you're the one on the field of battle, my Lady," Merric replied, his tone peaceful. "It's not a thing I want."

Caidy started down a steep stone staircase cut into the wall, making her way into the courtyard and past the temple. Weaving through tidy trees and blooming beds of flowers, she headed toward the great hall. On the step outside she paused, turning on her heel back to her bodyguard. "You know I didn't mean it," she said earnestly, looking at him. "As much as I might wish for adventure, I'd never want it at that cost."

Merric smiled at her. "Nothing to worry about, my Lady. If you're any later to breakfast, however, Lady Roussel may start a war of her own."

She yelped as she realized he was right and bounded through the door.

CHAPTER 4

3rd Day of the Harvest Moon

"Well, you certainly weren't this late to the dance last night. Do you find ruling a Province beneath you?" Caidy's mother, Lady Julianna, snapped at her as she skidded into the room.

Swallowing a sharp retort—the servants were *just* serving the food now and hadn't even gotten to her seat—Caidy curtseyed to her mother and slid into her uncomfortable wooden chair. Jealously, she watched Merric drift in silently and take his place among the other guards, evading her mother's wrath.

The Rose Guard waited to the right, between the dais where they ate and the other end of the great hall. The room was large and airy, with a high, arched ceiling and an expansive stone floor. Last night, the usual benches and tables had been cleared in favor of a space for dancing, but this morning the servants had returned the room to its usual state. A long carpet ran from dais to the main doors at the other end of the hall, and two fires crackled cheerfully in the hearths on either side of the room.

Sitting with her parents and the new Court Mage, Nolan, at the long wooden table on the dais, she politely thanked the servant who set food in front of her. Her back was perfectly straight as was expected. She had been taught, for as long as she could remember, that presentation was everything.

You can control you, her etiquette tutor had said a thousand times. *Act like your role.*

Caidy knew those words better than anything else, and she chanted them in her head often when she was in court. She was part of something much greater than herself. She held responsibilities beyond her own delights and pleasures. She was a princess first, a person second.

The scent of a steaming plate of sausage, eggs, stewed greens and caramelized onions tantalized her. Despite her earlier snack, she felt starved, as though she hadn't eaten in days. She forced herself to take small, ladylike bites as she had been taught although her stomach grumbled at the delay, earning a reproachful look from her mother.

Lady Julianna possessed something of a sixth sense for when Caidy violated even the most minor rules of etiquette. Her mother, of course, held herself with the grace of a queen and took minuscule bites. To everyone else her mother looked like perfection, but Caidy knew it was a miserable existence.

To her right, Nolan absently missed his mouth for the fourth time with his fork as he read intently from a scroll. She bit the inside of her lip to keep from laughing. Nolan wasn't much older than she was, and while she knew he possessed great power—or at least had been assured of as much by her parents—he was also one of the most forgetful people she knew.

He had been sent to Rosemoor earlier this year, the newest representative of the Aerian Lycantheum—the Imperial organization that managed mages and magic users across the Empire. She recalled vaguely that she had read about his abilities, but she'd filed that information away somewhere useful in her brain and promptly forgotten the details. He seemed to exist in a slightly separate world, which only barely touched reality, constantly lost in thought.

"Caidelene!" Her father, Lord Mattias, brought her back to the present.

She tried to swallow the chunk of sausage she was chewing on, nearly choked, and then worked quite hard to stop coughing. Her mother pointedly looked away, wrinkling her nose, while her father hid a smile. Nolan didn't notice. "Yes?" she gasped as she regained her breath.

"I hear Geoffrey discussed marriage with you last night." Lord Mattias speared a sausage, looking at her.

Her cheeks flushed. *Of course we're talking about this now.* "It came up," she replied, somewhat lamely.

Setting down her fork, her mother turned full attention on her. "And you said?"

Caidy sighed, tucking a stray curl behind her ear. Out of the corner of her eye, she saw Nolan watching curiously. "I said I'd give him a decision after the Harvest Festival. I've just got too much happening right now," she protested hastily, seeing her mother frown.

"Really, Caidelene, you should be ashamed of yourself. It's a smart match." Her mother sighed heavily. "The Valances would be good allies to have."

"I know. I know," she replied sulkily, returning her attention to pushing food around her plate so she could ignore her mother's glower. "I just need some time to think about it."

"See that you do," her mother's voice was cold. "Don't be rash."

An awkward silence stretched between them for a moment until her father spoke once more. "What matters are you attending to this week?" Lord Mattias looked pointedly at his daughter. "I assume you have more responsibilities than simply dancing the night away and frustrating your mother?"

"Um." Caidy paused, gathering her thoughts and focusing on the question. *Anything to change the subject.* "I'm meeting with the Market Council, Mayor Kluk asked for royal council in the city, the autumn festivities…" she trailed off. It felt like she was missing something. "All my normal lessons, of course," she finished lamely.

"Yes, can't forget about those." Lord Mattias nodded approvingly. Lady Julianna busied herself with shredding a chunk of meat into dainty, ladylike pieces, her mouth tight. "What does the mayor want?" he asked her.

"There's been some issue with crime. He petitioned to use the Provincial Guard contingent to supplement the Ierian City Guard." Caidy rubbed her nose with a finger, trying to recall details. "There've been a couple of prominent burglaries and attacks recently, if I remember correctly. A dancer in Honey District was beaten badly, and a merchant's warehouse in Dock was raided. It seems to be a manpower problem."

Lord Mattias frowned. "Why now? What's changed?"

She shrugged. "I think it's mostly that the Harvest Festival is going to be held soon so he feels like he has leverage."

"I don't like him trying to force our hand. You know we can't use the Provincial Guard in the city. They're—"

Her mother put a hand on his arm. "She knows, Mattias."

Interested, Caidy watched her father deflate before her eyes. Her mother had a unique ability to calm him, which was something Caidy had never been able to do. Indeed, her relationship with her father was rocky at best. Sometimes things were easy and friendly, but at other times the castle shook with their arguments.

"What's your strategy, Caidelene?" Lord Mattias asked around a bite of egg. Her mother wrinkled her nose but said nothing.

"Well." Caidy thought quickly since she had no strategy. "I think my first question is why the City Guard has a man-power problem. Is it a funding issue? Recruitment? Leader-ship? I don't know, but inevitably unless we eventually have more City Guard, any agreement we make is pointless."

Mattias nodded, rubbing his thick beard. "You really can't agree to using the Provincial Guard, you know."

Swallowing her annoyance, she forced a polite smile on her face. It felt like a grimace. "I know. The Provincial Guard are soldiers; they have no place catching pickpockets. That's why I think the solution rests in understanding why there's a problem in the first place."

Julianna set her fork down. "I think that's a good way to approach it." She offered Caidy a gentle, knowing smile.

Spearing a chunk of sausage, Mattias gestured with his knife, waving the meat in the air. "I was thinking Adept Nolan could accompany you into the city."

Nolan looked up from his scroll. "I'm sorry, my Lord?" he asked politely, clearly startled that his name had come up, or that Mattias knew his name at all.

Simultaneously, Caidy replied," I wouldn't want to be an inconvenience. I'm sure Nolan has plenty of ongoing work—"

"Don't be absurd, Caidelene. I don't believe Nolan has had the opportunity to see Iera City in full yet. It would be an excellent chance for you to show him our beautiful capital." Mattias chewed the sausage thoughtfully and then nodded. "Yes, I think that's an excellent plan."

Caidy glared at her father. She couldn't imagine a more boring way to spend the day, dragging the new mage around the city after meeting with the mayor. In the little time she had spent with him during court and a few meetings, Nolan had proven himself to be an insufferably dull companion.

"I don't know how long my meeting with the mayor will go. I wouldn't want him to waste his time," she tried a different tack.

"Nonsense," her father responded, his tone friendly but his eyes uncompromising. She knew she wasn't going to win the argument. "It would be good for Nolan to see more of Rosemoor, and it will give both of you the chance to spend some time getting to know one another. I also have it on good authority that the City Guard wants to meet with a representative of the Lycantheum, so he'll have plenty to do while you're busy." His tone left nothing up for discussion.

"As you wish, my Lord." Nolan looked as unhappy with the decision as she felt. She decided to try once more.

"Forgive me, but won't Nolan be needed to oversee the preparation for the Harvest Ball? I was under the impression he needed to create wards for—"

Her father's mood shifted in an instant from jovial and self-satisfied to thunderous. "I've made my decision, Caidelene. You'd do well to let it go."

Puffing out her cheeks in annoyance, she slumped back in her chair. Unfortunately, her mother caught her eye and sent her a withering look, forcing her back to straighten once more.

"The new Imperial Ambassador should be arriving shortly," her mother changed the subject tactfully as Caidy and her father glowered at one another. "I was thinking it would be nice to have traditional Mezrani dishes at the welcome feast."

As Julianna finished her sentence, the doors at the opposite end of the great hall swung open.

A young man sauntered in, unannounced. His gait oozed confidence, and he looked directly at the dais as he moved through the hall. From this distance, all Caidy could see was that he was dressed simply, in a white shirt open at the collar and loose black trousers tucked into dusty boots. A woolen cloak was slung over his shoulders, a silver pin flashing as it caught the light.

Caidy recognized his walk first. Her body moved before her mind fully understood what was happening. Jumping up, she darted around the long wooden table in front of her parents' seats and down the steps of the dais. She covered the distance between them in a few steps and flung her arms around his shoulders. "Alex!"

CHAPTER 5

———

3rd Day of the Harvest Moon
He heard her call his name in something between an echo and a dream. Her voice was filled with hundreds of emotions, and he felt his chest tighten. *What is she doing here?* Alex dug his nails into his palm, anchoring himself. Caidy flung her arms around his neck, slamming into him and nearly knocking them both to the ground.

He rocked back on his heels, absorbing the energy she catapulted into his body, and took a steadying breath. She smelled incredible, like sage and lavender and a hint of cinnamon. Her hair was just as soft as he remembered, and he itched to tangle his fingers in her curls, to kiss her and pull her off her feet, whispering promises of love and devotion.

She was more lovely than he remembered. Her thick, dark brown hair fell in graceful, shining curls over her shoulders, and a deep blue gown set off skin the color of fresh snow. Her gray eyes were overbright, framed with long, delicate lashes, large and dark in the graceful angles of her face.

A complicated set of emotions played across his heart in the space of a single beat: a shiver of fear, a jagged rush of anxiety, a flutter of joy, a tease of warmth and love. His breath caught in his throat, but in an instant, he forced himself back together.

Step back, he ordered himself. *Maintain your dignity.*

He stiffened, recoiling from her and from his own unruly thoughts. A deep, burning sense of guilt settled in the pit of his stomach and back of his throat as he felt her hesitate. Wanting nothing more than to wrap his arms tightly around her and never let go, he instead forced himself to fold his hands together behind his back. She stepped back, tilting her face to his, her cheeks stained red and her brows contracted.

"Alex," she said his name again, this time in little more than a whisper, and he felt his heartbeat in his throat. He knew for a moment—barely a moment—his raw emotions overwhelmed his control and shone through the lazy gaze he had spent so many years perfecting. But then, the moment passed, and he examined her with as much apparent dis-interest as he could summon. The refuge of cool, detached professionalism never failed.

Keep moving, he told himself. *Brush her off. Keep her at arm's length. Keep her safe.*

He looked down at her, dedicating all his energy toward carefully maintaining his apparent indifference. "Good day, Lady Caidelene."

Caidy's eyes, large and dark in her face, suddenly flashed with unshed tears, and sparked with anger. She searched his face for a moment and then took two abrupt steps back as she wound her fingers in her skirts. He noticed her hands shook. Caidy drew herself up to her full height in defiance. Even standing at her tallest, she still barely reached his shoulders.

She stuck her nose in the air—a painfully familiar ges-ture—and proclaimed, "And a good day to you. If you will excuse me, I have business to attend to." Her voice was no longer warm and vulnerable but tight with anger and hurt pride. She flounced past him, back rigid, her left arm barely brushing his right.

Alex remained quite still, his skin tingling where she had touched him, until he heard the doors behind him close with a dull thud and her footsteps faded. When the only flicker of her presence was a cloud of earthy perfume in the air, he turned his gaze back to the dais with his best studiously casual expression.

Lord Mattias' brows had drawn together, and his frown deepened the lines in his craggy face. Lady Julianna was watching carefully, her eyes slightly narrowed. The other man at the table—a mage, judging by his garb—appeared torn between running from the room and staying to see what was about to happen.

Lord Mattias solved the problem for him. "Adept, leave us, please." The mage bolted from his chair as though it had burst into flames, stuffed the crumpled scroll up one of his sleeves, and disappeared through a door behind the dais.

This is it. Establish yourself, show Mattias you've got backbone, and then leave. He had expected the Lord of Rosemoor to be less than welcoming: he hated reminders of the Imperial Authority. *Of course, I didn't exactly leave on the best terms.*

Deliberately calm, Alex strolled up the rest of the aisle, stopping when he reached the step up to the dais, which Caidy had launched herself off of moments before. He inclined his head toward the Lord and Lady but stopped short of bowing. It was an important distinction; he was an advisor to the Rosemoor Court now, not a subject. He answered only to the Imperial Authority.

"My Lord, my Lady." Alex straightened and stepped up onto the dais without invitation. Lord Mattias' eyebrows contracted almost imperceptibly, but Lady Julianna had recovered from her shock and wore an expression halfway between disdain and polite curiosity. He unhooked a scroll case attached to his belt, traced a finger around the cap, and then removed it to reveal a tightly wound piece of parchment with a flourish. "I come bearing an official message from the Imperial Authority."

Lord Mattias took the proffered scroll and unfurled it, his frown deepening as he read. Alex's stomach churned. He disliked the persona he had been trained to exude. He detested that demeaning authority gave him more independence, but he knew the importance. He understood that cockiness now would allow him to shed the expectations tied to his old reputation and create a new identity. He needed that freedom and flexibility to do his work, to protect the Empire, and to keep Caidy safe. His work was more important than anything else.

As Lord Mattias read, Alex studied the royal couple.

There were more glimmers of gray in Lord Mattias' brown hair and beard than there had been four years ago, and the lines around his mouth and eyes had deepened. He sat with his eyes narrowed, glaring at the missive. That wasn't a good sign.

Lady Julianna, to her husband's left, was in rare form, showing something resembling emotion for the first time Alex could remember. Her eyes were wide, and her painted lips clamped together in a thin line. She still held her fork and knife, and the tension in her jaw was nearly audible.

When Mattias finished, he folded the scroll tightly, running a finger across each seam to seal the document. Alex waited just as he would have during his training: hands clasped in front of him, feet braced shoulder's width apart, knees loose. He watched Mattias consider the situation and then select a course of action—all within the matter of a few, tense seconds. Alex's eyes flicked to Lady Julianna, who had collected herself and watched her husband impassively.

"Thank you, Master Laurent. Do you need directions to Raven House?"

"No, my Lord." The silence between them stretched taut. Alex waited it out, leaning into the discomfort and tension in the room. Lord Mattias glowered in his direction a moment longer.

"That'll be all then. Dismissed."

Alex raised one eyebrow a fraction and waited another moment as realization dawned. *He's testing me.* "My Lord," he finally began, "it is standard protocol for you to sign my orders, acknowledging that I have presented them to you in court."

Mattias' self-control snapped and the Lord bristled at him. "In court?" he asked tightly. "Is that what you call interrupting my breakfast with my wife and daughter—in court?" A vein stood out on his temple. Lady Julianna's fingers had tightened almost imperceptibly on her fork and knife.

He withstood the lash of Lord Mattias' anger calmly. Meeting the older man's furious stare with his best attempt at civil boredom, much like a parent watching a child throw a tantrum. Out of the corner of his eye, he was fairly sure he saw Lady Julianna's mouth quirk in a slight smile.

"Respectfully, my Lord, I represent the Imperial Authority, and my reassignment is considered of the highest urgency for the Empire." Alex chose his next words very carefully. There was a limit to how far he could push the Lord, and he was very close to it. "I've ridden for the past thirteen days straight from Danen to present myself before you. Wardens are integral to the safety of the Empire, and I consider it the highest honor to have the opportunity to work with you. I'm sure you can understand my haste in this matter."

As Lord Mattias continued to glare at him, he was struck by how different this conversation was than his previous interactions with Caidy's father. Years ago, the Lord had frightened him with his anger. Now, Mattias' rage had an almost energizing effect. Alex was ready for this fight, and he was in the right. Everything else faded away from their argument as his focus crystallized. The moment balanced on the edge of a knife.

Lady Julianna cleared her throat with a small cough, and the tension in the air snapped. Mattias muttered something and snatched a quill from beside Nolan's abandoned plate, dragging his sleeve through Caidy's congealing food. He scrawled his initials across the folded parchment and tossed the document, creased and somewhat worse for wear, back toward Alex.

With a fluid motion, Alex snatched it from the air. He inclined his head toward both rulers—again, stopping slightly short of bowing. Lady Julianna inclined her head politely in return as the vein on Lord Mattias' temple throbbed.

"A pleasure to see you again, my Lord, my Lady." Alex saw Lord Mattias' fingers curl into a fist and decided he should quit while he was ahead. He spun on his heel and briskly left the hall.

Her maid shrieked, jumped, and dropped the vase of flowers she was arranging as Caidy flung herself headlong into the safety of her suite, the door punctuating her passage with a bang. She ran past the maid into the bedchamber, hurling herself onto her bed in tears. Her hands shook uncontrollably—she hated that!—and her heart felt as though it was breaking all over again. Curling around a pillow, she buried her face and sobbed.

The joy she had felt that morning was gone, and the shift in emotions was overwhelming. She had imagined seeing Alex again many times although her dreams had always contained a joyous reunion. She'd lost count of the times she had imagined him sweeping her off her feet, spinning her in a circle, and holding her tightly; his hands tracing her cheekbones and spine, his fingers tangling in her hair. In reality he had been cold, as though carved from marble.

When he had left, Alex had been a tall, gangly youth, a good runner but a terrible wrestler. She had still seen some of her old friend in the way his eyes had flashed when she looked at him, in the instant before his calm facade reappeared.

Most of him, however, had been completely unfamiliar. He was taller than she remembered, and his sandy hair was thicker—though still messy, *probably from him running his fingers through it.* Her heart panged at the thought.

His eyes, the color of fresh pine needles, were still flecked with gold and encircled in black, shadowed by thick lashes, though the intensity of his look was new. Gone was the meek boy who followed her lead. He had caught her eyes with his gaze and held them, making her feel terribly vulnerable and open, as though he could read every thought tumbling through her head.

Her spirit ached for his crooked smile, the way his eyes used to dance when he laughed, his wry jokes, and his gentle devotion. He had always seemed to notice every motion she made, anticipating what she needed, supporting her, loving her. She was *sure* he had loved her.

She had clung to her painful memories for the past four years, fearing that he might never come home again. At first, a small part of her had hoped he wouldn't. They'd fought when he told her he'd put his name forward to join the Blades, but she had never believed he would actually be chosen. But then, he had vanished in the night, choosing a life of adventure over their life together.

Members of the Imperial intelligence service lived notoriously secretive and dangerous lives. She had imagined him hiking through the dark forests of Colmar, sailing the Pirate Coast of Danen, and exploring the Rainbow Mountains of Tanunt, the center of a rich tapestry of power and conspiracy—and never sparing a thought for her.

Despite her frustration, her heart had ached for him; she wanted nothing more than for him to return and sweep her off her feet. However, the years had slipped by and she had slowly lost faith that he would ever come home. He was lost to his new life of adventure and had left her behind.

When Geoffrey had started courting her, she had not been happy, but she had locked those feelings deep inside her heart. She painted on a face of delight for him, an aura of responsibility and maturity for her parents, and an attitude of inner peace for the world. She had embraced her new persona, had repeated over and over to herself: *Grow up, Caidy. This is your life. Everything is fine.*

Until now.

Now, nothing was fine at all. All of her painstakingly pent-up feelings bubbled up to the surface at once. Her entire body trembled as tears tumbled down her cheeks, and she couldn't think, couldn't breathe. It was all shattered, broken, melted. The precarious balance she had developed was collapsing. She was surrounded by people—counselors, servants, nobles, commoners—and yet she was utterly, completely isolated.

She couldn't remember ever feeling this alone before.

The weight of her life pressed Caidy into the pile of pillows, and she wept until she had nothing left at all.

CHAPTER 6

———

3rd Day of the Harvest Moon

Alex heaved himself onto his weary horse one last time, turning her head toward the palace gate. He sighed deeply, shaking the folds of his cloak around him. "That went about as well as expected," he said to her. His mount snorted, unimpressed. "Come on, girl. Let's get you settled."

Crossing through the gate and returning to the switchback road, Alex nearly halted his horse as all the nerves that had melted away when he confronted Mattias rushed into focus. Feeling as though he'd been punched in the stomach, he leaned over, bracing his hands on the edge of the saddle as his horse slowly picked her way down the hill.

He hadn't expected to see Caidy again so soon. She wasn't supposed to be there. She never used to take breakfast with her parents. *Idiot,* the voice in his head scolded, *things have changed.* It honestly hadn't even occurred to him that she might be taking on more responsibility, spending more time with her parents. *I'm not the only one who's grown up.*

In the struggle to maintain his composure as she did her best to knock him off his feet, all thought of emotion had vanished. He'd retreated deep within himself, focusing in a way only years of hard training and experience could teach. She had not been his mission. She had been a liability.

But now, riding down the rocky mountain road, overlooking a stunning, glorious vista with the city rising below, Feather Lake sparkled as fishing boats bobbed cheerfully, alpine falcons soared on the eddies of air near the snowy peaks, and she was once more the center of his world.

He knew, deep in his heart, he had never stopped loving her. And yet, he also knew that any chance they had was long gone. The ability to be closer to her, to protect her, was a big reason he had jumped at the chance to leave Danen and return to Rosemoor. It had seemed like a sign at the time, though now he wondered if it was just another divine joke.

"What a roll of Udo's dice that was," he muttered. The God of tricksters was famed for his weighted dice, designed to throw his opponent—or victim—off balance. "I don't think I could be more off-kilter if I was rolling down this mountain." He tightened his fingers once more on the reins, alert to his mount's footing in case the God got any more ideas.

Romancing her when he was a younger son of a Rosemoorian House was one thing. He could have brought wealth and political capital to her family and ensured stability when her father stepped down. Loving her as a Blade, a representative of the Empire, which *ruled* Rosemoor and controlled the Roussels? An Imperial spy, whose first loyalty always had to be to the good of the Empire, marrying a woman who would ascend to the throne of the most independent Imperial province? *Definitely not.*

Worst of all, he knew, was that if any hint of impropriety came into view, either party could ensure he would never see her again. Mattias could dismiss him, forcing the Blades to reassign him elsewhere and damaging already cool relations between the Empire and Rosemoor. The Blades could remove him from service, force him into a foreign posting, or—at worst—hand him over to the Shadows or the Glittering Hand.

"It just can't happen," he said aloud, for speaking the words had power. His horse shook her head and snorted as they continued their trek down the hillside.

The earlier chill had faded, and the city below them was alive, crawling with activity. The road was slowly becoming busier, too. Couriers jogged by, wagons of supplies trundled slowly uphill, and he passed at least one noble carriage making a precarious turn around a hairpin bend. The livery of the men-at-arms was the wine red and eagle gray of House Valance. The curtains of the carriage were closed when Alex rode by—likely a noble leaving after a diplomatic visit, a dance, or some other festivity.

When he reached the city, he passed through the Market Gate unimpeded and rode down the crowded streets around City Hill toward the Docks. The city had come alive while he'd whiled away the early morning at the castle, and he ended up dismounting, deciding it would be easier to lead his horse on foot than try and force his way through the crowd.

Thousands of souls lived in Iera, the largest city on the Empire's northern border, and thousands more visited each year for its fabled festivals. He recognized some of the faces as he passed, vendors who had been hawking their wares in the Ierian Market District since he was a child. The noble houses were walled compounds around the base of City Hill. If he rode south instead of north, he'd find his own family's home in Iera, a pretty place with thick ivy on the stone walls.

Theirs, not mine. That was another part of his life he would never—could never—return to. He'd been stripped of his nobility when he left for the Blades. Nobody quite knew what to make of the elite Imperial spies in the north. In Tanunt, the heart of the Empire, the Blades were seen as dangerously clever diplomats and lethal fighters, resources to protect the integrity of the Imperial Authority.

In Rosemoor they were much more the stuff of legend. Stories from his childhood had convinced him that Blades gained mysterious magical power, granted by the Goddess of secrets, Naia. It was just rumor—though one the Blades certainly let go unfettered, to add to their mystique. *In the end, it was nothing more than endless training and life-or-death stakes*, he reflected.

The wonderful smell of hot honeycomb tea wafted over him, and he turned his head instinctively, sniffing for the source. He quickly spotted it. Annabeth, one of his favorite tea merchants, had set up her cart where the road curved toward the Dock District.

Deciding he deserved some tea after a hard morning's work—he had promised himself, after all—Alex began to make his way through the crowd. Totally focused, he nearly walked into one of the City Guard, a man even taller than he was, with broad shoulders and sandy hair.

"Hey! Watch where you're—by Alun!" The guard cut himself off mid-thought as he stared at Alex through familiar green eyes. "Alex?"

He immediately recognized his cousin, Thom, who—if he remembered correctly—was a sergeant in the City Guard. He couldn't tell if the older man was happy to see him. He mostly looked confused. "Hey, Thom. It's, uh, been a while."

"Aye," the guard agreed, rubbing the back of his neck awkwardly. "Gods, Alex, what in the Hells happened?"

That seems to be a common reaction, he noted dryly—Bart had said nearly the same words earlier that morning. He found himself shrugging somewhat awkwardly. "I left."

"Really? I knew something was different." Sarcasm ran in the family. "Alun be praised, Alex. I thought you were dead." Thom clapped him on the shoulder, apparently getting past his initial shock.

Slightly offended, Alex frowned. "Dead? Seriously, Thom? D'you think I can't take care of myself?" Suddenly acutely aware they stood in the middle of the street and were causing a scene, he gestured to the opening of a side alley, regretfully far from Annabeth's cart.

Thom followed, chuckling. His cousin had to be in his late thirties by now with rough stubble covering his chin and a scar splitting one eyebrow in two. Nonetheless, his eyes still twinkled with familiar merriment. "I think you always had a nose for getting into places you weren't supposed to. The Blades make sense." He nodded at Alex's pin.

"I'm a powerful magician now," Alex lied, wiggling his fingers at his cousin. "Be careful or I'll turn you into a beetle."

"I'm sure you will," Thom snorted.

Alex was shocked by how good it felt to talk to his cousin. They'd never been particularly close, but now he had returned with experience under his belt—and pinned to his shoulder— he seemed to have somehow earned the older man's respect. "Are you still a sergeant?" he asked curiously.

"I wish," Thom sighed. "I was promoted to Watch Commander last year. Way more work, but it also means I actually talk to the Blades from time to time. Always asked about you, but you people run a tight ship. Never so much as a word."

That made sense. When someone joined the Blades, they left their old life behind. Not only would one Blade never reveal where another was, lest they be put in danger, but the concept of *family* no longer held sway. They only had one another.

"Speaking of, I should probably get going. I'm due at Raven House soon."

"Let me walk you," Thom offered, already turning back to the street. "I can fill you in, even if you can't return the favor."

Through Thom, Alex had his suspicions confirmed. His parents had returned to Everfall to tend to his sister, who had been sickly since youth. His older brother was serving with the Provincial Guard and was stationed near the Danen border. When he had left for the Blades, the family had done what all families did and began to erase him from their lives.

"My ma would kill me if she knew I was talking to you," Thom noted as they entered Guild District. "Her sister—your mother—is still furious you threw away a chance at the crown."

"It wouldn't have been my crown anyway," Alex said automatically. "It would have been Caidy's." It was an argument dredged up from the past but one he had made dozens of times before. "Besides, what's she want power for? All she wants is to stay home with her cats and her garden."

"Well, yes, but I think it's more the idea of power," his cousin remarked wisely. "It's easy to not want something when there's no chance of it happening. It's the temptation that'll get you."

A whistle cut through the air, and Thom stopped walking so quickly Alex almost walked into him a second time. "Hells. I've got to deal with that," his cousin said with a heavy sigh.

"Probably another recruit who got tripped by a lookout. Raven House is just at the end of the next street against the Hill."

Alex hesitated for a moment and then clasped his cousin's forearm. "It's good to see you, Thom. For what it's worth, I'm sorry."

His cousin grinned at him. "Naught to be sorry for. I got much of the same when I joined the City Guard instead of doing something more *worthwhile*. Just, erm, don't tell my ma we've been talking."

Snorting, Alex agreed. "Seeing as I'm a ghost to her, that would be hard to do."

"We'll grab tea or drinks some time," Thom promised, starting to jog away in the direction of the persistent whistle. "And welcome home!"

CHAPTER 7

3rd Day of the Harvest Moon

At last, he and his horse arrived at Raven House. The headquarters of the Amaranth Khmal—known to most outside Mezrani City as the Blades—in Rosemoor Dell was not an imposing affair. It was a three-story, stone-and-wood building with overflowing flower boxes tucked between a tailor's shop and an eating house. The building clung to the very bottom of City Hill. Further along the street, the steep Judgment Stair sloped up to the stone buildings that crowned the Hill. It looked more like the manor of a wealthy merchant than the provincial headquarters of one of the most powerful organizations in the Empire.

Sensing they were done traveling, his horse whickered and tossed her coarse mane twice, shaking off the day thus far. Alex tucked his gloves into his belt and extracted a carrot from one of his saddlebags. He snapped the dirty vegetable in two, tucked half back into the bag, and then presented the carrot to the horse. She lipped it off his palm, dousing him with horse slobber, and crunched down.

He wiped his hand on her mane and then led the horse down an alley beside Raven House to a small wooden lean-to with some hay, water, and enough space for two horses. Alex looped the reins over a wooden post, removed his horse's bit, and circled back to the front of the building. Stepping over the mud and muck in the street gutter, he ran his fingers through his hair again, twice, before opening the door.

Inside, three people stood glaring at each other. On the left, a young man with fiery eyes and a stubborn chin was braced, a collection of scrolls tumbling out of his hands. His fingers were stained with ink, and his hair stuck up in several, apparently unintentional, directions. Across from him, a woman in a purple silk tunic with short, black hair, and the dark skin of a Mezrani stood with arms crossed, her face made ugly by a sneer. Between the two, an older man with appraising eyes and a magnificently bushy mustache was leaning over a table, frowning. All three turned to look at Alex as the door thudded shut behind him.

The tension in the room was almost comical, and Alex resisted the urge to chuckle. Instead, he pulled out the crumpled scroll with Lord Mattias' smeared signature and tossed it on the table. "Alexander Laurent, Warden assigned to Rosemoor Dell," he said briskly, addressing the woman.

"Commissar Danila al-Mhir." She extended a hand toward him. From her imperious demeanor, he was unsure if he should shake it or bow over it. Some Mezrani expected the formality while others were offended by it. Knowing there was no winning, he decided to take her hand and incline his head slightly. If her face was any indication, it was the wrong decision.

"Archivalist Jakob Gesell." The Archivalist started to extend a hand, dropped three scrolls, and gave up. Alex knelt and collected the scrolls, handing them back with a smile. Archivalists were the Blades' researchers and analysts. They searched for patterns, put together reports, and spent most of their time buried in an office.

The large man behind the table walked around to the front of the room. Alex was tall, but he was still a head shorter than this man. "Lord Commissioner Rawley Hendrick, Warden." The large man engulfed Alex's hand in his, and Alex did his best to shake it firmly.

Hendrick was the highest Blade authority in Rosemoor Dell. He oversaw every effort the organization made within the province. Alex had been briefed on Hendrick before coming to Rosemoor. He was an impressive man with an expansive record of service. Rumors swirled within the Blades that he had been one of the Bandit Lords of Danen before, for some reason, he joined the Empire. Seeing him in person, Alex was ready to believe just about any wild rumor or exaggeration about the Lord Commissioner. His presence was imposing, to say the least.

Hendrick turned from Alex and glowered at Danila. "I'm sure you'll understand, Commissar, that I must cut this meeting short to meet with my newest asset. We can continue this discussion later. Archivalist?" He marched up a rickety staircase without looking back. Jakob immediately followed, nearly tripping on Hendrick's heels, and Alex shot Danila an apologetic look before climbing the stairs to the third floor. Her eyes smoldered.

The Bandit Lord led the two Blades into an office and settled behind a large wooden desk strewn with papers and maps. Jakob released his scrolls onto the pile and crossed to close the door. Alex leaned against the wall, folded his arms, and waited. Hendrick smoothed his mustache in thought and then leaned forward.

"She's not going to drop it, you know," Jakob commented, returning from the door. "We don't have a reason to keep her out."

"We absolutely do." The former Bandit Lord scowled. "The Authority can't just suddenly decide they want more control and send minders to make us do their bidding. That Mezrani has no idea what we do or why it's important."

"Yes, but she can also have any of us replaced with a letter," Jakob replied calmly, perching on the armrest of a chair and using a belt knife to clean the ink from under his nails.

"It's my problem. I'll deal with it." Hendrick waved a large hand, and Alex saw a long scar crossing his palm. "So are you." He turned his attention back to Alex. "You look young."

Alex looked up at his new superior, playing for time. Out of the corner of his eye, he thought he saw Jakob's mouth twist in a half smile.

"You've got nothing to prove in this room, Laurent. You've been assigned here. I don't have the time to reassign you anywhere else. And, frankly, nobody else wants your job. There's a reason the Warden Corps is so small." Hendrick's voice was brisk and final. He leaned back in his chair and propped his feet on his desk. "I know who you are but Jakob has better things to do. Give him the high points."

Alex had a funny feeling that he was being tested on something. He straightened, clasped his hands in front of his waist, and stood at attention as he'd been drilled. Jakob continued to clean under his fingernails.

"My name is Alexander Laurent, and I am a native of Rosemoor Dell. My parents are Lord Remon and Lady Amelia of House Laurent; I am the youngest son in my family. I spent my childhood in the Ierian Court and developed a close friendship with Lady Caidelene. I was recruited by the Amaranth Khmal four years ago and completed my training at the Citadel in the Capital District. My last training assignment found me shadowing a Vanisher in Swansea, and then I was assigned to aid the Warden in Danen. I've spent the past two years supporting our work there."

"And why were you assigned here, Laurent?" Hendrick laced his fingers behind his head.

He considered the question for a moment. "Wardens are responsible for garnering support for the Blades within provinces, for supplementing local investigations with Imperial resources, and advising the Provincial Lords. I'd imagine I was selected for this post because of my history here and because of my experience working with the Warden of Danen. We have such a small domestic retinue that any advantage can greatly ease our efforts."

Hendrick nodded once. It was a sharp, definitive motion. "And, since you've worked with Ingrid in Danen, you don't have the wool pulled over your eyes about your assignment." He glared at Alex under bushy eyebrows. "At least I hope you've got more sense than that. The Warden Corps isn't a glamorous assignment, especially not here. The Roussels don't like the Wardens, which makes your job much harder. The Citadel seems to think that your history with that family and your blood will make it easier for you to build bridges. I'm not sure that's true."

Alex couldn't contain a rueful grin. "I'm not sure it is either, sir."

The Lord Commissioner waved a hand. "We don't stand on formality here. There are too few of us. When we're with that Imperial witch downstairs, you can pull out the titles, but outside of those audiences, it's Jakob and Hendrick."

"Are Vanishers or Shadows assigned here?" Alex leaned back against the wall, relaxing.

Hendrick shook his head. "We've got one Vanisher deep under, but I think he's crossed into Colmar. His handler left, anyhow. No Shadows that I know about, but the Authority's been taking more control over those operations, so I'm not positive. Jakob's our main Archivalist. We can get another from the Citadel if need be, but I prefer to keep our shop small. Helps us stay out of the public eye."

Alex nodded thoughtfully.

"I want to be clear about one thing, Laurent." Hendrick leaned forward. "We follow the letter of the law from the Citadel here. It'll be very different than Danen. They're pirates chasing pirates. We face a different kind of problem here—a political problem. So it's by the book all the time. Don't try bending the rules, or I'll personally make sure the most important job you have is editing reports from other assets. Is that clear?"

He understood the threat, even if it felt a little superfluous. There weren't that many trained Wardens around, and Rosemoor had already been without one for a couple of months. They needed him. But Hendrick had a point. At his previous post in Danen, rules and laws had been viewed much more as suggestions. The corruption of the province ran deep into the Imperial presence and oversight. Ingrid, one of his old mentors, was the cleanest of the lot, and she could drink pirate captains under the table before torturing them for information. Not exactly in the typical Warden job description.

Rosemoor was a very different kettle of fish.

"Clear," Alex replied. "I like a little more structure in my life, anyway."

Jakob snorted. "You'll certainly have that here. Nothing but structure, reports, feasts, reports, meetings, murders, and political intrigue. And did I mention the reports? I've got forms for your forms."

Alex rolled his eyes. "Isn't that your job?" he jibed.

"Depends on whether or not I like you," Jakob countered. "And, more importantly, whether or not you can keep the Commissar off our collective asses."

The Bandit Lord waved a hand before Alex could respond. "We'll get into that tomorrow. Today, get settled in the city. I know you've been riding hard. You'll be living in Blue Trout Lodgings, in Dock District." He handed Alex a bag piled high with scrolls, papers, maps, and what appeared to be several uniforms. "Review this for tomorrow. I'll expect you here by the second bell of the morning. Dismissed."

Hendrick twitched two fingers toward the door. Alex suspected that was going to become a familiar motion. With a sigh, he hoisted the bag over his shoulder and wandered back downstairs. Danila had disappeared somewhere, probably to write up a report for the Imperial Authority. It was a headache he didn't want to deal with, but it didn't matter that the Bandit Lord claimed responsibility for Imperial relations. If the Mezrani were against them, everything would become infinitely more complicated. From the look of it, things weren't off to a fantastic start.

So much for a day off, he thought dryly.

CHAPTER 8

―――

4th Day of the Harvest Moon
It was too hot for Nolan to be this late. Caidy tapped her
foot impatiently against the flagstones, fanning herself with
one hand and glowering. The summer heat had returned
with a vengeance as they moved toward the autumn sol-
stice, and everything felt sticky. Outside the stables, her three
bodyguards stood in the shade of a juniper tree, wearing
leather jerkins.

They looked miserable, and she shuddered involuntarily.
Her cream linen shirt clung to her back. The bronze breeches
she wore—so wide they almost appeared to be skirts, as was
the fashion—felt scratchy and uncomfortable, and her toes
swam in her leather boots. She knew her hair was a hopeless
catastrophe, too. Margot had tried to braid it out of her eyes,
but small curls stuck to the sweat on her forehead and frizzed
out around her ears. She couldn't imagine wearing armor.

It's very hard to feel regal in this heat, Caidy fretted. For
a day in the city, she couldn't imagine worse weather. People would be *everywhere*, jostling this way and that. The
air never moved either since City Hill blocked most of the

wind off the lake. Riding would be miserably itchy from horse hair and sweat as they traveled to Iera, and she had to bring that foolish mage along with her, so she couldn't gallop. *Be on your best behavior,* her mother had reminded her over breakfast.

She had half expected Alex to barge into their meal once again and had been disappointed—then thoroughly annoyed with herself—when he remained absent. *There's nothing to be done about it,* she reminded herself stubbornly. *Clearly, things have changed.* The morning had been testing the strength of her self-discipline as she ordered her thoughts down more reliable paths and away from the way Alex had recoiled.

Nolan wandered into the stables at that moment, and Caidy snapped back to the present with a rush of anger. "Where were you? Mattias ordered you to accompany me, not make me melt! It's hotter than the Hells out here!" She narrowed her eyes, watching the mage. He raised both hands in a painfully familiar placating gesture, and she felt her mental discipline waver.

"I got caught up in my work, my Lady." He paused. She rolled her eyes and marched over to her horse, dragging the creature past Nolan without another word. As she walked out, she thought she heard him chuckle. "Don't get too *heated* about it."

But, when she rounded on him a second time, he was walking away from her toward his own mount. *Men are animals,* she decided as she mounted her horse.

The small party rode in silence through the main gate and down the switchbacks as Caidy stewed in her annoyance and Nolan seemed content to ignore her. She traveled everywhere with Merric—and often, like today, with two other guards. She was strongly divided on how she felt about her entourage.

Being escorted by Merric wasn't that bad. He had a remarkable ability to fade into the background. He rarely intruded on her adventures, but she also felt incredibly safe with him nearby. He possessed an understated competence, which she admired. She often ventured into smaller villages or wandered down mountain trails with him quietly on her heels, silent and uncomplaining.

There was something exciting about being surrounded by more guards, as though she was the empress of the lands beyond the Unending Desert, towering over her people. But the novelty quickly wore off, and she chafed at the number of them between her and the people—*her* people—they passed.

"Why do you call him by his first name?" Nolan eased his mount next to hers.

"Who?" she replied, rubbing sweat out of her eyes.

"Your father, Lord Mattias. You just called him by his first name. Is that a Rosemoorian custom?"

"No," she said shortly, annoyed that Nolan had been here for a month and had yet to learn anything. "And it's none of your business how I do or do not refer to my father. Don't forget your place." Even as she snapped, she knew there wasn't much heat in the words. She *wanted* to talk, craved the distraction—even if she would never admit it.

Silence stretched between them for a moment. "I can help with that, if you want," Nolan piped up again. She shaded her eyes with a gloved hand and looked at him.

"Help me with what, exactly?"

"The heat." Nolan gestured to the sweat dripping off what felt like every inch of her body.

She felt her eyes widen, forgetting her noble indignation. "Really?"

"Yep." Nolan grinned unexpectedly at her as he handed over his reins. "Don't let me fall."

Before she could respond, he leaned toward her very suddenly, and pressed a thumb to her forehead. Immediately, she felt the hot, heavy air around her start to move, as though a spring breeze was following them. She heard one of the guards behind her start at Nolan's movement. He was new enough to court that they did not yet fully trust him, but she held up a hand. The breeze seemed to cling to her skin as she gestured. It was a very odd sensation.

"Any better?" he asked, smirking.

"Much," Caidy said, her tone friendlier than it had been before. "What exactly did you do?"

"The spell forces the still air to move around you, as if there's a breeze. It takes a lot less energy to move the air than it does to actually cool it, and since wind has a naturally cooling effect…" he trailed off, looking at her. "What?"

She handed his reins back, still marveling at the delicious breeze and thankful that the conversation between them had veered to a safer territory. "It's just interesting, that's all. I don't know much about magic."

Though she'd spent the better part of her twenty-one summers in royal instruction, her lessons were decidedly bland. She could courtesy fourteen different ways, knew dozens of proper dances, could cook a four-course meal for fifty, and speak three languages—but when it came to magic, she was a novice. *Magic is best left to mages,* her tutors had claimed. *You will have no use for it.*

Nolan nodded, apparently unsurprised by her ignorance. "It's not that complicated, but unless you work with magic and the connection to the Winds on the Mystical Plane, most people don't really understand it."

Overcome by fascination, she spoke over the last half of his sentence. "There are different ways to do that, right? Connect to the plane?" Or so she thought she remembered—pretty much all her knowledge came from digging through old scrolls when nobody was looking. Beyond their world was the Mystical Plane, the source of magic and, according to legend, where the Gods originated. It was all very abstract, in her opinion. *Planes and Gods and magic—how does anyone keep it straight if you can't see it?*

She belatedly realized Nolan was answering her question. "There are three ways. The vast majority of mages are born with some sort of natural connection to the plane and the Winds of Magic. Most people have a very tenuous bond. They can perform small charms, make potions, that sort of thing. A lot of the time people won't even know they have the connection. They're just slightly better at certain tasks, like lighting fires or making bandages. Make sense?" Nolan's normally polite deference was overcome by academic curiosity, and his words flowed together quickly.

She nodded, settling comfortably into the moment for the first time all morning. The sweat on the back of her neck was drying, and it was a magnificent feeling. "Hedgewitches, right? Those aren't the kind of people who have to register with the Aerian Lycantheum, are they?"

Nolan paused. "Depends on who you ask," he replied, his tone more guarded. "According to the founding charter of the Lycantheum, anyone with any connection to the plane is required to register and serve the Empire."

There was an odd tension behind the words. Before she could comment, he continued, "Now occasionally, people are born with a much stronger connection to the plane. For whatever reason—there are many theories—they have more ability to control and manipulate the Winds of Magic to serve their needs. Those people are what you think of when you think of a 'mage.' In the Empire, the Lycantheum finds, registers, and trains these mages."

She got the sense he was shifting them away from a dangerous conversation. *Interesting*. Playing along, she replied, "What happens if a powerful mage isn't trained?"

He scratched his nose, appearing to consider the question. "You've heard of the Amarentine Guard and the Glittering Hand?" While the names sounded familiar, she couldn't place them. Her confusion must have been evident because Nolan clarified, "A group in the Lycantheum specializes in stopping rogue mages. Mages have to be trained to control their power, or they become consumed. They'll cause massive arcane accidents, or summon Rakatash's monsters from the Divine Realms.

"Usually it's unintentional, but sometimes it's malicious. The Lycantheum finds these mages and stops them from hurting innocent people. In theory, anyway. As you might imagine, in practice it's a little more complicated." He looked like he wanted to continue talking, though he paused instead, pursing his lips.

She remembered where she'd heard the name before. According to her history lessons, the Glittering Hand had been the personal magical assassins of the Emperor nearly eighty years ago, in the time just before the Cleansing. After, when the Lycantheum was created, the Glittering Hand had been given broader authority across the Empire.

"What's the third way?" she asked, as Nolan let the silence stretch between them. They were almost at the bottom of the hill now, approaching Iera. The road opened through a patchwork of fields to the solid walls surrounding the city.

Flowering bushes and trees were everywhere, and Caidy watched a flock of shockingly purple butterflies flutter through the stagnant air. Her skin was pleasantly cool now, and her mood had significantly improved with both the magic and conversation.

"Hm?" Nolan looked at her, cocking an eyebrow.

"You said there were three ways," Caidy replied, ticking the points off on her fingers. "You told me about hedge-witches and regular mages. What's the third way?"

"Oh, that. Temple Orders. Some people swear allegiance to a God or Goddess. Of those worshippers, a small number are given divine powers. It's different from people with a connection to the Winds."

"How's it different?" There were more people on the road now, and the guards they rode with made a tighter circle around them.

Nolan sighed heavily. She frowned at him, and he raised a hand. "It's not a bad question. It's just complicated. Temple mages don't have to register, because the Imperial Authority is afraid that forcing them to join the Lycantheum will offend whatever God gives them power. See?"

"So Temple mages don't have any connection to the Winds and the plane? Their power is just from the Divine Realms?"

He shrugged. "That's what we think, anyway. We're not sure since nobody has actually seen a God in centuries."

The guard on Nolan's left looked shocked. "That's blasphemy," he muttered, drawing the divine sign, a clockwise spiral, on his chest. From the front of the group, Merric made a small gesture—a twitch of his fingers, really—and the guard who had spoken fell back a pace. Nolan appeared supremely unruffled by the guard's reaction, fidgeting with a pouch at his waist as they rode.

She tucked a struggling curl behind her ear as she considered. She, like her parents, worshipped Caldir, the Patron God of Rosemoor and the Tender of the Earth. There were festivals in the fall and spring, and plenty of ordinary services. Her mother attended worship services every dawn. Caidy only went when she was ordered to.

The Gods had vanished from the mortal plane hundreds of years ago, long before the Cleansing, just as Nolan had said. Faith was comforting, and certainly served a purpose across the Province, but she could see the value in his points. *Why spend time and tithes on a creature no one could prove still existed?*

Considering, she absently looked around. She itched to dismount and go wander through the crowds, meeting traders, buying sticky cakes, and splashing fountain water on her cheeks. She loved spending entire days in the city, drinking strawberry twilsey in the Silver Maiden eating house, catching performances of jugglers and magicians in Honey District, buying trinkets, and visiting businesses. That was what she and Alex used to do before he'd left and life had gotten complicated.

For a brief moment, her heart beat painfully once more and she found herself blinking away sudden tears. *Gods cursed feelings*, she sniffed to herself. *I didn't ask for you and I don't want you. Leave me be.* If he wasn't interested any longer, neither was she. She was the heir to the throne of Rosemoor, for Caldir's sake! One of the most powerful nobles in the four provinces! *I have more important things to do than be heartbroken.*

She fixed a pleasant smile on her face and followed the path her bodyguards cut through the bustling streets. Regretfully, she waved forlornly to Annabeth, her favorite honeycomb tea seller, as their small group made their way to City Hill. *Maybe after this meeting, if it goes well, I'll stop,* she promised herself.

CHAPTER 9

———

4th Day of the Harvest Moon

Iera was built in a semicircle on the lakeshore, snuggled between the Somber Mountains and Feather Lake. A hill rose in the center of the city, upon which the mayor's house and offices were. City Hill hosted most of the administrative efforts for Iera, including the magistrate courts. Noble homes were built into the terraced sides of the hill, great city manors that sprawled into one another.

They had just ridden through Market District, one of the busiest areas of the city in the morning. It was also one of Caidy's favorite places in Iera. She loved how confetti fluttered through the air during festivals and how there was always *something* happening.

Honey District, to the south, was vibrant. It was the home of entertainers, of ribbons of magical light threaded between buildings too close together, of masquerades and pastries soaked in brandy. Caidy had only spent two evenings there—one with Alex before he left, and another with Valarie, Geoffrey's older sister. Both nights were a blurred haze of wine, music, dancing, and sparkling light. She and

Alex had snatched breathless kisses behind a shrine and then danced under the stars as lute music wove through the summer breeze. The memory still sent light shivers down her spine.

Lately, when she came to the city it was to Guild Quarter or City Hill. The former housed the powerful trade cartels, merchant guilds, and shipping magnates who controlled the economy of the province. Guild Quarter was the business district of the city. People bustled about, moving goods, negotiating shipping costs, and bribing workers. She had wasted many hours in meetings with influential guild leaders, learning how to say one thing and mean another.

Her nose wrinkled at the memories. Caidy dreaded meetings with the guilds more than just about anything else. She chafed at the delayed diplomacy and struggled to bite her tongue for the sake of argument.

Though now that she thought about it, she was fairly sure that Raven House, the headquarters of the Blades, was somewhere in Guild, near the Dock District. *I could ask Merric to check up on Alex, see how things are going*, she contemplated briefly. Then, just as hastily, she discarded the notion. *He made it perfectly clear he wants nothing to do with me. Two can play at that game.* She fixed her gaze straight ahead, purposefully ignoring the lump in her throat.

The small group continued through the busy streets, winding up High Road, a wide thoroughfare that curved around the hill. Two stairs led directly to the top of City Hill, bisecting the road, but they would have had to climb them on foot. High Road was beautiful, lined with blossoming flower bushes, the occasional street vendor, and ribbons fluttering in the late summer air. It was designed to show off the cleanest, shiniest parts of Iera to visiting dignitaries.

"See that?" Nolan pointed into a small square off the road to the left. In the center, standing on an old wooden box by a fountain, a young man dressed in garish colors was making the clear waters contort into fascinating shapes. A small watery horse galloped through the air around the square, leaving translucent flowered vines in its wake. Children giggled as streams of water danced through skirts and sleeves, and the small crowd gasped in wonder.

Caidy smiled. "That's one of my favorite things about Iera. All of the street performers."

Nolan shrugged. "Sure. It's a great example of someone who has a connection to the Winds but nothing more than a link. He doesn't have any control over the actual power behind magic. That performer is just a conduit for the Winds."

"It's still beautiful," Caidy said, watching the performance until their horses rounded a curve and it faded from view.

"I suppose," Nolan replied. "It's not very useful, though."

Bristling, she frowned. "Does something have to be useful to have value? That seems like an awfully limited perspective."

He held up a hand. Instinctively, she opened her mouth to keep talking to argue with him the same way she and Alex used to bicker. Before she could gather her thoughts, the mage started speaking. "That's not what I'm saying. My point is, based on our discussion of the types and uses of magic, that's an example of weak, useless magic. It still has arguable value, sure, but nothing compared to the power that could exist."

"What determines how much power exists, then? What makes one mage more powerful than another, or one act of magic more worthy?" She did her best to ignore the prickle of annoyance at his dismissive tone.

Rubbing his chin, the mage took a few moments to answer. "You've managed to ask one of the most complicated questions in magical studies," he said finally. "There's a lot of debate on the subject."

"How do you not know how much power someone does or doesn't have?" *Mages*, she decided, *are wholly impractical.*

"So, the most common mages are in the Temple Orders. They get their powers directly from whatever God they're sworn to. In theory, it can be an infinite amount. In practice, well, nobody's actually talked to a God in a millennia. We haven't had any prophets or God-touched walk among us for centuries." He appeared to ignore her guardsman who again drew the sign on his chest. "So practically, their magic is limited to whatever their God is best at. Fritha's Maidens can do some pretty powerful healing spells, but that's constrained by a lot we don't understand."

Even more confused, she stared blankly at him. With a sigh, he continued, "It's like this. Orders need their God to give them power. Right? Except nobody knows if the Gods are even still around. So, they pray, and they build up faith. They make tithes, hold holidays. The High Priests claim that at certain times of the year, their Gods are more powerful— closer to the Mortal Plane. So, they can only perform truly great feats of magic at certain times. Most of the time, they can do small magics, make trinkets, those sorts of things. You follow?"

"I think so," Caidy replied slowly, all thought of annoyance once more overcome with curiosity. "So that's the Temple Orders. Their power depends on whoever they worship. What about the others?"

"Everyone else gets their power from their connection to the Winds, which we don't really understand. I mean," he corrected himself. "We kind of understand. We don't know *what* gives people a stronger or weaker connection, but we know some mages are much more powerful than others. It's a double-edged sword, though, because the more powerful a mage, the more unstable they tend to be. That's what the Glittering Hand spends their time dealing with—mages who've lost themselves in the Winds, or gone mad, mostly."

Her head hurt, and she sighed heavily. "I don't understand what all this has to do with how powerful someone is or isn't."

"Think of it this way. Mages who are close to the Winds tend to be very dangerous but not very versatile. They can pretty much only do very big acts of magic, but they don't have tight control. If a mage with a close connection to the Winds was doing that," he gestured back behind them, in the direction the performer had been, "there would probably be a waterspout ripping up cobblestones, or a sudden thunderstorm flooding the market."

"Okay, that sounds definitionally very powerful."

"Well, yes. But the thing that's hard is telling *within* the different groups who is more or less powerful. Who's to say if that water magician is more powerful than an illusionist at a carnival? You see?"

Deciding it seemed like a very academic distinction—and that she had endured enough of Nolan's slightly hard-to-follow explanations for the morning—Caidy was relieved that they had just arrived at the mayor's offices on the top of City Hill.

The summit held a stunning view. Administrative buildings crowned the western side of the hilltop, closer to the castle, while the eastern side opened toward Feather Lake. A grand plaza lined with manicured trees led to the magnificent panorama over the cliff where the ground fell away to Dock District below. Caidy could smell the fish-scented, freshwater breeze as it whipped through the air. It was much cooler up here above the city, with nothing between them and the wind.

Far below, a fleet of fishing boats bobbed cheerfully toward the center of the lake, and she could hear the shouted instructions of dock workers. Across the lake, farmland and small towns curled along the shores, leading into the foothills and woodland beyond. Everything was bright and sunny, bathed in the nostalgic light of a fading summer.

Regretfully, she turned away from the sparkling lake, dismounted, and handed her reins to one of the guards. *Business first.* Flanked by Merric and Nolan, she led the way into the mayor's office.

Mayor Eldon Kluk reminded Caidy of a lazy, sleepy cat that had just woken from a nap in a bad temper. He was settled on a poofy purple chair behind a desk covered in useless shiny trinkets, his fingers steepled underneath his beard. When she entered, he smiled and opened both arms toward her in greeting but did not stand.

The meeting did not improve from that point on. She *hated* trying to reason with the mayor. He was a decidedly unreasonable person, who gave her the vague impression he thought she was not very bright.

"We don't have the guard contingent you're asking for," she snapped, nearly losing her temper and drumming her fingers on her hip. "I'm not hiding anything from you."

"You just don't seem to *understand* the problem I'm facing, my Lady." She detested how the mayor seemed to chew thoroughly on each word before spitting it out. "Crime is up. My City Guard doesn't have the support to keep our people safe. It's as simple as that." A disdainful sneer colored the words. She felt her cheeks flush.

"And as I've explained to you," she replied, speaking with measured patience, "I can't just supplement your forces with the Provincial Guard at will. The Guard is stationed across the province and is the sole authority protecting many of our smaller towns. Iera has hundreds of trained guards and the barracks from the Castle in the event of a disaster. You'll just have to make do. Talk to the Lycantheum," she pointed at Nolan. "They might be able to teach your guards some tricks to make their jobs easier."

The mage, who had been observing the conversation, cocked an eyebrow. "Maybe..." he said. "There should already be mages embedded in the Guard though, based on the Lycantheum reports I've read." The look she shot at him could have melted steel. *Useless.* He smiled blandly back at her, apparently unimpressed by her anger.

"Precisely the problem!" Kluk shifted his attention back to her. "I've used the resources I have. Ierian citizens aren't safe. Just yesterday three dancers in Honey District were assaulted. The nobles are up in arms."

Something sparked in the back of Caidy's head. She felt her eyes widen, and then her words tumbled out, faster than she could think. "Good! If they're up in arms, that solves everything!" She reached across the mayor's desk without invitation, grabbing a scroll and piece of charcoal, and started to scribble notes. "There are what, five major houses and at least ten minor houses with property in the city? Each house keeps their own guard detail, and they patrol the area around each estate."

She roughly sketched City Hill, starring the map as she listed the names of the houses. Nolan looked over her shoulder, curious. "Between the houses, they can cover the entire hill, and a few streets out from the base at least. You put the City Guard further out, in the outskirts of Iera and work with the noble guards to protect the city. You'll still be short, but it'll be less thin if this is an intentional partnership rather than happenstance."

Kluk leaned over the paper, combing his beard with one hand. His bushy eyebrows rose to his thick hairline as he reviewed the notes. "That… could work," he admitted, grudgingly. "I'll have to talk to the Noble Council."

Caidy flapped a hand, new energy coursing through her. "I'll speak to our head steward and have my house make the announcement. That'll bring the major houses in, and the minor families will fall in line. It's in everyone's interest." She stepped back from the table, folding her arms. It would work. She felt it in her gut. It wasn't a perfect solution—they needed to increase recruitment efforts for the City Guard—but they had thousands of ways to do that.

Her mind buzzed with possibilities. Vaguely she heard Kluk clear his throat and thank them for the meeting. She nodded politely and then marched out of the room, Nolan in tow. "Do you…" she started, but Merric wordlessly handed her a sheaf of paper and charcoal. "Thank you." Caidy absently started sketching down her thoughts, smudging her fingertips with charcoal. Merric silently led the pair out of the mayor's office and back toward the city plaza.

Nolan and Merric whiled away an hour while Caidy sat cross-legged under a juniper tree overlooking Feather Lake, engrossed in the flow of ideas from thought to word to scroll. While she couldn't conjure more City Guard out of thin air— her mind briefly flitted to Nolan, wondering if he would be able to—perhaps she could fix the bigger problems facing the force that protected Iera.

When she was finished, she rolled up the papers tightly and handed them back to Merric. Ideas still fluttered around her head, a calming sensation rather than an overwhelming one. Her veins hummed with a pleasant, tickling energy. Spinning on her heel, she tapped Nolan on the shoulder.

The mage, who was arguing animatedly with one of the other guards, stopped mid-sentence and turned around. "Yes?"

Caidy bounced on the balls of her feet. "I'm ready to walk," she announced. "Want to join me?" She heard Merric sigh behind her and chose to ignore it. "Come on! We can take the Noble Stair." Without waiting for an answer, she spun and skipped toward the northern side of the summit.

"I'm willing to bet nobles never use the Noble Stair," she heard Nolan mutter under his breath, and Merric snorted. The two men followed her toward the staircase, Merric ordering the other guards to attend the horses with a gesture.

The Noble Stair was one of two ancient sets of steps that served as a quick way to reach the top of City Hill. It was a nice idea, but the hill was steep with houses built nearly on top of one another, the layers of history like rings in a tree. The estates at the foot of the hill sprawled, with delicate gardens and ivy-covered walls, but the higher up the hill, the smaller the houses became. Near the top, where they currently stood, houses leaned into one another and receded back into the stonework, carving away the land itself to make way for humanity. The Noble Stair was a precarious path, weaving in between these houses down to the base of the hill.

It was one of her favorite places in the city. She loved the poetic crumble of stone and the winding of vines, the little puffs of dust and the snatches of hidden conversation that drifted from homes as you descended. Years ago, when she and Alex had explored Iera together, this was one of their hideaways. Nobody used the stairs. There were just too many to be practical. So they had clambered up and down, hiding behind walls, playing bandits and guards, and skidding down the hill.

An uncomfortably familiar pang settled in her chest as she thought of Alex. She had done a remarkably good job putting him out of her mind since he had humiliated her yesterday. Her cheeks flamed red at the thought. The awful moment had played out, over and over, in her mind for the rest of that morning. Try as she might, she couldn't figure out why he had been so cold. The last time she had seen him—the last time they had been together—everything had been perfect.

It had been the third day of the Spring Festival, and they had spent the morning exploring the fairgrounds, sampling delicacies, and listening to music. Alex had gripped her hand, running a finger over her knuckles, and tugged her away. Following old game trails, they had climbed a mountain to a small pond tucked away near the summit. They had splashed and doused each other in fresh mountain water and curled together in the clearing as the afternoon sun sloped through the sky. Hours had slipped away, vanishing in whispers and laughter.

The sunset that evening had gilded the clearing. Caidy remembered how her tunic had dried slightly stiff, the fabric itchy. Her skin tingled with the echo of Alex brushing against her collarbone. She could feel the warm late summer breeze from the mountains spinning around them, her hair tangling over her eyes, Alex's magnificently windswept smile...

She had relived every second of those last, precious hours a thousand times. When he had been gone the next day, she had written down, as clearly as she could recall, the time they had spent together. It was important that she not forget, she knew. She was terrified of losing those warm moments, where time had frozen around them.

Caidy felt tears build in the back of her throat as the memories washed through her. Swallowing painfully, she focused back on the stairs in front of her.

"We should stop by Annabeth's cart on the way to the castle. She has the best honeycomb tea in the city," she explained to the mage.

"Lead on then, my Lady." Nolan winked at her, and she saw Merric stifle a smile. The other two guards turned, beginning to guide their mounts back down the main road to meet them near the gates. Ignoring the men, Caidy pointed her nose in the air haughtily and started down the stairs, each one helping her bury the emotions trembling just under her confidence.

CHAPTER 10

———

5th Day of the Harvest Moon

This, Alex decided, was how he was going to die. The piles of papers on his desk seemed to loom higher with each passing hour. His shoulders ached from hunching over the scrolls, his vision blurred with exhaustion, and Jakob—Alex had discovered—had a grating habit of humming softly as he worked.

Alex had spent the past two days pouring over the minutiae of life in Rosemoor in the second-floor office he shared with Jakob. Crop estimates and market reports were in a disorganized heap to his left. Stacked neatly behind him were rows of maps, both large and small. To the right, garrison reports dating back every month for the past three years were organized chronologically. Scattered on the desk in front of him intelligence requests and analyses from across the Empire tumbled together.

Cracking his knuckles loudly, he rolled his head a few times. His neck creaked in a very satisfying manner while his stomach grouched with hunger. He'd been working all day, cramped in his wooden chair, and he had a horrendous headache settling in behind his left eye.

Swallowing a tremendous yawn, Alex reached for another scroll. He would call it a night after this one, he promised himself. He'd do some exercises to stay fresh and get the blood pumping, grab a couple of fish kabobs on his way home, and curl up under a blanket in bed. Eventually he'd dig himself out from under the piles—just not today.

Catching up on the reports was the worst part of his job. He'd forgotten just how bad it had been when he had arrived in Danen although then he'd been finishing his training, which made it more reasonable. A year ago, he had still been in training. The Danen Warden, Ingrid, had read the incoming reports. His job had been writing out the details of their investigations while she added supporting intelligence. Now, with the responsibility of the province on his shoulders, he was struggling to bring himself up to speed.

If that weren't bad enough, he read slower than a pirate three drinks in and found himself constantly returning to papers he had already read, skimming for a fact or weeding through to a hidden insight. Rosemoor was very different from Danen. The problems were more political, and the crime was less overtly violent. Finding patterns in these reports and bringing that intelligence to his work was half his training, and he knew it was important. But that didn't mean he had to enjoy it.

As he tried to decipher a map depicting something like rural Provincial Guard patrol areas, the door opened. Jakob had left a few hours ago to bring a stack of reports up to Lord Mattias, and Alex stifled a moan, anticipating the tuneless humming.

Jakob stuck his head through the door. He looked as though he had been swimming. "So it's raining," he remarked conversationally as Alex grinned in spite of his mood. It had been pouring for the past day and a half, bucketing down sheets of rain in one of the last truly terrible thunderstorms of the late summer. Alex loved gloomy weather. The past two nights he'd gone wandering outside Iera in the rain, examining the swollen rivers and rivulets coursing down the streets, and enjoying the cleansing sound of thunder. Those nighttime explorations were half the reason he was having so much trouble focusing today.

"I can see that," Alex replied, taking the conversation as an excuse to lean back and prop his ankles up on the desk between two messy piles of paper.

Jakob used a spare uniform to towel off his hair, shaking his head much the same way a horse shakes its mane. Balling up the damp linen, he chucked it into a corner and then turned back to Alex, his forehead wrinkling in a slight frown. "You look like you're about to be hanged."

Alex rubbed his eyes and scraped his fingers several times through his hair until it stuck up at odd angles. "I hate reading," he confessed. "I have a terrible time with it." His eyes were itchy with exhaustion from staring at Jakob's meticulously tiny writing.

Jakob shrugged. "Makes sense. That's why you're not an Archivalist." He crossed and knelt to pick up a jumble of scrolls that had fallen off the table in an unceremonious heap. Untangling them, he rolled each document and placed it back on the desk. When he'd finished the careful, practiced work, he rapped the top of Alex's boot with a knuckle. "Let's get moving."

"Moving where?" Alex was on his feet before he had finished the thought. He would take any excuse to get out of this room.

"We're going to go grab a bite and talk." Jakob picked up a coin purse and fastened it to his belt. "You need a break."

Alex nodded and followed Jakob downstairs. The two men wrapped tightly woven woolen cloaks about their shoulders, and Jakob settled a wide-brimmed, oiled hat on his head. Alex double checked that he had, in fact, repaired the hole in the sole of his boot before he'd left Danen and followed the Archivalist out into the lashing rain.

"Follow me, I know a place in Honey with the best apricot-stewed boar in the city." Jakob pitched his voice above the patter of rain so Alex could hear and then set off toward Market District, rounding the base of City Hill. A pair of guardsmen in the livery of House Myreall huddled under an awning, nearly hidden behind sheets of rain. A woman hurried past them across the street, heading toward Dock District, her head bowed against the storm.

"Where's a mage when you need one?" he called to Jakob over the splatter of rain. "Could do with a shielding spell right about now."

The Archivalist's laugh echoed over the storm. "One of the many downsides of the Cleansing. If only Emperor Asim had remembered the storms, perhaps he wouldn't have ordered all the mages slaughtered."

"It's because Tanunt is a desert. They don't get rain." Alex did his best to wipe water out of his eyes. "Asim never realized how important mages are to quality of life."

Hints of the Cleansing still scarred the world, though nearly seven decades had passed since that dark age. He had never realized how strange the Empire was until he'd spent several months in Swansea. The Free City had no such laws against the unlawful use of magic, and as such, mages flocked there. It was the only place south of the Somber Mountains on this side of the Unending Desert where mages could live without fear of persecution.

The Imperially sanctioned hunt and slaughter of every mage living in the Mezrani Empire had shattered confidence and faith in the Imperial Authority—trust the Empire was still struggling to rebuild. Alex remembered his shock when he learned that Rosemoor had sheltered magicians fleeing the magical assassins of the Glittering Hand, smuggling them through mountain passes to refuge in Karath, or on ships in the Viridian Sea. The Lycantheum's mage hunters had scoured the Empire, ruthlessly butchering anyone they encountered with magical powers.

Since that time, tensions between Rosemoor and the Empire had risen to fever pitch. Lord Mattias had never made any secret of his dislike and distrust of the Imperial Authority, and Alex knew it was a matter of time until the Imperials decided to stop tolerating the Lord of Rosemoor and installed their own puppet ruler. Really the fact that the Roussels still ruled the province at all was nothing more than an accident of fate. The Valance family estates had been attacked by a band of mages, and the only children old enough to rule had been killed.

In Rosemoor, Alex had come to understand that the Blades held a precarious position. They represented the Imperial Authority to all who lived here, but according to the law of the land, the Amaranth Khmal was independent from the Empire. While this worked better in some cases than in others, it gave them much-needed flexibility and the ability to gain the trust of the ruling family. *That's the critical piece, trust*, Alex thought. If the Roussels didn't trust the Blades, their advice and influence were severely limited.

They splashed down a back alley of Market District into Honey. The rain had slackened as they walked, and more people were out and about as they entered the entertainment district.

It didn't seem to matter what time of day it was, Honey District was always shimmering with energy and crowded with revelers. The buildings leaned together as though they had a secret to keep. It was early evening, and as the stalls in Market District were shuttering for the night, Honey was coming alive with jugglers, dancers, magicians, and the tantalizing, mouth-watering smell of fried dough and elderberry wine.

Underneath the gilded atmosphere in the shadow of rain, the underworld lurked. Alex watched a band of pickpockets dip their fingers into the purses of at least three different, unknowing victims before melting back into the wet shadows. A lovely woman with full lips and a flimsy dress gazed at a rotund merchant with a predatory smile that didn't reach her eyes. An older man passed a small pouch across his stall counter, handing it and a steaming apple bun to a customer in one fluid gesture.

Alex loved the way this other world, one of trickery and deceit, intermingled with the gaudy dazzle of everyday life. He always had. Caidy saw glitter and laughter and magic, but he saw intentions and darkness wherever he went. Now, it was a hazard of his work since his job was to keep his finger on the pulse of the underworld to protect people like her from danger. His natural distrust was an asset.

Jakob shouldered through the crowd filling the streets despite the light rain. "Did you come to Honey much when you used to live here?"

"Mostly for the festivals," Alex admitted. "Not as often as I'd have liked."

The Archivalist flashed a grin at him. "You ever been to the Bustling Mushroom?" When he shook his head, Jakob clapped him on the shoulder. "You're in for a treat."

CHAPTER 11

5th Day of the Harvest Moon

Anyone who, like Alex, had grown up in Iera knew about the Bustling Mushroom. The place was an infamous institution in Honey District, as old as the Imperial Age. Built over five hundred years ago, the crowded little tavern used to be called the Honey Emporium. But, a century back, a fire had ripped through Honey District, burning the upper stories to ash. When the building had been rebuilt, the upper floors ballooned over the stone foundations, making the little tavern look distinctly fungal. Its good-natured owners had renamed the building the Bustling Mushroom, painting a new sign to hang above the bright blue door and adding a plethora of fungus-inspired foods to their menu.

The small tavern had a decidedly comfortable atmosphere, Alex decided as they stepped inside, like the hug of an old friend or the smell of dinner after a hard day's work. It was the kind of place where thousands of patrons over hundreds of years had worn smooth seats in the hard wood benches, carved initials on the walls, and nicked the tables with eating knives. And best of all, in Alex's opinion, it was a predominantly local affair. Iera's visitors tended toward larger and cleaner—or flashier and dirtier—taverns closer to the heart of Honey District. The patrons of the Bustling Mushroom all had their own tankards, tables, and chairs they returned to night after night.

Jakob, apparently, was one of those regulars. A sparkling, fiery-haired server winked at him, brushing his arm with her own and placing two tankards full of amber beer and a platter of fried asparagus drizzled with some sort of fish sauce on the table. The Archivalist nodded his thanks with a shadow of a wink in return and turned his attention to Alex. "So what pieces are you missing?" he asked conversationally, taking a swig from his tankard. A smudge of froth clung to his nose, though he didn't seem to notice.

Alex tapped the handle of his tankard, thinking carefully. "I'm mostly working to get a good idea of the big picture," he said slowly. "It's a very different perspective on Rosemoor than I'm used to having."

Jakob nodded, smearing some fish sauce around the plate with an asparagus prong before crunching down on the fried vegetable. "My reports say you only spent time in Danen before coming home. Is that right?" It sounded like a casual question, but Alex had an itch that Jakob was probing for some sort of information.

"I did my training at the Citadel and supported a Shadow mission in Swansea before being assigned to the Warden Corps. My first official work was in Danen, supporting the Warden contingent." Alex sipped the beer cautiously and then heartily. It was very good with a hint of apple and honey in the hops.

"Well that makes good sense." Jakob swallowed another asparagus trident and then twitched a finger toward their server. "Keivah, love, are they cooking up anything new?"

The redhead approached their booth and leaned over the table conspiratorially, again brushing Jakob's arm. A bouncing curl slipped over her shoulder as she spoke animatedly, moving her hands to complement her words. "We're working on a new spring mushroom and chicken roast, if you want to try it for us!" Her voice was soft and teasing.

"That sounds delightful," he grinned broadly at her. "You always know how to treat a man, love."

She straightened and tossed her head back in a laugh. Every motion she made was fluid and sultry, like a draft of perfectly aged whiskey. "Anything for you, Jake." Keivah smiled the words and flounced away from them toward the kitchen, twitching her hips back and forth. Alex looked at Jakob with raised eyebrows and sipped his beer.

Jakob snorted. "As you've probably noticed, Hendrick keeps Raven House as bare as possible. It means we both do a lot of different jobs. We've both got our own, unofficial Whisperers, like Keivah, outside of whatever you come up with formally."

"How long has Rosemoor been without a Warden?" Alex sampled the asparagus. It was very good, perfectly crispy and not dripping with oil.

Pausing for a moment to think, Jakob absently whistled through his teeth. "It's been several months. We've gone through two since Dunbar left. He was Warden when you were still here."

Alex vaguely remembered a middle-aged man with salt-and-pepper hair and a beaked nose in the halls of the Citadel.

"Mattias drove both out," the Archivalist continued, "I think partially out of spite. He and Dunbar got on well, but Dunbar was pushed out by our first Commissar. The Authority decided they wanted to forge a new relationship with the Roussels, which was a little less chummy."

"But the whole point of the Warden Corps is to foster goodwill and build relationships," Alex mused. "It doesn't make sense to antagonize the ruling family of a powerful province."

Jakob shrugged, raising his hands. "You're telling me. Anyway, mission accomplished; the trust Dunbar built up for us has eroded. Hendrick and Mattias get along alright, but the Commissars have made it exceedingly difficult for them to spend any time alone. Official channels say that a Commissar must be present at any conversations." His tone was flat and dry.

Alex chose his words carefully, knowing he was treading in dangerous waters. He did not yet have a sense of whether or not Jakob liked the presence of the Mezrani. "Do you have any idea why the Imperial Authority has increased its presence in the Provincial Kingdoms? We saw something similar in Danen."

"Yes, we got the report on that from Danila after the fact. Hendrick was furious that the Imperial Authority hadn't bothered to tell any of the Blades what they were doing until the coup was over."

"You mean the Lord Commissioner in Danen had no idea?" Alex was surprised. He didn't know the Lord Commissioner in Danen very well. The Blade presence in the southern province was much larger than in Rosemoor, and he had spent most of his time in the countryside with Ingrid. "You're kidding."

"Not according to Hendrick," Jakob took another swig of beer. "I thought he was going to strangle Danila on the spot when she gave him the news. I haven't seen him that furious in years. I mean, I can't believe it either—the Blades backing a coup in Danen to place a competing trade cartel on the throne? It never would have happened a decade ago. But to your question," he rubbed his thumb along the smooth edge of the table. "I don't know. I've got my own opinions, of course, but I can't say for certain. I also haven't been to the Capital District in years. I don't exactly have current information about what the current whims of the Imperial Authority are."

It was a guarded answer, and Alex sensed he had more than a hunch. Jakob, after all, was in close contact with the Archivalists at the Citadel, near Mezrani City. It seemed highly unlikely that he didn't have good information. But, in his position, Alex knew he would have made the same calculation. He was a fresh face in Rosemoor, and an unknown actor. Jakob had no reason to trust him with his opinions on the Authority. Alex could well be on the payroll of one of the many powerful noble families of Tanunt, gathering information about traitors to the Empire.

Keivah returned, carrying a steaming platter of chicken so tender it was falling off the bone drenched with tiny button mushrooms in a thick, savory sauce. She expertly slid the dish onto the table and refilled Jakob's beer with a pitcher held in her other hand. "Anything else I can get you?" She pitched her voice over the burbling crowd, bracing her free hand on her hip.

"This looks delicious, love." Jakob smiled at her. "Hear anything interesting today?"

Alex watched Keivah's large eyes flick to him and then back to Jakob. "He's the new Warden," Jakob said softly, his voice just loud enough to reach the pretty maid's ears. She took a worn cloth from her apron and leaned closer to the men, running the cloth absently over the table.

"I've got three tidbits," her voice was hushed with a dramatic secrecy. Alex resisted the urge to roll his eyes; Keivah clearly relished sharing the day's gossip with Jakob. People became Whisperers for the Blades for all sorts of reasons, but the sense of drama and grandeur working with the Blades carried was one of the more popular motives. "Rumor is that the noble houses are being forced to contribute to the City Guard permanently, for one.

"That pretty dancer down in Dock—Esmeralda—was attacked after a show last week, also. No one knows who got her, but she's beat pretty bad. Word at the bar is that she tried to leave one of Rafe's folk and they jumped her." Keivah shook her head and clicked her tongue sorrowfully. "Always better to leave the rogues alone," she remarked wisely, making eye contact with Alex.

He raised his eyebrows skeptically. "Do I look like a rogue to you?"

Keivah tossed back her head in another laugh. "Nah. You look like you've got the fires of Iya in you, though, that's for certain. I'd bet you've got women lined up outside your lodgings, one for each night of the week." Jakob snorted into his beer, and Alex couldn't decide if he was offended or tickled by Keivah's comment.

"I've got a sense for these things," Keivah continued, unfazed. "I've half a mind to turn to matchmaking later this year. I'm much too pretty to wait tables the rest of my life. Isn't that right, Jake?" She looked at Jakob through lowered lashes.

"Couldn't have said it better myself, love." Jakob squeezed her hand. "You're the most beautiful woman in Rosemoor."

Her cheeks sparkled in a blush, and she twinkled a smile at Jakob once more. "You're too sweet."

The expression was painfully familiar, and images of Caidy's pretty blush rose, unbidden, to the front of Alex's memories. Grinding his teeth in frustration, he interrupted the casual flirtation. "Did you say there was a third piece of news?"

Sticking out her lower lip in a pout, Keivah sighed deeply. "You're all business. Aren't you? Jake, I liked the last one more. He was fun." She tossed her hair, red curls bouncing before continuing, "I've heard whispers that the dockmaster is going to increase supply bribes. With the nobles supporting the City Guard, that'll almost triple bribe money businesses have to pay out. I know our tavernmaster is in fits about it."

A man across the room raised his voice for a waitress, and Keivah tousled her curls as she straightened. "I'll be back for you later, Jake," she murmured with a hint of a wink and a flash of dimples.

"You know she's not wrong. You are a bit of a bore. Our last Warden was a blithering idiot, though," Jakob said in an undertone as Keivah sashayed off through the crowd. He grinned at Alex. "I like you much more."

"That bit about bribes is interesting," Alex replied absently, only half listening as he turned over the tidbits of information in his mind.

Jakob slurped mushroom sauce loudly and then spoke around his food. "It'll be interesting if it actually happens. Rumor's just rumor."

"Very wise," Alex replied sarcastically, and Jakob chuckled.

The Archivalist skewered a piece of chicken slathered in sauce and offered it to him. "I suspect we'll get along just fine, Laurent."

The two men spent another hour in the Bustling Mushroom. Jakob wanted to hear about the Citadel and his training. Alex probed him for more information on the Roussels and the state of the province. He discovered that Jakob was no lightweight. The slender Archivalist matched him drink for drink with no signs of slowing.

When he grew tired and decided drinking himself into oblivion wasn't his brightest idea, Alex made his excuses to leave for the night. He stepped out of the warmth and chatter of the Bustling Mushroom, sloshing out into the downpour. Little rivers of water spiderwebbed through the cobblestone streets, and most of the revelers in Honey were huddled under awnings or crowded into entertainment houses.

By the time he made it to Dock District, the Honeypots who usually lounged near the edge of Honey had decided no profit was to be made that evening and returned to their pleasure houses. His head spun with drink, and he resigned himself to wandering the docks for a few hours until his brain cleared enough to sleep. The rain slackened, turning into a gentle shower rather than a painful attack.

Dock District was one of the rougher areas of Iera, haunted by the working class and sailors, not young noble-women and their escorts, but Alex found that suited him just fine. He'd always liked seeing places at night when stalls were shuttered and the only people out and about were up to no good. He lived in this shadowy world. He understood the surreptitious movements of street urchins out to find a meal and the weary, nervous paces of men who'd been held late to finish an urgent job.

He explored the back alleys, which curved around the base of City Hill—the fastest way through Dock District but also the most unguarded. Eventually finding his way to his lodgings, tucked away near a fish market and the gate to the main city, Alex stumbled up the stairs and fell, face-first, into a dreamless sleep.

CHAPTER 12

———

5th Day of the Harvest Moon

The past day had been an enchanting swirl of activity. Caidy was swept from meetings to court to dress fittings, expertly shepherded from appointment to appointment by Margot. The Harvest Festival was quickly approaching, and as the heiress of House Roussel, Caidy was expected to play a prominent role in the festivities.

Every year, the ruling family attended the Festival, quenching Iya's flames with Erius' autumnal moon. Great effigies were burnt in Iera City on the first night of the celebration, and visitors flocked from across the Empire to eat, drink, and be merry. It was one of her favorite festivals, and she delighted in meeting newcomers, appearing at parties across the City, and lighting the first effigy to herald Erius.

According to tradition, the second evening of the Festival was the Harvest Ball. Caidy was itching to see the final gown the tailors had spent months creating. In the tailor's quarters of the castle she waited eagerly for Octavio, the head tailor, to finish lacing the bodice of her undergown, vibrating with anticipation.

"My Lady," Octavio began patiently for at least the fourth time as he missed the last eyelet and nearly stabbed her in the back. "Please hold still."

Caidy rocked back slightly from where she had been hovering on the balls of her feet. She held very still for an instant—just long enough for the experienced tailor to expertly thread the last lace and tie an efficient bow—and then began to bob up and down again.

"And your arms, my Lady." Octavio slipped the silken dress over her head, fussed with the hem for a moment, and then tied a sash about her waist. "What do you think, my Lady?"

She spun, quickly at first, and then more slowly as she caught sight of herself in the mirror. Her hair was a nest of matted curls and her cheeks flushed, but despite how unkempt her appearance was, the gown was breathtaking.

The undergown that Octavio had so painstakingly laced up her back was a delicate blush of orange, which shimmered with fiery red and sunlit gold as she swirled to a stunned standstill. A hint of orange teased at the very top of her bodice, drawing the eye to her sharp collarbones, and at her elbows, the dress opened like the mouth of a lily, revealing ruched folds of golden tangerine cloth.

Her second layer, the over-gown, was a nearly iridescent shade of white, with gathered skirts opening to reveal a smudge of orange, and nipping in with a wide, old-fashioned sash, drawing the eye to her waist. Across the bodice, small shards of blue—she couldn't identify the stone—were arranged in a careful, triangular pattern. It was at once elegant and flirtatious, dignified and full of delight.

The true masterpiece, Caidy realized, as she stepped closer to the mirror, was how the tailors had stitched the dress as an offering to Erius the Arbiter himself. The God of Justice was most often depicted wrapped in the white robes of a magistrate, bearing a heavy golden medallion with his sign—three dots, the points of a triangle—inscribed upon it. As her skirts shifted, the light caught the same delicate triangle pattern in the iridescence, and she gasped.

"It's incredible, Octavio!" She smacked the tailor on the arm in glee. "It's like something out of legend!" She twirled, lifting her arms gracefully overhead. "I could be an acolyte, ready for temple—or a noblewoman preparing for a summer picnic!"

"You *are* a noblewoman," Margot muttered, and Caidy laughed.

"As you never let me forget." She smiled back at the maid. "It's beautiful, Octavio. You and your staff did an amazing job. I can't wait to show off your work."

Octavio bowed, bobbing his head like a hummingbird toward nectar. "You are too kind, my Lady." He paused and then continued, "We would be honored to keep it safe for you until the ball, of course."

She snorted. "I see you haven't forgotten how I ruined the midsummer gown you created." As Octavio opened his mouth in protest, she waved a hand with a forgiving smile.

"Caidy! You look like a consort worthy of Erius himself!" Geoffrey Valance barged into the fitting suite, bringing with him an air of drama. Bowing over her hand, he kissed her fingertips. "Words fail me."

"It's the dress," Caidy felt herself blush. "Octavio did—"

"You are truly breathtaking, my dove." Geoffrey straightened and tweaked one of Caidy's curls.

A sudden rush of righteous annoyance filled Caidy, making her fingertips tingle. Geoffrey *always* did this. Nobles were praised for the hard work of their servants. It didn't seem to matter how often she challenged him. He seemed incapable of understanding why it made her want to crawl out of her skin.

Biting back a retort, she turned toward Octavio. "I'd love if you could keep this safe for me until the ball," she murmured to the tailor, who bowed politely. "I would hate to damage such a masterpiece."

Octavio and Margot both politely ignored the interruption and made short work of the ribbons and ties that laced her into the gown. Geoffrey made a show of looking busily out one of the large windows across the room as Caidy quickly changed into her normal attire—a pretty lavender gown with a lace underskirt. While she changed, Margot tenderly packed away the festival dress, collected the various sashes, pins, and fabrics scattered about the room, and wisely disappeared out the servants' door.

As Octavio made to leave, Caidy caught his arm. "Thank you," she said, so softly it was nearly a whisper. "It's the most beautiful thing I've ever seen. Please tell the entire staff—you have my gratitude."

The head tailor blushed from his beard to his eyebrows and bowed deeply. "Yes, my Lady. You are too kind."

When the door latched with a gentle *click*, Geoffrey turned back to face her. Caidy, feeling his eyes on the back of her neck, did not turn, instead opting to try and finger-comb her curls into some sort of order.

Geoffrey creaked across the floor and wrapped his arms around her waist, kissing the side of her head in what she was sure was supposed to be a surprising, romantic gesture. "Thank goodness they're gone!" He hugged her tightly.

In another world, the Dreamworld, perhaps, Geoffrey was as kind and generous as the heroes of legend—the noble princes and brave travelers of her childhood fairytales, who listened intently to the problems of those well beneath their station in life. But in this world, she found him disappointingly similar to the other noblemen and merchants' sons she knew, more interested in his own social status than anything else. Sometimes shards of the man she knew he could be shone through the noble exterior, in the way he would thank a stable-hand or barter with a merchant. Most often, however, his noble sensibilities were firmly in place.

She tilted her head back to look up at him. Geoffrey was a good head and a half taller than she was—taller even than Alex, she thought ruefully. She felt the blush on her cheeks deepen, and her stomach churned with guilt at the thought. Geoffrey was attractive enough, in a very bland sort of way. When they had first met, she had convinced herself that he had the jawline of an adventuring sea captain and the strong eyebrows of a knight seeking justice. But, as the months had slipped by, Geoffrey had become decidedly less interesting. He always wore his brown hair combed the same direction, and his shoulders slumped in a slightly defeated manner.

His eyes frustrated her the most. Caidy loved seeing complicated emotions play out behind the sparkle of a glance—motivations and intentions dancing, evident to the discerning eye. When she looked at him, she most often saw a vague disinterest and contempt. He feigned it well, but she had quickly learned that he only ever listened to half of what anyone said—less, if he believed his station to be above the speaker. He spent lots of time choosing his words but rarely directly responded to people. She had spent much of the past few months attempting to move past his boredom, to connect deeply.

Caidy longed for Iya's spark, for the reassurance she and Geoffrey were made for one another, body and soul. And yet, despite the yearning in the pit of her stomach, no mountains moved when she looked at him. She felt nothing at all behind his gaze.

"You're going to be the talk of the ball." Drawing back slightly, he smiled at her. "I cannot wait to have you on my arm."

"*You'll* be on *my* arm," she replied, disentangling herself from him and starting to gather her hairpins, discarded on a dresser.

"Your what?" Geoffrey trailed after her, like a lost puppy. There were moments he reminded her irrepressibly of an overgrown hound pup with paws too big for its body and a tail that bashed into expensive vases. She swallowed a laugh.

"I need to eat dinner." Caidy began to thread the pins through her curls. "I don't have time for this."

He gripped her arm again, his fingers gentle. She felt herself reflexively harden with anger at his touch. "It's a compliment, Caidy. Most women would love me as their escort."

She felt her cheeks grow warm as she pulled away a second time. "I am not a prize you have won, Geoffrey." Her tone was sharp, and she leaned into the edge of her annoyance.

"No of course not. You are a prize I already have!" Geoffrey smiled at her as she turned back toward him.

In the back of her head, Caidy knew he meant it as a compliment. However, it was a very small, cool voice, and she ignored it readily. "Already have? Do you own me, then? Am I just some pretty thing for you to parade about?" She could feel her face flushing with anger and knew her hands trembled.

Taking a deep breath, she made to walk past him toward the door. He wouldn't follow her into her rooms—and if he tried, Margot would stop him. She had seen the normally reserved maid halt men before, telling them it was supremely ungentlemanly for a man to be in Caidy's rooms without express permission. *If only her powers extended to neutral ground, like the tailor's suite.*

"Well, you do look lovely by my side." Geoffrey sounded confused, and she watched his eyebrows meet at the center of his forehead. It looked as though he was chasing a just-out-of-reach thought. "Come here, dove. Let's go for a walk." He offered his arm, and Caidy drew herself up in indignation.

"We are *not* betrothed, and I am *not* some younger daughter seeking to make her name at court." Her voice, so recently hot with frustration, was chilled. She clenched her right hand in her skirts and felt the hairpins dig into her left palm as she tensed. "I have no interest in going for a walk right now, thank you very much."

His confusion flashed to anger. "What in the Hells are you talking about? By the Gods, Caidy, one moment you're happy and the next you're furious. I never know what you're going to attack me for!"

The familiar wash of rage swept through her. She felt slightly lightheaded and then very hot as her vision blurred. Geoffrey had a knack for making her furious. *You can't do this*, she reminded herself, fighting back fury. *Get control of it. This isn't worth destroying an alliance over.*

Her fists relaxed subconsciously, and she took two deep breaths through her nose. Geoffrey smelled of roses and soap—a very odd smell for a man. She focused on it. As she breathed, her vision sharpened again, and the ground beneath her feet felt steady. *Just ask him to leave. Give yourself space before you do something you regret.*

"It's nothing. I overreacted." Her voice, she knew, was colder than it should be. But she could only control so much. "It's been a busy week with Festival preparations. You know how it can be." The words felt unfamiliar, foreign, coming out of her mouth.

Geoffrey's face softened. "I'm sorry, darling, I know how draining court engagements are for you. What can I do?"

"I'm sorry. I haven't slept well. I may take an afternoon nap." It was a white lie, she told herself.

Her explanation seemed to make sense to him. He hugged her tightly for a moment and then stepped back and bowed. "Of course, you need your beauty rest, dove. I'll see you tomorrow."

CHAPTER 13

———

5th Day of the Harvest Moon

Caidy stood very still until she heard the door close and Geoffrey's footsteps echo down the hall before releasing a breath. Gathering her remaining hair pins, she left through the servants' stair, heading directly back to her rooms. The two servants she passed bowed, but she ignored them. When she finally entered her suite, she leaned against the door, closing her eyes.

When she was younger, she used to fly into explosive rages at the slightest frustration. Her temper was one of her biggest vulnerabilities. Ironically, Geoffrey, more than anyone else, had taught her that. She was angry with him often, frustrated by his lack of ambition, disappointed in his selfishness, and infuriated by his arrogance. But anger with Geoffrey never led anywhere. He was convinced, completely, that he was always in the right. It had taught Caidy very quickly to diffuse the situation rather than fight it.

She opened her eyes, smoothed her skirts, and wandered into the dining room. Margot was laying out a light dinner and smiled at her mistress. "Fresh trout, caught this morning, my Lady."

Returning the smile, Caidy sat. "Have you eaten yet?" It was a pointless question. Of course, Margot had not eaten. She would never dream of eating before her mistress.

"No, my Lady." Margot set out a basket of warm bread rolls and a small bowl of buttery sauce.

"I can't possibly eat all this. Please sit with me." Caidy watched Margot consider the suggestion for a moment before settling beside her. The young noblewoman placed a portion of fish and asparagus on the maid's plate before buttering a roll. "Thank you, Margot."

The maid's smile was rueful this time. "I love trout. I grew up in Maret, on the coast, and my ma made the best trout in the village. She roasted it in some sort of sauce. Bartholomew's trout recipe is a close second, though."

Caidy laughed. "I have no complaints. Are your parents still in Maret?" Margot had been serving Caidy for a little over a year but rarely talked about herself. *It makes sense,* she thought sourly, but she didn't have to like it. She loved getting to know other people.

"My ma is the village matchmaker, a Flame of Iya. My da worked escorting barges and caravans with Bertrand's Company, for the Riverlords, until a few years ago. Now he does odd jobs on the docks." Margot smeared a roll in the savory sauce dripping off the trout.

"A matchmaker? Maybe she could help me find a better nobleman to marry." Caidy's tone was more bitter than she would have liked.

Margot appeared to be considering what to say next. Saving her maid from an uncomfortably formal response, Caidy continued, "Please speak frankly, Margot. I listen to dozens of people every day talk for hours and rarely say anything of substance."

The maid shredded the remainder of her roll into small pieces. "I think it's a smart marriage but not necessarily a happy one, my Lady." Her voice was quiet and hesitant.

"You're right." Caidy twirled a curl around her finger. "Sometimes I wish it was easier."

"I think it's a very noble thing, putting the alliance before your heart, my Lady."

Caidy forced a laugh. "At least he's my age. I could be promised to Lord Felix." Lord Felix, the heir to House Commorel, was fourteen summers her senior.

Margot's laugh was natural, and the invisible tension eased. Comfortable silence stretched between them for a moment as Caidy built a miniature castle of fish and rice. "May I offer you advice, my Lady?"

"Please do." Caidy set down her fork, looking at the maid.

"My ma always said, it gets easier when you accept what the relationship is." Margot didn't meet her eyes.

Caidy's brow furrowed. "I'm not sure I understand what you're saying."

"I'm saying…" Margot paused and then plowed on, as though she had suddenly made up her mind about what to say. "I'm saying that you're right. It's a strategic marriage. It's not likely to be more than that. You'll make yourself miserable trying to make Lord Valance something, or someone, he isn't."

Caidy sawed an asparagus prong in half as she considered the advice. Deep down, a small part of her knew Margot was right. Geoffrey would never be the hero from her daydreams, and continuing to dream was impractical. However, accepting the way things were, accepting that *this* was her grand adventure, was an equally unpalatable choice. The room seemed to wobble around her, and she rubbed her eyes.

"Thank you, Margot." Caidy forced a polite smile. She felt as though she was trapped, dizzy and nauseated. Carefully, she stacked her utensils on the still half-full plate of food. As the maid started to rise, she waved her away. "Please don't stop on my account. I'm just not as hungry as I thought. I'm going to go unwind and retire early, I think. I'm feeling quite tired."

An hour later, Caidy found herself sprawled on the flagstone floor among scattered paints and papers, her fingers dyed with deep jewel hues, dozing off on folded arms. Painting let her relax and unwind in a way few other activities could. She could be completely alone, immersed in a private world, free from her duties and responsibilities. Yawning, she stopped wrestling with consciousness and let sleep overtake her body.

In the Dreamworld, Caidy's mind raced, galloping on a thousand adventures. She was at once a plain and unassuming cobbler's apprentice with a knack for fortune-telling, a daring pirate drinking her enemies into a stupor at the infamous Edo's Retreat in Swansea, a beautiful enchantress locked away in the icy ivory towers of Rhiamor College, and a Freelark plotting to overthrow the tyrannical rule of Nicholas Herdegen, Lord of Colmar.

She explored the farthest reaches of the Unending Desert, meeting nomads and slaying dragons with an opalescent sword, and painted caves with the Asaka warbands. She sampled delicate honey liquor on the bluffs of Morrani Isle in the Viridian Sea and sailed on to the Western Kingdoms, to see a world where women led great armies into battle.

The swirling tapestry of her dreams suddenly sharpened with surprising clarity, and she found her dreamself standing in an airy library, surrounded by bookshelves stuffed to bursting with books. Books! She ran her fingers over the leather bindings in stunned amazement. Never had she seen so many books before in one place. Something deep within her heart fluttered, and she spun around, delighting in the smell of old ink.

Turning, she caught sight of a woman, curled in a window seat, watching the world spin around the library. All Caidy could see was a long, shining braid, the color of moonlight, and a plain robe. Crossing the yards between them in a few, bouncing steps, she approached the woman cautiously. At her approach, the woman turned, and eyes the color of the night sky strewn with stars met her own.

"You came." The woman's voice sounded like wolves howling at the moon and water tumbling over rocks. She stood, and Caidy was forced to her knees by an invisible wave of irresistible power. "There may yet be hope."

Though nothing else in the room had shifted, Caidy felt as though she stood on the edge of a great precipice, the yawning chasm opening beneath her feet. A glowing power seemed to radiate from the woman, enveloping them both in a mist and blocking out the color and light from the world.

She felt two icy fingers under her chin, and she looked up into those terrible, awe-inspiring eyes. Squinting, as though staring straight into the sun, Caidy saw something flicker within the starry gaze.

"Save us," the strange woman whispered.

Beneath them, streaks of magical light shattered the world. Sparkling explosions of color and energy ripped through the very fabric of the universe. A great whirlwind swept the earth clean, taking with it all life and joy. Harsh, unfriendly light scorched the barren world, and a thousand screams tore Caidy's thoughts from her mind. She jerked her head back from the woman's icy grip, and the world shuddered to a jarring halt.

Falling backward, she braced herself against the soft carpet of the library, looking up at the unknown woman. "Who are you?"

The woman's infinite gaze caught and held Caidy's own. "We are all that ever was." The words echoed, as though shouted down a distant canyon.

"Why am I here?" Though her head spun and her hands shook, Caidy's voice was firm. The question demanded an answer, the voice of a future queen.

The towering woman seemed to shrink—or perhaps the world grew around them—and the silent howl tearing through Caidy's head ceased instantly. When the woman spoke, her voice sounded like a mountain after an avalanche: peaceful and dangerous, all at once. "You are all that ever will be."

Wind whipped around them, and in an instant Caidy was on her hands and knees on the hard flagstone floor of her rooms, wide awake. The window in her studio was cracked open, misty rain frosting the gap. Gasping and clutching a stitch in her ribs, feeling as though she had just sprinted for miles, she rolled onto her side. A shaft of moonlight drenched her face in silver, and she took several deep, steadying breaths, slowing her frantic heartbeat.

Thoughts skittered across the surface of her mind faster than she could keep up with them. Closing her eyes and settling back on a pillow, Caidy let the tangle play out behind her eyelids, specks of white dancing across the darkness. A deeply uncomfortable sense of foreboding sank into her bones, the piercing gaze of the strange woman imprinted behind her own eyelids. There had been a feeling of ancient power in the dream, if it had even been a dream.

Struck by an idea, she leapt to her feet, hopping back and forth on the chilly flagstones. She wrapped herself in a robe and padded over to a bookshelf, rifling through the scrolls and tomes by watery moonlight. *Where is it?* She could see it clearly in her mind—a thin storybook, bound in leather with beautiful illustrations. She had not looked through it since she was little.

After a few moments of desperate searching, she nearly whooped when her fingers found the narrow book. Hurrying to the window seat, where moonlight painted the cushions silver and rainy air misted through the small opening, she began flipping pages frantically until she found the passage she was looking for.

Regarded by many as an oracle or soothsayer, the High Priestess traveled from village to village, sharing her wisdom with all. Some folk claimed to be haunted by strange dreams after she left, of a strange woman with eyes the color of a midnight sky and a voice like the roar of the ocean.

That was the end of the story, a fable about one of the High Priests of old that must have stuck in her thoughts as a child, only to resurface now. Caidy rubbed her forehead, trying to puzzle through the problem. *It could be a coincidence*, she told herself. The description in the story was hauntingly similar to the woman she had just…witnessed? Met? Dreamed of?

Shuddering with a sudden chill, she made her way to bed, curling under the warm covers with relief. Tossing and turning, she struggled to find comfort until finally, she slipped into a dreamless sleep.

CHAPTER 14

———

6th Day of the Harvest Moon

His still-damp clothes were carefully laid out across the small table in his lodging. It was the only thing he'd bothered to do before falling into bed. With a groan, Alex slumped to his feet and dragged a fresh shirt and breeches on, rubbing his eyes and willing his head to stop pounding. Rain still pelted his wooden shutters, and he wrapped an oil-slicked cloak about his shoulders before setting off toward Raven House.

He stopped at a cheap vendor near the gate to Guild, buying three apple cinnamon turnovers. He wrapped the hot pastries in a handkerchief, which he tucked into his tunic, in a half-hearted attempt to keep the food dry. His midriff was pleasantly warm and smelled deliciously of cinnamon sugar by the time he unwrapped his dripping cloak in the main room of Raven House. He attempted to finger-comb his wilted hair with one hand as he pulled out the handkerchief.

Setting the pastries down, Alex took the stairs up two at a time to the second floor, grabbed a pile of scrolls off the desk he had abandoned last night, and then returned to his breakfast. Pinning the first report flat with a tankard, a glove, and the two uneaten turnovers, he took a satisfying mouthful of hot apple and butter.

At that moment, the front door banged open, and a man barged into the room. He was very tall and very thin, like the raka from children's tales. His hair was magnificently silver, and though his clothes spoke of flashy wealth, he was unkempt. His eyes were swollen and bloodshot, and he was hunched despite his height, as though he carried a great burden.

Swallowing his turnover with great difficulty and scalding his throat, Alex bit back a string of explosive curses as he leapt to his feet.

As he opened his mouth to speak, he caught sight of the three wavy lines on a broach the newcomer wore on his shoulder, and he changed tack mid-sentence. "What in the Three H–How can I help you, sir?"

Shocked, he watched Riverlord Sylvester Alamay, patriarch of one of the most powerful trading cartels in Rosemoor, sway as though drunk, rain lashing through the open door behind him. "It's my daughter, Evaline." His voice cracked in anguish as he spoke her name. "She's been murdered!"

Whatever he'd expected, that wasn't it. The burning sensation in his throat forgotten, Alex stepped forward. "Sir, do you want to come in? You can tell me all about it."

Alamay lashed out, a man possessed by grief and anger. "How *dare* you! You're just like the others. You don't give a damn about her. You only care about my *money*!"

Alex opened his mouth and then closed it again, deciding against arguing. Cautiously, he took another step toward the Riverlord where water was now pooling by the door as Alamay leaned heavily against the doorjamb.

"Sir, I'm very sorry to hear about your daughter. I want to help you. I need you to tell me what's happened." He found himself speaking very slowly and clearly, as though to a child.

Sylvester Alamay ignored him. He rocked back and forth so violently Alex worried he might fall over. He'd never understood when people grieved so publicly and openly. It made him deeply uncomfortable. *Be professional*, he ordered himself, even as Alamay let out a howl of grief.

Heavy boots tramped down the stairs, and Hendrick's bulk appeared in the main room. Without pausing for explanation, the Bandit Lord folded his arms and addressed the Riverlord directly. "Alamay. Stop letting the storm in. You'll ruin the carpet."

Alamay drew himself up in an odd cross between indignation, outrage, and exhaustion, and Hendrick's eyebrows met at the center in a silent thunderclap. When he spoke, his voice was calm but left no room for argument. "I understand you're upset, sir, but nothing'll be helped by this weather. Come in, and have a seat." He glanced at Alex. "Laurent. Fetch my waterskin from upstairs."

Grateful to have an excuse to collect himself, Alex scampered up the stairs to Hendrick's office. The Lord Commissioner was tidy. Reports were neatly stacked on his desk, a collection of books and journals were shelved, and there was not a dust mote to be seen. He took the only waterskin he could find—leather, with small embroidered violets around the border—and returned to the first floor.

Hendrick had settled across from Alamay in Alex's vacated chair. Twitching two fingers at him, a signal to stay put and stay quiet, Hendrick took the waterskin. His steaming turnovers were sadly abandoned beside the Riverlord, and Alex briefly considered retrieving them. However, as his stomach growled longingly, Hendrick caught his eye and glared.

Resigning himself to hunger, Alex leaned near the stairs, listening carefully. He was outranked. The Riverlord was one of the wealthiest men in the entire Empire and would expect to be treated as such. Hendrick shouldn't have to waste his time with people who had mistaken the Blades for the City Guard, but politics made every situation more complicated.

Using his belt knife, the Lord Commissioner speared one of the untouched turnovers and dropped it into a handkerchief he handed Alamay. "Eat. You look like you're about to keel over." Hendrick glowered at Alamay until the crumpled man took a bite of turnover.

As their visitor ate, Hendrick caught Alex's eye and nodded nearly imperceptibly. *What in the Hells is that supposed to mean*, he wondered, painfully aware he hadn't been here long enough to understand all of Hendrick's nonverbal signals. When he didn't move, the frown in the Bandit Lord's eyebrows returned, and he flicked his gaze to another chair and then back to Alex.

Decidedly confused, he stepped forward and settled himself in the chair near Hendrick, keeping his eyes on Alamay. After several long, uncomfortable minutes, color returned to the Riverlord's cheeks, and he looked a little less like the living dead.

"Alright, Alamay, let me set something straight for you." Hendrick leaned forward, bracing his elbows on his knees and staring intently at the Riverlord. "You know who the Blades are and what we do. You also know that a murder is usually the purview of the City Guard. Why don't you tell me what happened, and we'll sort out the best way to get you help."

Alamay wiped his eyes on his sleeve and sniffed dramatically before speaking. Alex resisted the urge to roll his eyes. "I've been to the City Guard, thank you very much. I've been everywhere—the Guard in Iera, the Provincial Guard, I've even petitioned the Roussels for help. I wouldn't come here unless I had no other choice."

When Hendrick remained silent, Alex decided to try playing off the Riverlord, to cajole the story out of him. It was a strategy he knew could work well. He just hoped Hendrick wouldn't skin him for it later.

"Sir, I'm Rosemoor's Warden, Alexander Laurent. I'm sorry you've had such trouble so far. Can you tell us a little more about what happened? I can't look into it if I don't know what I'm looking for." He chose his words carefully, trying to both not commit himself to anything and not shift blame to other organizations. There was always the risk it could get back to them, jeopardizing their working relationship.

The Riverlord looked at him unsteadily, eyes bloodshot. "You'll help my Evaline? You'll find her killer?"

Alex heard Hendrick clear his throat in warning, though he didn't need the reminder. "Start by telling us what's happened, sir."

The story came amid hiccups and dry sobs. Evaline had left on a trip to see a childhood friend in Torren, one of the busiest port cities in Rosemoor on the coast of the Viridian Sea. When she did not return last week, he had sent two guards to bring her back to Iera.

Alex got the distinct impression the Riverlord was not surprised Evaline had been late coming home. He knew very little of the family outside what everyone knew. They monopolized trade on the many rivers of Colmar, Rosemoor, and Danen. But from the familiar, exasperated tone, which hinted itself through Alamay's grief, it seemed like Evaline's journey had been the continuation of a tired argument between father and daughter.

A little more than a week ago, the guards he'd sent to find her had stopped to spend the evening in Pheant, a settlement on the main road to the western coast. The town was awash with rumors and fear. A young woman had been found dead a few nights previously. The guards had soon returned to Iera with the news, and ever since Alamay had been distraught, convinced the dead woman was his daughter.

Furious and grieving, Sylvester Alamay had knocked down the door of any guards he could find, seeking to avenge his daughter. The City Guard of both Pheant and Iera had assured him the murder was being investigated, and they would notify him if the victim was confirmed to be Evaline. The Roussels declined to get involved, despite Alamay's clout at court, and Alex didn't blame them. There was nothing to justify royal involvement in the matter. Nobody other than Alamay was convinced the girl was Evaline.

As his story wound to a close the man began to sob uncontrollably again. Alex exchanged a look with Hendrick. It was clear to him that the former bandit agreed with his impressions. Not only was there no proof Evaline had been murdered, but there wasn't really a good reason for the Blades to get involved. Usually, Wardens reserved their support for particularly complex or dangerous crimes, and it was nearly always because the local guard requested help.

But money spoke, and Alamay knew it. He was clearly distraught, but Alex wondered how much was genuine. The Riverlord was very clever and a shrewd businessman—the kind of person used to getting what he wanted. He knew if pretty much anyone else had come in with a wild story about a missing girl and no proof, they would be turned away, yet now, both the Lord Commissioner and Warden of Rosemoor sat, giving their undivided attention to the story.

The hypocrisy grated on his patience.

"Alright, sir. Do you know who in Pheant is responsible for the investigation? We can certainly reach out and offer our support." Hendrick's voice rumbled.

"I don't want an offer of support!" Alamay exploded with anger. "I want you to find the bastards that killed her!"

There it is, Alex watched the fury flare, unbothered by it. The Riverlord hadn't come here as a desperate man seeking guidance. He'd come to flex his power and wealth.

Hendrick watched impassively until the Riverlord settled back in his seat. "If you want us to get involved, you need to tell us who to speak with about the crime," the former Bandit Lord explained patiently.

It seemed to mollify Alamay. "Some country bumpkin named Elk is leading the investigation." He sniffed at the thought, clearly convinced if a Constable was from the countryside, they weren't good enough for him or his daughter. "He's in Iera now, trying to get help from the City Guard. You have to meet with him!"

Alex jumped at the chance to leave politics to Hendrick. "Do you know where he's staying?"

"Some poorhouse in Market. The Ivory Marigold." Alamay sniffed dramatically again.

Exchanging another look with Hendrick, and gaining—he thought—the Commissioner's tacit approval, Alex retrieved his cloak and headed out once more into the rain.

It was still early, and days always seemed to start more slowly with dreary weather. There were no crowds to avoid on his way to the Ivory Marigold, only a few sodden shopkeepers looking distinctly disgruntled.

His stomach grumbled again, reminding him he'd only enjoyed a bite of breakfast, and Alex stopped at another stall, purchasing a small loaf of hot, fresh bread and some honeycomb tea. He settled himself on a bench under an awning swollen with rain, watching the children of a trader chase each other up and down the street as he waited for the Constable from Pheant to emerge.

The Ivory Marigold, a slightly lopsided lodging house with lavender shutters and a neatly swept yard, was sandwiched between a large general store and a specialty armory, both of which were shuttered against the rain.

One of the children shoved the other into a puddle. From the looks of the flapping woman who screeched at the pair, they were brothers. At the same time, a portly man slipped down the steps of the Ivory Marigold, nearly falling flat on his face in the gutter muck.

The man straightened and brushed at a tunic which had fit better many years previously, and Alex caught sight of the scarlet ribbon that denoted a city guardsman. Leaping to his feet, his boredom forgotten, Alex splashed across the street, catching the man as he turned to walk toward Honey District. He tapped the Constable on the shoulder.

"Constable Elk?" He smiled brightly. It was usually better to start friendly and then get mean if the situation warranted. He'd learned that the hard way trying to bluff into a gambling den in Swansea.

Up close, the man was an oddity. Elk had thinning brown hair which he wore slicked back with some sort of oil, and a feeble attempt at a mustache on his upper lip. A generous person would say Elk's eyes were green, and his eyebrows were almost comically bushy. His Constable's uniform—similar to the City Guard, but with the Star of Alun embroidered on his shoulder—was well-worn and loved. The man was shorter than Alex by several inches.

"And who might you be?" Elk's voice was lower than Alex expected, a soothing bass, which seemed to resonate through his chest.

"Warden Alexander Laurent, Constable. Is there somewhere we could talk?" Recognition flashed in Elk's eyes when Alex used his title. It usually did.

"Of course, Warden, I'd be happy to help however I can. Not to trouble you, but I've a meeting with the City Guard this morning. Could I come find you later today?"

"Not a problem." Alex reeled off the address to Raven House. "I'll be there whenever it's convenient for you to stop by."

Elk scratched the back of his head and nodded. "I certainly will, Warden. Do you know of anywhere I can get some of that famous honeycomb tea? Thought I might partake while I'm here."

A genuine grin breaking across his face now, Alex raised his own wooden mug. "I need to bring this back to one of the stalls. Come with me, and I'll point you to the fastest way to the Guardhouse after."

CHAPTER 15

———

6th Day of the Harvest Moon

Later that day, around the third bell of the afternoon, the Constable was sitting in the second-floor office Alex and Jakob shared as rain continued to patter against the building. Alex had pulled his chair around next to the Constable and propped his feet on his desk. Elk was digging into a second steaming flagon of honeycomb tea and a fresh hunk of bread stuffed with nuts and raisins. Jakob had obligingly taken a pile of scrolls downstairs so he could have relative privacy in the small office.

He busied himself looking at a map to give the Constable a few moments to wolf down his lunch. When Elk leaned back in satisfaction, Alex carefully rolled up the map and turned his attention to the man.

"I'm sorry for surprising you outside the Marigold, Constable," Alex began.

"Rodney," Elk interrupted. "Rodney Elk, I suppose, but everyone calls me Rodney." He tore off another bite of bread. "I'm not real used to standing on ceremony, so you'll forgive me if I'm too forward, Warden."

A smile—this time, a real one—broke across Alex's face. It was always a relief to speak man-to-man rather than play politics. "In that case, it's Alex. To be honest with you, I'm not used to my own title quite yet."

Rodney's eyes wrinkled in what Alex suspected was a subtle grin. "You do look quite young, but you've got the right uniform for it." He had a slight burr buried in his deep voice. Pheant, Alex knew, was only a few days south of Iera, but it was a world apart.

"Fresh out of recruitment." Alex chuckled. "I should hope I look young."

The Constable gave a booming belly laugh. "Aye, nothing to fear there, lad. What can I do for the Blades?"

"I had an unexpected visit from Master Alamay. Do you know him?"

Rodney's eyes widened, and he seemed to grow paler. "Aye, I know his reputation and I've met his men."

Alex watched the knob in the Constable's throat bob up and down as he swallowed hard. "Master Alamay believes his daughter was murdered in Pheant a fortnight ago." As he finished speaking, he feigned disinterest, examining his fingernails.

To his surprise, Rodney's reaction was not subtle. "Raka's shadow," Elk swore loudly, slamming his fist on the desk and nearly upsetting his flagon of tea. Feeling it would be rather obvious if he continued to clean his nails, Alex looked directly at the Constable in surprise.

"My apologies," Rodney muttered angrily. "It's just... I told his men we didn't know if it was the girl or not. It's about his daughter Evaline?" Alex nodded. "His guards couldn't give me anything to identify the girl by. They just insisted it must be her. Right age, right hair, but the body we have..."

she's beaten badly. I couldn't tell if she was my own daughter, you see?"

His tone was pleading, and in a flash, Alex understood. Rodney Elk was terrified that he was about to lose his job because of the word of a powerful trader. He'd seen it happen too often in Danen. Hells, he knew exactly how the Constable felt. The wealthy and the powerful seemed to take pleasure in making the lives of the common folk more difficult. With effort, Alex swallowed the bile that rose in the back of his throat.

"Rodney," he started slowly. "I'm not here on Alamay's orders. I'm asking if I can lend a hand to see who this girl is, help her soul to the Pleasure Lands." He raised his hands, palms open. "I've got no interest in ruining your job; and if I did, I don't honestly know if I could."

The Constable, who had been sitting rigidly on the edge of his chair, relaxed almost imperceptibly, an invisible tension leaving his frame. "My apologies," he began again, but Alex waved a hand.

"None of that. I'd be anxious too; the Riverlords are powerful. But they don't have a chokehold on this city. You're a City Guard. That means something, especially in Raven House. Hells, I couldn't do my job without your help. I've got nothing to gain by sticking my nose in your business." Alex interlaced his fingers behind his head. "Just tell me what happened."

Elk nervously rubbed his thumb along the ribbon sewn into the cuff of his sleeve as he began to speak. Alex noted the information—understanding how contacts behaved under pressure was always useful—before devoting his attention to the story.

"A little before dawn two weeks ago, a fisherman tossing fish guts into the river caught sight of a lump caught under the docks. His curiosity got the better of him and he investigated and, well, started shrieking so loud Rakatash heard it in the Nightmare Realms. Our guards got there and discovered the body." Rodney paused and rubbed a hand over his eyes. His eyebrows stood on end, pointing in several directions.

Alex waited the silence out. After a moment, Rodney continued, "It was bad, Alex. It *is* bad. The body is so bloated from water it looks more raka than human. Our mage is sure it's female, but that's about all we know. Nobody saw nothin', nobody heard nothin'." Another pause. "Long dark hair, like Alamay's daughter, Evaline. That's all I can tell, though. His men—they were looking for a dark-haired girl, and they found one. But that don't mean it's his daughter. From what I understand, she's supposed to be in Torren, not Pheant, anyway."

Alex tapped one thumb on top of the other behind his head. It certainly did sound like Alamay's guards had jumped to several conclusions and not bothered to even go to Torren to see if Evaline was there. "Do you know who this girl might be, if not Evaline?"

Rodney huffed loudly and leaned back in his chair, scrubbing his hands over his face again. "Not a puff of smoke. None of the locals are missing anyone, nobody at the taverns hasn't returned. Since she was trapped under the docks, poor thing, I thought the body might've floated downstream so I traveled north. Nothing in any of the fishing villages, and Iera's the biggest city on Feather Lake. I got in late last night, and was heading over to the Guardhouse when you caught me."

Nodding slowly, Alex sorted through his thoughts. He could see now why Alamay had been turned away by the City Guard and the Roussels. There just wasn't enough there to warrant interference with a local matter. And yet, something itched at the back of Alex's brain. He couldn't tell what it was, but it was a lesson he'd had beaten into him, quite literally, in a back alley of Swansea by his old trainer, Starling. *Trust that itch; it means something doesn't make sense, even if you don't know it yet.*

Abruptly taking his feet off the desk and leaning forward, he braced his forearms on his knees, looking intently at the Constable. "Describe her to me. I know what drowning does to a person, so just do your best. Anything you remember."

Rodney ran his thumb along that ribbon again, his face screwed up in concentration as Alex waited patiently.

"Long, dark hair, like I said," Rodney began, closing his eyes in concentration. "Pale skin, a northerner, not one o' the Imperials. Probably skinny once. Maybe."

"Clothes?" Alex prompted, sensing he was losing focus.

"Traveler's clothes. A cloak; that was tangled about her neck and chest caught under the dock. A pain to dig out that was. Plain clothes, worn. Naught identifyin' that I could see."

"Boots? Sandals?"

"Aye, good leather boots now you mention. Expensive, for a peasant."

Alex frowned. "Why do you say she's a peasant?"

"Well, she didn't have any of the sparkles or fancy clothes nobles and merchants like. And there was the tattoo. Only nobles I've seen with ink on their skin like that are Imperials, and she ain't them."

A tattoo? Alex considered. Elk was right; the Mezrani wore tattoos, often denoting clan ties. Northerners didn't tend to, unless... "Rodney," he said slowly, putting significant effort into shielding excitement from his voice. "Where was the tattoo?"

Elk's eyes popped open, and he looked at Alex. "On her wrist, just here." He tapped an area Alex would call a forearm, not a wrist. "Of some sort of flower. I remember I was surprised we could make it out at all, her skin was so stretched and bloated."

Alex sat back, mind working fast. An excited tingle lit in his belly. He only knew of one group that tattooed its members. And he hadn't the slightest idea what a dead Freelark was doing in a nothing town like Pheant.

Two hours later, Alex was back downstairs. He'd promised Rodney a dinner at the Bustling Mushroom and sent him off with a tip to speak with Thom Laurent, Alex's cousin and one of the City Guard Shift Commanders, since the Constable hadn't had much luck getting help that morning. Alex was putting the finishing touches on his report of the meeting, and Jakob was happily piled under scrolls, his quill scratching in a constant, soothing way while he hummed tunelessly.

Leaning back and rolling his head around, Alex considered heading out for an early dinner as he skimmed the notes he had taken. In Danen, he had quickly learned that writing things down sooner, rather than later, was always worth it. And so, no matter how painstaking or inconvenient, he dutifully recorded his meeting with Elk—the content, his impressions of the man, and some general observations.

In this case, it had most certainly raised more questions than answers. The Freelarks were a complicated blend of humanitarians and anarchists, dedicated to harmonious life with the natural environment. For many, that meant maintaining Hearth Halls to house travelers and feed the hungry;

for some, it meant plotting to bring down cities and nations. He hadn't a clue what they would be doing in Pheant.

Deciding he'd done good work so far, and that he deserved a snack, he made to get up. At the same time, Hendrick came in from the street, and Alex collapsed back in his seat, attempting to look as though he had been stretching. Hendrick raised one eyebrow.

"Did you meet that Constable, Laurent?" The Lord Commissioner joined the two men and sat, resting his left ankle on his right knee and observing Alex impassively.

"Yes. Just finished my report, actually." He offered the parchment to Hendrick, who took it and started reading. Alex winced when he saw how fast the Commissioner's eyes were moving. *Didn't anyone else read slowly?*

He took out his belt knife and started scraping a lump of muck off his boot as Hendrick read. More quickly than Alex anticipated, the older man was done. "Well done writing this up so quickly. It's a good report, Laurent." Hendrick handed the scroll back to him.

"Thank you." Alex was startled. He didn't think Hendrick was the kind of man who gave compliments.

"You think Alamay is wrong, then? Did you think that during the meeting this morning or only once you met with the Constable?"

"Something stank this morning," he replied. "His grief was real, but he was also entitled. He wasn't nearly as distraught as he wanted us to think."

Hendrick nodded. "That's a good instinct. You should always be careful of what the rich say."

"It's hard to be skeptical of the powerful sometimes," Jakob commented. Hendrick glared at him. He shrugged. "Just saying."

"Why aren't you and your damned humming upstairs?"

Jakob ignored Hendrick's glower. "Because I kindly gave up my desk so Alex could meet with the Constable undisturbed, and now I'm comfortable."

Hendrick rolled his eyes and returned his attention to Alex. "Tell me more about the Freelark angle."

"I don't know how it fits," he confessed. "But the only northerners I know with tattoos are criminals or Freelarks. And sometimes they're one and the same. A flower? If that's a coincidence I'll eat my boot."

"Spare the hyperbole, Laurent." Hendrick frowned, but Alex had a niggling suspicion he'd discovered the man's sense of humor. "What's a Freelark Dandelion doing in Pheant?"

"Jakob, any Whispers?" Alex redirected the question at their Archivalist.

"Naught but the usual," Jakob replied, not looking up from his scroll. "I'm waiting on a report from the Citadel but that could take weeks."

Hendrick nodded. "Stay on it, Gesell. If the Freelarks are sneaking around, I want to know. So what's your next step, Laurent?"

Alex was ready for this question. "I sent Elk to meet with the Guard, and I'm getting dinner with him later. I want to know if our City Guard have anyone local missing, which could tie this up neatly. If not," he shrugged, "I figured I'd travel back to Pheant with Rodney to see if I can lend a hand. At the very least, you'll be able to tell Master Alamay we're chasing it down."

Smoothing his mustache, Hendrick nodded. "That's the important piece. I don't need a Riverlord up my ass about his missing daughter if I can help it. Did you send him to meet with your cousin?" Alex couldn't keep the surprise off his face, and Hendrick waved a hand. "It's my job to know the local players, and a Shift Commander in Iera is important enough for my attention, Laurent."

"Yes, I did. I can take Thom out for drinks if I need to know how his conversation with Rodney goes."

"Good plan. Following this trail, at least back to Pheant, is a—" Hendrick was cut off before Alex could find out what the rest of his sentence was going to be.

Their front door burst open for the second time that day, and Danila al-Mhir, their Mezrani watchdog, dripped over the threshold. She unwrapped a heavy, oiled cloak from her shoulders and draped it over the back of a chair before turning to face the three men, hands braced on her hips.

Her hair, Alex noticed, was not actually as short as he had thought, but rather braided tightly to her scalp, similar to some of the fashions he had seen in Mezrani City. Today she wore a long tunic of deep maroon with golden embroidery and soft leather sandals, which were soaked through. A belt drew the tunic into her waist, and he noticed a gold ring with the Imperial sigil flashing on her left middle finger. It was a slightly exotic style, which felt both sophisticated and entirely inappropriate for the late summer storms of Rosemoor.

"Lord Commissioner." Her voice whipped across the room. There was no hint of arrogance, Alex noted with interest, but rather an expectation to be listened to.

Hendrick raised both eyebrows at her but did not stand. "Yes?"

"Why have you skipped the past three meetings regarding security at the Harvest Festival?" Alex could feel the heat of her glare and busied himself with his report.

"I've got quite a lot to do outside of your meetings, Commissar." Hendrick replied coolly. "I'm responsible for an entire province. Me, and my men, safeguard the realm. We don't stop pickpockets."

Danila folded her arms. "You most certainly do when you are ordered to."

"We've just gotten a request to assist a murder investigation." Hendrick glared at her. "If *you* want to go explain to the Riverlords that we just don't have time to help them because we're chasing petty thieves around the city, I'm certainly not going to stop you."

Danila held up a palm, and Alex was shocked when Hendrick's jaw snapped shut in response. Glancing at Jakob, Alex saw him watching the exchange, eyes wide. The Mezrani reached into a fold of her tunic and extracted a scroll, sealed with wax. "I've just gotten a report from an interrogation in the Capital District; the Freelarks are planning an attack on the Harvest Festival. Paying attention yet?" She tossed the scroll on the table and then stepped back.

Hendrick broke the seal with the hilt of his dagger and read the message. "Why didn't this come through my Archivalist? You don't have access to our secure messages."

"No, I don't. But Imperial couriers are faster than yours, and this was sent at top speed. I have the right to read anything handled by an Imperial courier, *your* messages included," she remarked flatly.

Behind the backs of the two titans, Alex exchanged a shocked look with Jakob. *The Imperials are reading our messages now?*

"I'm not here to debate sources with you," Danila continued. "We've got a real threat, and I want to know why you aren't doing anything about it."

"Well, now that we know about it, we'll do something about it," Hendrick replied testily. "I don't have the manpower to waste chasing possibilities. That's for the Lycantheum."

Something in Danila's eyes snapped, reminding Alex of the crackle of flames in a bonfire. "See that you do. Those anarchists aren't worth the ink in that intelligence report. However, if they manage to disrupt the Harvest Festival, we will have no choice but to address them directly, lending credibility to a juvenile cry for attention." She lowered her voice, and Alex heard tight anger in the way she bit off the syllables of each word. "We're not going to give these tree-scummers a stage to make fools of us all on. The Harvest Festival is important to Rosemoor, and the stability of Rosemoor is important to the Empire."

Hendrick stood. "I don't appreciate your insinuation that I have an interest in letting civilians die on my watch. Unless you have something useful to say, get out. You've delivered your message." Alex and Jakob very purposefully avoided each other's eyes.

Danila's cheeks flamed red. "If the attack happens, I'll serve your head on a platter to the Imperial Authority," she said with a sneer before snatching her cloak from the chair and slamming the door. A thunderclap from the storm echoed mournfully in her wake.

Hendrick stood in silence for a moment, breathing heavily through his nose. Alex and Jakob exchanged a stunned glance. Taking a deep breath, Hendrick returned his attention to Alex. "Laurent, go to the City Commander up on the Hill. He'll be the one overseeing security for the Festival. Take this." He offered the scroll. "Read it and share the intelligence. I know the officer who wrote it. It's good information. We've got two weeks until the Harvest Festival to come up with a plan. That Freelark body in Pheant just got a whole lot more interesting."

Alex's eyes widened. He nodded and took the scroll, tucking it into an inner pocket of his tunic, as he started to fasten his cloak about his shoulders. Hendrick continued speaking. "Jakob, talk to your Whisperers. See if they've got anything. If you have time to meet with our informant in the Freelarks, do it. Figure out if this is the report you were waiting on, or if we've got more coming. We need to know what we're missing." Jakob was already standing, moving toward the door.

As Alex fastened the catch on his cloak and made for the storm, Hendrick's voice caught him.

"It's on your head, Laurent. The Authority will want blood if something happens at the Festival." Hendrick's blue eyes were as cold and unfriendly as shards of glass. "Don't let it."

"I won't." Alex raked his fingers nervously through his hair, his body tingling with anxious energy. He met Hendrick's eyes and swallowed hard. "I'm ready."

Hendrick looked at him appraisingly. "Let's hope so. Lives are riding on that bravado, now."

CHAPTER 16

———

8th Day of the Harvest Moon

"I really hate these formal gowns." Caidy scratched at her neck, fussing with the high collar of the moondust-and-ruby dress she wore. In the mirror, she saw her maid purse her lips, straightening the collar she'd just displaced.

"I know I have to," Caidy replied to herself, deciding to carry on both sides of the conversation. "And I know it's a gift from the Valances, and I know Geoffrey will want to see it. I *know.* It's just so uncomfortable."

Patting her mistress on the shoulder, Margot walked around so she was face to face with Caidy and began fussing with her curls.

"I am excited to meet the new ambassador, though. Alaim was *boring.*" She sighed heavily, dramatically raising a hand and faking a yawn. "The new one is…" She searched her memory, sorting through documents she'd reviewed in the past few days. "Farah. Farah al-Kalim. A woman! I bet she doesn't have to wear itchy clothes."

Margot snorted. "If you think Rosemoorian styles are dramatic, my Lady, you should see those of the capital. I'd imagine the new ambassador wears her own fair share of uncomfortable clothes. A curse of womanhood, unfortunately."

"I'll change it," Caidy declared, stepping back from her maid and starting to pace the room. "I'll outlaw dresses and itchy fabric. Nothing but loose shirts and comfortable boots for me."

"I'm sure you will, my Lady." Margot stepped in front of her, forcing her to stop pacing. "But right now I need to finish getting your hair to stop frizzing. The welcome lunch will start soon."

Forcing her body to be still, she let her mind wander. The last few days had been a blur—working hard, from sunrise to sunset, and then falling into a deep, dreamless sleep. *Dreamless.* That was a hidden blessing. Her strange dream—vision?—of a few nights ago still lingered in the back of her mind. It had felt so real but so bizarre at the same time. Dreams weren't supposed to be like that. The Dreamworld was firmly fantastical. *Unless...*

"Margot." Caidy spoke suddenly, and the maid nearly stabbed her scalp with a pin in surprise.

"Yes, my Lady?"

"Don't the Temple Adepts have visions sometimes? Masquerading as dreams?" She watched Margot frown in confusion in the mirror.

"I'm not sure I'd know, my Lady. I don't have many dealings with the Temple Orders."

"I don't either," Caidy mused. "But I could have sworn there's some country fable about dreams being some sort of connection to the Mystical Plane, to the Winds. Am I making that up?"

"No, it sounds familiar." The maid spoke slowly, clearly deep in thought. "I know those who worship Cami and

Rakatash claim to visit the Divine Realm. But they rule the Dreamworld, so that would make sense."

"I took lessons on religion for *years*. How do I know the proper way to light incense in all four provinces but I don't understand the Dreamworld?" Caidy complained.

At that, Margot chuckled. "My Lady, I think even Adepts who spend their whole lives in service to the Gods don't understand the Dreamworld. Perhaps you should take it up with them."

"Maybe I will," Caidy began to bounce in her chair, impatient with how long her hair was taking. Margot patiently ignored her and worked three different creams through her curls until they lay smooth and silky.

Stepping back, the maid looked satisfied. "You're beautiful, my Lady. That should last you through lunch."

"I don't understand how my hair gets so tangled so fast," Caidy replied, scratching at the collar again as she headed toward the door. She didn't wait to hear the maid's answer as she stepped into the hallway and made her way to the great hall, her steps shadowed by Merric.

Her parents and Geoffrey already sat around the table on the dais. Julianna was resplendent in cream and coffee, her hair coiled sleekly back and her lips painted a muted pink, while Mattias wore his regular uniform of a maroon tunic with gold brocade and brown leggings. Geoffrey rose to greet her with a bright smile.

"My dove! I'm so glad you like the gown my mother sent. It was handmade in Juniper Meadows just for you." He hugged her and then drew out the chair beside him.

"It's lovely." She smiled politely back at him. "She really shouldn't have."

"Nonsense," Mattias rumbled across the table. "The woman has good taste, and it's natural to give gifts in courtship. Excellent, Geoffrey."

While he beamed at her father, Caidy struggled not to roll her eyes. *Men.* They were constantly praising one another for things the women in their lives did for them. Glancing at her mother, she detected the barest glimmer of hidden laughter in Julianna's mild gray eyes.

The doors at the end of the hall opened, and the castle steward cleared his throat. "Presenting Ambassador Farah al-Kalim, of Mezrani City," he proclaimed.

The woman who entered and walked toward them was beautiful. Farah had dark skin and long hair she wore in a complicated braided bun at the nape of her neck. Her eyes were large and soft, her skin unlined and clear. She wore a gown in traditional Mezrani style with a short bodice in deep navy, decorated with golden accents. Golden fabric, skintight, flowed from breast to hip, where a long navy skirt rippled to the ground. Her neck and wrists were adorned with gold bangles, and earrings flashed at her ears.

She approached and inclined her head respectfully. "Lord and Lady Roussel, it is my pleasure to be here. Iera is a beautiful city."

Caidy rose with her parents and curtseyed deeply. "Ambassador al-Kalim, the pleasure is ours," she heard her mother say. "Please, we would be honored if you would join us for lunch."

"I'd be delighted." Farah smiled warmly, stepping up to the dais. Her eyes swept over the small group and then settled on Caidy. "You must be Lady Caidelene. An honor to meet you."

Deciding to err on the side of formality, Caidy curtseyed again. "The honor is mine, Ambassador." When she looked back up, the woman was smiling broadly at her, her eyes dancing with joy.

"And Lord Geoffrey, if I'm not mistaken. I've met your father in Mezrani City before, a generous man." Farah stepped toward Geoffrey and offered her hand. He brought her fingers to his lips for a kiss.

"My father always speaks highly of Mezrani City whenever he returns from business. I've heard incredible things about the seafood," he replied politely.

"There's none better," Farah agreed. She settled in the open chair. "But if it's not too forward, I'm very much looking forward to a hot meal. I've been traveling for weeks."

Retaking her own seat, Caidy waited for her parents to say something. When silence stretched, she glanced up. Mattias looked angry, his face a thundercloud, while Julianna politely sipped tea, watching her husband over the rim of the mug. Farah appeared unbothered by either reaction, accepting a bowl of onion and venison stew with a slice of thick bread from a servant with a word of thanks. Next to her, Geoffrey busied himself with his food, apparently impervious to any tension.

Uncomfortable with the silence and unsure what silent conversation was happening between her parents, she spoke up. "Ambassador, would you mind telling me a little of Mezrani City? I've yet to have the opportunity to visit, and I've heard the most wonderful things."

"Farah, please. No need for titles now the formalities are dealt with." The beautiful Tanu woman waved a hand. "I was born in Reza, one of the Tanu fiefdoms where my family rules. I've lived in Mezrani City since I was a girl—no more than eleven or twelve summers old, I think. It's truly a metropolis like no other."

Caidy swallowed a spoonful of stew. "Is it true the buildings are carved from marble?"

Farah nodded. "Tanu craftsmen love to work with the natural stone, whether it's marble or sandstone. Our buildings are often carved from these materials. Near the Imperial Palace, the streets themselves are paved with complicated stonework, remnants of battles long since passed. In some of the smaller markets, the buildings have stood for a thousand years."

"I can't imagine," she replied slowly, imagining the dwarfing grandeur of the city.

"My father always said the marble architecture was incredible," Geoffrey commented helpfully before returning to his stew.

When her parents still remained quiet, Caidy asked the ambassador, "What's your favorite thing about the city?"

"I think the dock market," Farah replied thoughtfully, her dark eyes focusing on Caidy's intently. "Yes, our docks are famous. There are always battleships from the Imperial Navy drydocked, massive trading ships loading goods on and off. You can find anything you imagine—exotic teas and cloth from the tribes of the Unending Desert and wine from the Morrani Isles. When I was younger, I used to beg my parents to take me walking through the market so I could see all the treasures from the world collected in one place."

"That sounds amazing." Caidy slowly tore her bread into strips. "I've only been to Torren, our own port city, a few times, but I've always been stunned at the variety of goods sold. It must be an amazing place to grow up."

"Certainly," Farah smiled at her. "And you, Caidelene? What do you love about Iera?"

"So many things." She laughed. "I love the way the sunlight bathes the city in the morning and evening, washing everything with gold. When I visit the city, I love hearing from our people, listening to their stories and goings-on. I've been working on preparing for the Harvest Festival—one of our largest celebrations—in a few weeks. I think that's perhaps my favorite time of all. The city is so full of joy."

"Then I cannot wait to experience it." Farah turned her gaze to Mattias, who had regained control of his temper with some effort. "Mattias? What do you love about Iera?"

"I love our people's sense of freedom and independence," he replied. "Rosemoorians take care of themselves and one another. I couldn't be more proud of their hard work."

It was a strange response, Caidy realized. Of course, her people *were* hardworking and independent, but Mattias seemed to be alluding to something much more than self-sufficiency.

Farah's face remained smooth, though her smile seemed more polite than genuine now. "That's one of the things that makes the Empire great, the industry of her people," she replied, her tone gentle.

"Industry, yes, but I appreciate how Rosemoorians value their freedom more than simply hard work," Mattias pressed. Caidy saw her mother frown slightly as he spoke, and next to her, Geoffrey looked confused. "They want to care for themselves and their families and don't bother with complicated politics or unnecessary laws."

Something flared in Farah's gaze, though her tone did not change. "There is certainly a time and a place for independence, as long as it does not conflict with law and order."

Before her father could continue, Julianna spoke. "Farah, have you met many of our people?"

Turning her attention to the Lady of Rosemoor, Farah offered her a winning smile. "I had the pleasure of becoming rather close with one of the younger sons of House Laurent a few years ago. Alexander—last I heard he was assigned to Danen with the Blades."

Caidy felt her body stiffen at Alex's name. What did she mean she'd become *rather close*? How long had he been in Mezrani City? And when? Her mind raced, though years of schooling kept her face impartial.

"Yes, Alexander recently returned to Rosemoor as our Warden," Julianna replied carefully. "He was a common sight at court when he was growing up."

An understatement, Caidy thought ruefully.

"Is that so?" Farah's elegant eyebrows arched. "I'd wondered if he wouldn't eventually come back to Iera. He used to tell me the most wonderful stories about the city. I've wanted to visit since. I couldn't believe my luck when the Diplomatic Corps assigned me to the province."

"I didn't realize Blades had free time during their training," Caidy commented, a pang of jealousy in her heart. *If he had time to visit Mezrani City, why didn't he have time to write?*

"He spent some of his time with his mentor in the city. After all, the Citadel is only a days' ride from the capital. It's not a hard journey." The ambassador's bright smile returned.

Talk turned to other things, and Caidy found her mind wandering. She had no idea what had happened to Alex when he'd left Rosemoor. The Blades were notoriously secretive, and since he'd returned, he had made no effort to speak with her. Watching the beautiful, charming Tanu woman happily chat with Geoffrey about the prospects of his family's vineyards, the jealous pang grew stronger.

It would be easier, she decided, if Farah was ugly, or unpleasant, or both. But, unfortunately, the new ambassador was delightful, quick with a joke, easy with stories, and unfailingly polite. Mattias still watched her warily, though Caidy didn't find that surprising. Her father made no secret of his dislike and distrust of the Empire. She didn't really see his point. Now that the Tanu had united the four provinces under one flag, their borders were relatively safe, and trade flowed freely.

"Well," Farah said after they finished a delicious dessert of hot cherry pie and vanilla cream. "I'm afraid I must be going. I've lots of reading to do to catch up on the affairs of the province."

Caidy, Julianna, and Geoffrey all stood as Farah did. Mattias remained seated for a moment, then joined them, folding his arms.

"Lady Caidelene, I'm very excited for us to work together," the ambassador continued. "I know you are going to do great things for both Rosemoor and the Empire, and I cannot wait to be part of it."

Taken aback, Caidy blushed. "I...thank you. I do hope you enjoy the Harvest Festival in a few weeks. It's my pride and joy."

Farah smiled at her again and clasped both Caidy's hands in her own. "I've no doubt it will be wonderful."

As they dispersed, and she made her way back to her rooms, her thoughts turned to the Festival. A seemingly endless number of things needed doing before the twenty-first. The various guild leaders needed to be cajoled into finalizing preparations. They were still waiting on a shipment from Torren. And she hadn't even begun to think about the speech she needed to give before lighting the Great Effigy ablaze.

CHAPTER 17

10th Day of the Harvest Moon

Slowing his horse at the top of a rolling hill, Alex shaded his eyes with a gloved hand and looked south. He had to be getting close to Pheant—the country village was only a few days' ride south of Iera. Elk pulled up next to him. The Constable rode a short, stocky horse but had proven himself to be a companionable riding partner. Unlike Jakob, Elk didn't hum tunelessly.

The Constable had been surprised when Alex had offered to ride back to Pheant with him, and his startled pleasure gave Alex the sense Elk had been prepared to be ignored and sent back to the countryside. As they had ridden together, he had toyed with telling the Constable about his suspicions— that the girl, while likely not Alamay's daughter, was tangled in a Freelark conspiracy. He'd eventually decided against it. Though he liked the Constable just fine, he'd been trained to keep secrets as close as possible.

Last night the pair had opted to camp in a small grove of trees near the road rather than pay the exorbitant rate inns charged this close to the capital city. It had been a blissfully quiet evening with a soothing breeze and the chirp of crickets. The day so far had been surprisingly cool, the chill of autumn haunting the air with each step along the road.

If nothing else, Rosemoor was picturesque. It didn't have the glittering danger of Swansea, or the dwarfing marble magnificence of Tanunt, but Alex rather preferred Rosemoor's understated beauty. It reminded him of how he felt collapsing into a chair with a hot dinner after a hard day's work—remarkably satisfied and at peace. For miles, the hills rolled, fields fading to small villages and then back to farmland. The Twin River burbled cheerfully along, and the smell of animals and soil floated on the breeze.

In front of him, the gravel-and-dirt wagon tracks they followed threaded between two fields. A village—really nothing more than a small cluster of farms—lay tucked beside a pond to his right. Off to the left, beyond another hill, he could hear the dull roar of the river slipping over rapids. The track led past a fruit stand through the valley and up another gentle incline. The Somber Mountains loomed in the background, impossibly high as their snowcaps scraped the autumn skies.

Seeing mountains everywhere he went was very reassuring. Danen was almost all plains and coastline with a small range in the south encircling the Free City of Swansea. It was one of those things he hadn't realized he missed until he'd come home. Something was soothing about the size and security of the mountains, about their constant presence, protecting the idyllic valley.

Nudging his horse forward once more, Alex rode past a worn sign pointing toward the village of Wheat Hollow. At the fruit stand, he purchased two apples from an excited child, munching on one and tossing the other to Elk, who offered it to his horse. Wheat Hollow was little more than a footnote on the maps he had reviewed before starting the ride, but it oriented him. He knew they were no more than a few hours from Pheant, which meant a hot meal and time to explore the new town before dark. Gesturing to Elk, he urged his horse to a rocking canter, and relaxed into the saddle as the distance melted away.

Surrounded by a sturdy, if somewhat overgrown, wooden palisade and nestled against the Twin River, Pheant was a cheerful collection of stone, wood, and thatch buildings. They entered through the northern gate and nearly collided with two merchants who were in animated discussion.

"There's just no way," the merchant with thick silver sideburns was saying to the other. "I don't believe it."

His partner, a bulky man carrying a sack of flour, shrugged. "I don't rightly care if you believe me. It's just what I heard."

"She'd have to be Udo's fool!" Sideburns leaned back against a crate burying his face in his hands. "Fritha's Maidens, they came through said she might have what it took to join the Temple next year."

Flour Sack clapped him on the shoulder. "I just thought you should know."

Watching the conversation, Elk dismounted and sidled up to the two men. "We both know Arabel's destined for the Temple. Let the gal cut loose a little," he consoled Sideburns. "She'll spend a year or two travelin' and then come back to the Maidens. You'll see."

"And you." The Constable rounded on Flour Sack. "You know better. Don't wind him up because nobody's buyin' your wares today."

Sensing the conversation was drawing to a close, Alex dismounted and looped the reins around his hand. Bidding the two men farewell and joining Alex, Elk began to walk his own horse down the muddy street. "Albert's niece is off to join the Players in Juniper Meadows," he explained. "Her mother doesn't mind, but old Al had his heart set on her joining the temple, becoming a Maiden."

"I think being a Player would be more fun anyway," Alex replied, startling a chuckle out of the Constable as they made their way through Pheant.

The Constable, he quickly discovered, knew everybody in the small town. But, more than that, he seemed determined to introduce Alex to every single villager before the sun set. He allowed himself to be swept along in a stream of introductions, handshakes, bows, and polite nothings. It took them nearly an hour to make their way down the main street of Pheant and to the inn where Elk introduced him to a smiling, round-faced woman named Felicity.

Felicity assured him that there was room in the inn and stoutly refused his offers of coin. "Absolutely not, Warden," she said sternly, shoving the coins back across the counter. "Folk'll think I've gone mad! It's my honor to serve you and yours."

As she bustled up the stairs, the Constable opened his mouth again, and Alex spoke quickly, hoping to avoid another introduction. "Rodney, is there somewhere we could eat? I'm famished, and I'd love to see a little bit more of the town. Since I'm here officially for the murder, I should stop by the guard house to introduce myself."

Elk nodded, smoothing the patchy mustache on his upper lip. "We'll have to find Captain Harold for that. He usually takes drinks at the Broken Cup near the docks."

After unsaddling his horse in the small stables adjacent to the inn and depositing his saddlebags in the room Felicity had prepared, Alex followed Rodney toward the river, passing the local Hearth Hall, an herbalist's shop, and the delicious smells wafting from a bakery. The Dock District of Pheant was not large—more a street than anything else—but it boasted a fishmonger, some lodging houses, a bait shop, and a drinking house. The tavern spilled light and the stink of cheap ale out onto the street. As the shadows lengthened and dusk started to descend on the village, dozens of men gathered to share the day's gossip and drink.

Alex drifted behind Elk as the Constable made his way, painfully slowly, through the crowd. He clapped many of the men he passed on the shoulder in greeting and seemed to stop every few steps to have a snatch of conversation. Alex supposed that was the way things were in small towns everywhere and wondered privately how anything ever got done.

He also noticed with interest that, while Rodney greeted everyone with a warm smile and friendly word, most people pulled away rather quickly, turning to other groups of friends or keeping the dialogue short and clipped. Nothing seemed to fluster Rodney's implacable, easy-going spirit, however, and he chatted away with gusto. Alex did his best to remain unobtrusive and uninteresting.

They finally made their way into the tavern, the Broken Cup, and toward a round table in the back corner where a large man with close-cropped hair conducted animated conversation with several men and women in guard uniforms.

"Captain Harold!" Rodney called over the hubbub as he approached, Alex in tow. "I've a guest for you to meet!"

The large man raised a hand toward Rodney and continued his story, "So she looks up at me with these big eyes, right—"

Clearing his throat and stepping around the Constable, Alex extended a hand toward the man. "Warden Alexander Laurent, Captain. A pleasure." His voice was friendly, but he kept his gaze cool and steely, forcing an abrupt shift in the conversational tone. Harold cut himself off mid-sentence and glared, appearing to size him up. Alex met his eyes evenly and held out his hand until the guard captain reached around and clasped his elbow.

"Warden, eh? Elk, what's this about?" From the frown in Harold's bushy eyebrows, he did not think much of this development.

"I'm here assisting an investigation, Captain." Alex smiled politely.

"You're doing what?" The captain glowered at Rodney. "I didn't think we had any open investigations that needed the Blades involved."

"The Alamay girl—" Rodney began, but the captain cut him off almost immediately.

"You mean that drowned wench we found under the docks? The girl that the Riverlord guard couldn't identify as their own? *The case we let the ink dry on weeks ago?*" The last words were said with such intensity Alex could feel the venom radiating from the guard captain.

"With all due respect, sir, you sent me to Iera to—"

"I sent you to Iera to shut your blathering mouth!" Harold stood, and his bulk made the corner seem small. The man was built like a giant with a thick neck and belly. "Not to drag the Blades into a closed investigation!"

"Captain." Alex's voice was soft but carried an air of authority that cut through the bustle of the bar. The guard captain was a good head taller, and certainly much larger, than he was, but that wasn't a concern. It just meant that if this came to blows, he couldn't let the larger man get him in a grapple. "I assure you that it's no bother for me to look into it."

Harold took a menacing step forward, and Alex stood his ground, hoping the surrounding men couldn't hear how fast his heart was beating. "We don't need any damn Imperial sticking their nose in our business." Harold leaned in, closing the distance between them.

Alex decided indifference was the way to go. His gut said heat would only get him into a fight, and even if Elk was on his side, he was badly outnumbered. He'd learned the trick through several terrifying encounters with bandits and thugs in Danen. Bullies never expected you to ignore them.

"I don't particularly care what you need or don't need," he replied, keeping his face calm and tone level. Harold looked as though he'd just tasted something rather unpleasant, but Alex held the larger man's glare evenly.

For four tense breaths, nobody moved, and Harold leered over him. When the guard captain stepped back with a frustrated *huff*, Alex made a show of wrinkling his nose and stepping forward to fill the space.

"It's not even dark outside and you're as drunk as a pirate," he commented, his tone dripping with contempt. "No wonder a woman was murdered on your watch."

The guard captain turned a rather interesting shade of puce. "You dare…" he sputtered, making to step forward again.

Alex held up a hand, stopping the other man in his tracks. "I don't want any more of your stink on me, thanks much." He pivoted on the heel of his boot to address the table where a small group of men and women, Harold's cronies, clustered.

"I can mind my own business while I'm here, or I can— how did you put it? *Stick my nose in your business* and drag the lot of you to Iera for contempt of duty and endangering the safety of this village." Several of the guards looked away. A few even appeared properly ashamed. One woman with a thin face and square jaw narrowed her eyes at him. He returned the glower with a steady, flat gaze.

He let the silence stretch until it became uncomfortable— another trick he had learned in Danen. Most people hated awkward pauses and would say just about anything to fill the gap.

Finally, the woman looked away. Alex swept one more look across the lot of them. "You've gotten ale on your tunic, guardsman," he snapped at one at the table, who jumped.

Turning back to Harold, a small warm knot of pride unfurled in his belly when he saw that the older, bigger man had kept his distance, eying him warily. Stepping close—and trying not to wince at the stink of the man's breath—Alex firmly stuck his nose in the man's face. No harm in really driving the point home.

"I will haunt you like a raka if you cross me. Every bribe you've taken, every innocent you've abandoned, I will find them all and I will drag you before Erius' judgment myself." He saw a spark of real fear deep in the guard captain's eyes. "Understand me?"

Harold nodded almost imperceptibly, and Alex stepped back. There was nothing in continuing to humiliate the man beyond satisfying his own ego. He'd made his point.

Turning, Alex nodded to Elk. "Know anywhere we can grab a bite that doesn't reek of incompetence and greed?"

Poorly stifling a grin, the Constable nodded and gestured to the door. "After you, Warden."

CHAPTER 18

———

11th Day of the Harvest Moon

The next morning dawned too soon for Alex's liking. The innkeeper, Felicity, had left the curtains open, and the sunlight woke him up as it dripped across the tidy bedspread. Groaning, he splashed some water from a pitcher on his face, and raked his fingers through his hair.

After the confrontation at the bar, he and Rodney had walked back to the inn in what Alex would call a stunned silence. The Constable, who had been chatty and chipper before, seemed cowed by his sudden display of nastiness. It had taken two tankards of local ale before Rodney confessed he was worried that Harold would retaliate against Alex. Doing his best to conceal a self-satisfied smirk—as if a local guardsman could stand a chance—Alex reassured the Constable he could take care of himself.

This morning, the first order of business was to see the girl's body. Pulling on his change of clothes and leaving his old uniform in a soiled pile, Alex rifled through his packs for a number of supplies: magnifying lenses, a set of clinking vials, and a jar filled with iridescent powder. Stuffing the items into a pack that he slung over his shoulder, he locked the door to his room and tramped down the creaky wooden staircase.

Felicity smiled brightly when she saw him and waved him over toward the bar. "Your partner—is that the word?—is here already!" she remarked cheerfully. "Can I bring you some eggs?"

"Partner?" Alex turned, distracted, and saw to his utter horror that Danila had seated herself in a corner of the main room, near the smoldering fireplace.

"Yes! You know," Felicity lowered her voice to a stage whisper, "I think I can count the Imperials I've met on one hand!" She wiggled her fingers for emphasis.

"Is that so?" Alex said absently, mind racing. Whatever she wanted, it couldn't be good. He had a sinking, nauseated feeling in the pit of his stomach. The last thing he wanted was to be dragged into the conflict the Blades had with their Imperial oversight. That was one problem he'd gladly leave Hendrick to deal with.

Realizing Felicity was still talking though he had no idea what she was saying, he patted her on the hand. "Eggs would be lovely." He kept his tone as light as he could. She bustled away behind the counter and he made his way through the worn tables and tired couches toward where Danila was perched.

As he approached, she looked up at him over a mug of hot, black coffee. Her hair was braided tightly to her scalp still, though the pattern seemed to have shifted. Her clothes were relatively plain—a long, indigo tunic and dark leggings tucked into soft boots. The Mezrani, he knew, often wore rings on every finger and stacks of bracelets, but Danila wore only a few small golden hoops in the flesh of her right ear and a braided golden band on the middle finger of her left hand. No emotion was betrayed in her gaze beyond mild interest in his appearance.

"You look like you slept in that shirt," she remarked as he settled himself across from her.

"Well, it's a pleasure to see you too, Commissar," Alex retorted. "I'll have you know this is my clean uniform."

"I certainly hope you are less careless with your work than you are with your clothes," she fired back, but there was no bite in her voice. It was a very strange interaction, all things considered. The Commissar seemed almost friendly.

"How can I help you, Commissar?" Alex folded his hands on the table, drawing on his limited patience.

She took another sip of coffee before replying, "It's Danila. Nobody knows me here, so the formalities don't matter."

He raised an eyebrow, constantly surprised by the arrogance, which seemed inherent in every Mezrani he had ever met. "Everybody knows you here. You don't exactly blend in."

"I am an Imperial in the Empire, Laurent. I blend in where I like."

Opening his mouth, Alex reconsidered what he was about to say before he got himself in trouble. Deciding against a sarcastic comment, he continued, "How can I help you, Danila?"

"It's a matter of how I can help you, Alexander." She leaned forward, across the table. "The Imperial Authority has a vested interest in keeping the Riverlords happy, and currently Sylvester Alamay is anything but happy."

"You're here to make sure I don't make a mess of things," Alex interrupted.

"With that kind of investigative prowess, we should have the case solved in no time," she snapped back.

"And the threat of a Freelark attack wouldn't have anything at all to do with it, I imagine," he replied dryly.

Danila eyed him, wrapping one delicate hand around her coffee. He had the distinct impression he was being sized up. "You're a newcomer, but you certainly aren't a fool, Warden. I go where the Imperial Authority has an interest. Take from that what you will, and don't ask foolish questions."

Alex held up his hands in surrender. It seemed like a bad idea to needle the woman who held the fate of his career in her hands. "I'm going with Constable Elk to examine the girl's body soon. Would you like to come?" Felicity bustled up, carrying a plate laden with eggs, thick country bread slathered with some sort of fruit preserve, and some charred sausages.

It smelled delicious, and Alex said as much to Felicity, who blushed and fluttered away. As Alex dug in to the hearty breakfast—it was just as good as it smelled—Danila sighed theatrically. "I'm sure there are worse ways to spend the morning, though none come to mind."

An hour and a half later, Danila, Alex, and Rodney were all crowded around a stone slab in a chamber underneath the village temple. There, preserved with a bit of magical trickery Alex vaguely remembered from his training, was the bloated corpse at the center of this mess. At first glance, taking in the hair and rough body shape, Alex supposed it was a safe bet that it was a woman. More than that, he could not tell: her skin was stretched and shiny, her features buried and blurred.

To her credit, when Danila saw the body, she did not throw up. However, the dark-skinned Mezrani woman looked decidedly pale, and she covered her mouth with a handkerchief. The smell didn't bother Alex nearly as much. One hazard of his work was unfortunate amounts of time spent in the company of the dead. The preserving spell took away the worst of the stink, in any case.

"She was found under the docks?" Alex leaned in close, examining the clothing the dead woman wore. The cloth was stretched tightly against swollen mounds of skin, but it looked as though it was some sort of tunic and leggings, as Elk had reported. The tattoo Rodney had mentioned stuck in the back of his mind, but he forced himself to be methodical. The last thing he needed was to overlook something important.

"Aye." Rodney too had a handkerchief out. "We fished her out last moon."

"Anyone missing from the town?" Danila asked, her voice tight.

"Nope, none of our folk are gone, and the only traveler we had was a merchant, who left town several days later."

Alex removed one of the magnifying lenses from his pouch and carefully examined the skin of the dead woman. Much of it was bluish-green, as though bruised. Underneath, she appeared to have a pale complexion, similar, he admitted to himself, to that of Sylvester Alamay.

"The Riverlord guardsmen said she's the right height and build?" he asked, circling the woman to examine her other side.

"Aye." Rodney nodded again and then shrugged. "But they saw what you're seeing. I don't know how much you can tell about her build."

"They weren't alone with the body?"

"I was here the whole time."

Alex nodded and turned his attention to the girl's wrists, where Rodney had mentioned the tattoo. Freelark radicals— Dandelions—marked their own with flowers on the inside of the left wrist. Indeed, as he leaned close and studied the warped skin with his magnifying glass, Alex could discern an inky splotch that, he supposed, could be a flower. The bloating was too severe to make out the details.

Replacing the lens carefully in his belt, he turned to Danila. "Do you know what the Alamay girl looked like?"

"I've seen a painting in the Riverlord's estate," Danila replied slowly.

"Alright come here." Alex beckoned her closer, and she took a few steps toward him, wrinkling her forehead in disgust. "You wanted to come," he reminded her and received a glare for his efforts.

She held the handkerchief over her nose and mouth as she reached his side and kept her eyes focused on him, rather than the body on the slab. "What could you possibly need?"

He resisted the urge to roll his eyes. "Have either of you heard of Rakatash's Scales?"

Both Rodney and Danila shook their heads, nearly in unison. He nodded, unsurprised. "So, when we die, we either go to Cami's Pleasure Lands or Rakatash's Three Hells in the Nightmare Realms. Temple mages and scholars believe that Rakatash chooses what souls must stay with her and who may pass to Cami's lands unmolested. With me?"

Despite her discomfort, Danila managed to look impatient. "What does this have to do with the girl?"

"Well, to determine what happens to a person after death, Rakatash has to know who they are and what they look like. Temple mages believe Rakatash can track the very essence of a person—what makes us, well, *us*, and use it to identify who they are."

Rodney whistled through his teeth and made the sign against evil on his chest. "I don't like messing with the domain of the Gods."

"We're not," Alex reassured him. "Some Temple mages came up with this powder—an alchemical way to identify the essence of a person, drawing on their connection to Rakatash. I think that means it's God-approved."

Neither Rodney nor Danila looked totally convinced, and Alex wasn't sure he'd done a good job explaining himself. He reached back into his bag and pulled out the jar of iridescent powder he'd taken from his rooms earlier and held it out. "Danila, when I use this, we'll see an image of the girl, the same way Rakatash saw her in life. I need you to tell me if it's Evaline. I don't know what she looked like."

The Mezrani woman gave an unsure nod. Unscrewing the top of the jar carefully, Alex took a generous pinch in gloved fingers and then tossed it over the corpse between them.

When the iridescent powder touched the corpse, a wisp of pale energy appeared, hovering over the body. Features came into focus: a strong jaw and high cheekbones, imperious eyes and long, dark, wavy hair. Even before Danila spoke, Alex knew it was Evaline Alamay. He could see echoes of Sylvester in the sharp slant of her nose and stubborn lips.

"It's her." Danila's voice was resigned. Behind them, Rodney watched, eyes wide in his round face. Alex examined the glittering figure carefully, looking for any detail he might have missed before turning to the wrist. Through the shimmer of magic, he could make out the tattoo plain as day: about halfway up the forearm, where it would be easy to conceal under clothes, a dandelion, crowned in fuzzy strands, three of the seeds dancing away toward the crook of her elbow.

Not good, Alex thought. Dandelions were marked based on their commitment to the cause. Every direct, dangerous action against society earned another seed, to symbolize the unstoppable spread of their ideas and violence. Three seeds meant Evaline hadn't just been searching for a cause—she had been committed to one. *How did a wealthy merchant's daughter wind up with the Freelarks? And what in the Hells had she been doing in Pheant?*

"I need to send word to the Riverlords," Danila muttered, stepping back from Evaline's body as the shimmering figure faded to nothing.

"As soon as Alamay knows we've found her, his people will be all over this town," Alex replied quickly. "We need the time to investigate before word reaches them."

Danila paused. When she spoke, her voice was measured. "If the Riverlords find out this is Evaline by some hand other than mine, it won't be good for either of us."

"Nobody knows yet but us," Rodney spoke up, and they both turned toward him. "I don't have to report it for a few days."

Alex nodded. "If you can keep it under wraps for a little, let us work, Danila can send word the same day you tell Captain Harold. Our messenger will leave before anyone else knows, which means the information should reach Alamay by our hand." He looked at Danila.

She drummed her fingers absently on her arm for a moment and then seemed to make up her mind. "We'll do it your way, Laurent." Her tone was abrupt. "We need to solve this murder quickly."

Alex put his tools away and stepped toward the door, looking at the Constable. Rodney looked nervous, but settled. *He wouldn't be an issue*, Alex thought. "Then it's settled. We'll chase down what we can while we still have the benefit of silence. Let's get to work."

CHAPTER 19

12th Day of the Harvest Moon

"It just doesn't square," Alex muttered, tapping his nails on the worn wood of the breakfast table the next morning.

Across from him, Danila arched one perfectly tailored eyebrow. "Oh really? I wouldn't have noticed if you hadn't mentioned it." It seemed that most things she said dripped with sarcasm.

"That's why I pointed it out," he replied calmly. "I've been told I have excellent powers of observation."

Danila rolled her eyes and then moved her plate aside and folded her hands on the table. "What are you stuck on?"

Swallowing a draft of hot coffee, Alex puffed out his cheeks as he thought. "I feel like we have all these pieces but I still can't see the big picture."

"So walk through the pieces." The Mezrani leaned back, lacing her fingers across her stomach.

"Our intelligence says the Freelarks are planning an attack on the Harvest Festival. We don't know what the attack will be or exactly what part of the Festival they're targeting. Freelark attacks tend not to be very sophisticated—slicing through a crowd with swords or destroying a symbolic building or location. Occasionally they get a mage on their side, usually to hurt the Lycantheum rather than society itself, which is always dangerous."

"The Glittering Hand aren't tracking any rogue mages in the area," Danila commented. "At least not that I'm aware of."

Hiding his relief, Alex nodded. The Glittering Hand were a terrifying group, the elite mages of the Lycantheum assigned to track down and imprison rogue mages. It was a necessary job, to be sure, but they were a frightening lot. The stories he'd heard during his training had given him nightmares for a week.

"So a mage is less likely, then. That's a relief." Alex rubbed his nose. "That's one piece. The other big one is the Alamay girl. We still don't know what she was doing here."

"Whatever it was, I'd bet you she bribed her guards to spend a few days in Iera and then catch up to her on the road. Her father said she traveled to the Viridian Coast regularly to help oversee their trading empire; probably used the trips as some sort of excuse to do whatever she did for the Freelarks." Danila bit into a slice of bread.

"Isn't that awfully bold though? What if word got back to the Riverlord?"

Danila shrugged. "Sometimes the best secrets are those that are kept in the open," she said wisely.

"What, exactly, is that supposed to mean?" Alex took another gulp of coffee.

"It's an old Imperial saying." She waved a hand. "Everyone has secrets, but the best secrets are those that are wrapped in the mundane. The secrets that are shrouded in subterfuge are often not nearly as interesting as the details of people's lives." He didn't really follow her explanation, but it did sound like the kind of vague platitude he had heard frequently in the capital.

"Well, if she was here doing something for the Freelarks, we should pay a visit to the Hearth Hall." Alex dragged his fingers through his hair and swallowed the last of his coffee. "Ready?"

Together, the two of them made their way through dusty streets to the center of town where the Hearth Hall stood. Outside, they met Rodney, who greeted them with a wave from his perch by the town well.

The Hearth Hall was a large, warm building with long wooden tables, a cheerfully snapping fire, and the delicious smell of fresh stew and homemade bread. A ladder in the corner of the room led to a loft in the rafters, where Alex knew anyone was welcome to bed down for the night.

The legend of the Hearth Hall predated the Empire by several centuries—something Alex knew the Mezrani were touchy about. Hearth Halls were scattered across the Empire and provided food and shelter to the downtrodden wherever they were built. Supposedly blessed by Valdon the Steward, the Hearth Hall had been wound into the fabric of the world as long as anyone could remember.

Hearth Halls were how the Freelarks had gained a popular following. They began as Hearthminders, the tenders of the Halls. To most people, the Freelarks were known for providing free food and shelter, and they were protected by the Gods. To be fair, most of the Hearthminders were not directly involved with the illicit, anarchistic activities of the Freelarks, but it made the Imperial battle against the group all the more difficult.

"Rodney! Good to see you!" A short and portly man bustled across the room and clasped the Constable's arm. "Are these the visitors I have heard so much about?"

"Warden Alexander Laurent of the Blades, and Danila al-Mhir, from Mezrani City." Rodney gestured to each of them as he spoke. "This is Glynn, the Hearthminder of Pheant."

"A pleasure to meet you both!" Glynn gripped Alex's hand in both of his as he shook it fervently. He returned the enthusiasm with a smile, though he saw Danila's nose wrinkle. "I heard you were in town looking into that dreadful situation at the docks!"

"Rodney asked for a second opinion," Alex responded casually. "Have you heard much about it?"

"It seems like every rumor there is comes through these doors. Part of the business, I suppose. We get all sorts in here." Glynn chuckled.

Danila seated herself on one of the benches, and he turned abruptly to her. "I've forgotten my manners! Can I get you some bread, fresh from the oven?"

"Valdon bless you, Glynn." Rodney nodded, settling himself next to Danila.

When the Hearthminder left them alone, Danila drummed her fingers on the table. "It's foolish, these Halls. Just another opportunity for the Freelarks to spread their vile, anti-Imperial message to the public. It's nothing but trouble." Her tone, usually so measured, was a sharp staccato.

"Tell me how you really feel," Alex replied dryly.

She glanced up at him and then around the room. "I know you learned this too. We have countless cases of the Hearth Halls shielding Freelark Dandelions from Imperial justice. I cannot understand why we permit the Freelarks to operate so openly in our society."

"I'm not going to argue with you." Alex's voice was calm. "Rodney, is this what Glynn is normally like? So friendly?"

Elk rubbed his chin. "I suppose so. I've never met a Hearthminder who wasn't, though. All sorts come through Hearth Halls, and their minders greet each one. I've never met a soul who didn't like Glynn. He's doing the work of the Gods."

Alex ran his fingers through his hair and scanned the room. A few small clumps of people were enjoying the free meal, and Glynn had not yet returned from the kitchen door. Nobody was paying them much attention. He made a snap decision. "I'm going to go poke my nose in it. Back in a moment."

Without waiting to see if Danila had snide remark, Alex left the Hall through the main door. The building was positioned on the edge of the central town square. A small cluster of merchant stalls dotted the area, and two children splashed in the fountain. Alex slouched casually around the side of the building.

The alley that encircled the Hearth Hall was just wide enough for a wagon to squeeze through. Crates, spare wooden planks, and other clutter were stacked haphazardly in the dust against the building, and a steaming pile of kitchen scraps perfumed the air. Alex hooked his thumbs through his belt and walked, scruffing his boots in the dirt. Nearing the back of the Hearth Hall, he heard hushed voices echoing slightly in the narrow space. Crouching down beside a crate near the corner, Alex narrowed his eyes, trying to focus on the conversation.

"—have to be more careful!" Glynn's voice, so friendly and warm a moment earlier, was clipped and hurried. "I've got the Constable just inside. I told you we'd meet later."

"Your problems are not my concern." The voice was male, smooth and silky. "You are stalling."

"I am not!" There was a whining note in the Hearthminder's voice. *Was it fear?*

"Careful. You would not want the Dandelions to doubt your dedication to our cause." The voice remained light, a jarring juxtaposition to the threat.

"What do you want from me, Drake? I can't give you what I don't have."

"That is not my problem. My problem is that you promised me this shipment last moon, and I am becoming less and less convinced you can deliver."

Glynn mumbled something Alex couldn't make out.

"I do not give a damn if killing the girl ruined your plans." The slippery voice turned cold. "She will be remembered as a martyr. Her sacrifice was the last piece to our success. Other, of course, than my shipment. And that brings us back to you, *Hearthminder*," Drake spat the word like an insult.

"I swear to you that it's coming." Now Alex was certain he heard fear in Glynn's voice. "Tomorrow, I promise you."

The silence stretched so long that he wondered if the two men had left. As he tried to decide what to do, he heard Drake speak once again. "Meet me at the usual place tomorrow evening. And if you don't have what I need by then, don't bother coming. I will just hunt you down and kill you." The threat sent a shiver down Alex's spine. He thought he could hear a hint of a laugh in Drake's tone.

When he realized the conversation was breaking up, he also realized he had no way to get out of the alley without being seen. He dove behind the pile of kitchen refuse, slowly composting in the hot sun. Holding his breath against the stink, he lay curled in a ball, praying to every God he could think of that he was hidden. He heard quick steps pass him without pause and then waited an extra twenty count to make sure nobody else was coming.

Exhaling through his mouth, Alex straightened and grimaced as he tried to brush the muck from his tunic. Hurrying to the end of the alley, he peered out into the square but saw no one out of the ordinary. Glancing down, he realized he had failed magnificently to remove the stains of rotten food from his clothes, and flies buzzed around him. Letting out a heavy sigh, he took off at a quick trot back toward the lodging house for fresh clothes.

It took him a little over twenty minutes to change and return to the Hearth Hall. By the time he sheepishly slid onto the bench beside Danila, the table was laden with fresh bread, thick venison stew, and apples. Danila was tearing the bread into strips and using it to scoop stew while Rodney chomped an apple. When he returned, she raised an eyebrow at him. Signaling he would fill them in later, he smiled sheepishly at Glynn as the Freelark bustled over looking decidedly pale.

"Are you feeling alright, Warden?" The Hearthminder smiled warmly, but Alex saw the hint of fear in his eyes. The Freelark was clearly shaken.

"I'm actually feeling a little under the weather. Do you have somewhere I could lie down?" He thought quickly. If he could get Glynn alone, he could probably force him to confess to whatever Freelark plot he was tangled in.

"Of course, Warden. There's a private room upstairs I can show you to." Glynn's smile was just a little too forced to be genuine.

"You didn't say anything about feeling—ow! What'd you do that for?" Rodney glared across the table at Danila, who tore off another strip of bread.

"I'm sure I don't know what you're talking about," she replied in a bored tone.

"You kicked me!"

Danila glared at the Constable. "Ladies do not kick. I would recommend you shut your jaw before you say something that offends my honor."

"To be fair," Alex chimed in, steering the conversation to relatively safer territory. "She has an awful lot of honor you can offend. Throw a dart and I'm sure you'll hit something." He stood, making a show of moving slowly, as though he felt ill. "After you, Glynn."

The Hearthminder led him up the stairs to the second level of the Hearth Hall. Most of it was dedicated to communal sleeping quarters. Bunks three high were built into several walls, and mismatched chairs and tables were strewn about. Glynn guided him through the chaos to a small room off the main area.

As soon as the door closed, Alex positioned himself between Glynn and escape. "I know about your deal with Drake, Hearthminder."

Fear and disbelief fought for control of the Freelark's features. Alex watched him struggle to stay calm and come up with an excuse.

He chose a classic. "I don't know what you're talking about." Glynn tried for defiance but ended up sounding unconvinced.

"Okay, let me lay out for you what I know. Sit." Alex pointed to the bed and then folded his arms. Once the Freelark, looking entirely miserable, had settled, he began to speak.

"I know that Evaline Alamay was a Freelark and got herself tangled up with the Dandelions. I know she was helping

Drake smuggle something, and I know you somehow got pulled in as the middleman." He watched the weak indignance on Glynn's face fade to shock until the man buried his face in his hands. "If you want to come out of this, you need to tell me everything you know, and you need to do it now."

CHAPTER 20

13th Day of the Harvest Moon

Walking into the Broken Cup tavern was like walking into a wall of heat, noise, and stale ale. It wasn't actually that big of a place, but its popularity with dockworkers, guards, and townsfolk in general packed it tightly. The bar wrapped around one side of the wall, and tables were stuffed into the rest of the room. So many chairs dotted the floor it was hard to make his way through the tavern without stepping on feet, cloaks, or egos.

Alex had settled in a shadowy corner behind the door several hours earlier. After he had confronted Glynn yesterday, the Freelark had snapped. He didn't know as much as Alex had hoped. It seemed that Drake was planning something, but the Hearthminder didn't know what. Glynn had been Evaline's contact. When she smuggled goods for the Dandelions, she brought them to Glynn, who then held them until another Freelark could come ferry them to wherever they were going.

The Hearthminder had also confessed that he didn't have whatever shipment Drake was looking for. Evaline had come to town, yes, but she had not visited him as she usually did. And then, a few days later, her body was found under the pier. Glynn claimed he didn't know who had killed her, or why, but Alex had the distinct impression he blamed Drake. And, after overhearing part of their conversation, he could understand why.

The Freelarks were supposed to be meeting in the Broken Cup tonight, and Alex was waiting. He was glad he'd cornered Glynn and convinced him to meet with Drake. The Hearthminder had been ready to run for it and take his chances disappearing.

He hadn't quite decided if he believed that Glynn was truly caught in the wrong place at the wrong time and forced into helping the Dandelions. His gut leaned toward no. Rodney had told him Glynn had run the Hearth Hall for over a decade, and it seemed unlikely that someone who had been in the Freelarks for that long had simply been taken advantage of.

The front door pushed open again, and Alex watched as Glynn entered, looking nervously around. He went straight for a booth near the door to the kitchen, nearly opposite where Alex was currently settled, and tucked enough away it would be hard to overhear any conversation.

Scanning the room, Alex searched for a good perch. With a sigh, he resigned himself to the corridor that led to the latrines out behind the building. It adjoined the booth where Glynn sat, and men had been drinking long enough that a queue had formed. The stink from the latrines didn't quite reach the tavern—at least not this early in the evening. Swiping an empty tankard from a wobbling tray held by a sleepy-eyed server, Alex tossed his cloak across the back of a chair, untucked half his shirt, and blended into a knot of men singing a bawdy song about wenches and ships.

When Alex's makeshift group of drinking partners neared Glynn's table, another figure joined the Freelark, sliding onto the bench in a fluid movement. Alex watched carefully through the jostling crowd, craning his neck to get a good look at the newcomer.

The young man had shockingly pale hair, hard eyes, and a dark green tunic as he leaned across the table to grip Glynn's arm at the elbow as a way of greeting. His clothing was somehow exotic. It was not the traditional layers most Roosemoorians wore or the long tunics favored by Mezrani men. Rather, his garb reminded Alex of the pirates he had met in the Free City of Swansea on the southern coast. From this angle, he couldn't make out any weapons—though Alex would have bet a favor from a God the man was armed.

Assessing his options quickly, Alex edged forward, turning his back to the table and positioning himself on the edge of the line. He swayed back and forth absently to the nonexistent rhythm of a drunken song and furrowed his brow, listening carefully.

"—taken so long." Alex could hear the nerves in Glynn's voice.

"I am not known for my patience." He recognized the voice as Drake's—silky and smooth, like melted butter. It made Alex's skin crawl. "We are both working toward the same goal, you know."

"Y-yes. Yes. I know. I was just shaken by the girl's death. I had to find another way to move the goods for you."

"Glynn, perhaps I was not clear when last we spoke." Drake had a slightly strange way of speaking, Alex observed. It was very formal, nearly old fashioned. "I have been working on this for *years*. I do not care if you have cold feet. I need that shipment."

"I don't even know what I'm looking for!" Glynn sounded truly panicked now, and Alex weighed whether or not to step in. Deciding to let it play out a little longer, he tried to edge closer. "I don't know how you think I can get what you need when I don't know what it is!"

"Evaline was not your only contact in Torren, of this I am certain," Drake replied. It sounded as though he swished each word around his mouth before letting it dribble out. "And your decision to stay out of Dandelion affairs is your own business. I still expect you to perform your duties or you can be...replaced."

"Is that a threat?"

"Oh good, so you *do* understand Common. Given the number of times we have had this conversation, I was not quite sure." He sounded very patronizing, Alex realized, which struck an odd chord given Drake's obvious youth— especially when compared to Glynn. "I promised you would regret failing me, and I intend to make good on that promise. Remember, Glynn, there is not a place in the natural world you can hide where the Dandelions won't seek you out."

A particularly loud chorus sounded near Alex, and he lost track of the conversation in the disjointed tune. Half turning, he watched Drake move like water and glide out the kitchen door to leaving Glynn behind, looking as though he was about to pass out.

Making a snap decision, Alex darted past the line outside, shouldering his way into the kitchen. He dodged around a bored-looking cook and narrowly avoided upending a pile of dirty dishes. Barreling out the door in the back of the kitchen, he collided with the tall man dressed in green.

His instincts kicked in, and he threw his weight into Drake's midriff. Caught off guard, the man tumbled but managed to react, his leg snapping out and hooking Alex to the ground as well. Alex landed hard, gasping as the air was nearly knocked from his lungs. That was a fighter's move, and a dirty fighter's move at that. He'd learned it himself during his training.

Regaining his breath—and ducking another swing—Alex sharpened his focus on his opponent. He needed to end this quickly. If the scuffle lasted much longer, he would be out-maneuvered. Drake had the reflexes and power of someone who didn't carry weapons simply for show. The last thing he needed was a knife between his ribs.

They plowed into the muddy alley, rolling and scrambling for purchase. Alex took two hard punches, one to the stomach and the second to his kidney. The world nearly went black, and pain lanced through his torso. Flickering toward darkness, a voice in the back of his head that sounded suspiciously like Starling, his trainer, echoed. *Finish it, or he will.*

His breath gone and vision blurry, Alex clawed his way back to consciousness. With an animalistic grunt, he thrashed out, clawing at the taller man who pinned him to the ground. He felt his nails sink into soft flesh, heard a shriek, and felt Drake's weight shift backward. Seizing the moment, he slammed his knee between Drake's legs, bucking the man off him. Rolling up, he straddled the taller man, gripped the sap he carried at his belt, and slammed his fist into Drake's chin.

It was a perfect nap-tap. Drake's cold eyes rolled up in his head, and his fingers went limp around Alex's collar. Gasping, Alex muttered a string of colorful expletives as he rubbed his side, swaying with pain. With his other hand, he reached for a set of rawhide ties tucked inside a pouch and forced himself to bind Drake's hands and ankles. He wouldn't win a second round.

When he pushed the man's sleeve up to tighten the knot, Alex saw the same ink flower that had marked Evaline's wrist tattooed on the pale skin—though this one was surrounded by a thick cloud of dandelion seeds rather than just three. Through the muddle of pain, Alex knew that was the final connection he needed. It was enough to justify a detainment, perhaps even arrest, though he couldn't definitively prove much. The final decision would be Hendrick's, back in Iera. Regardless of the outcome, it would buy him more time to uncover the truth.

Once the ties were secure, Alex allowed himself to slump back and the pain to take him. Leaning to the side, he let himself be sick. His throat was raw, and his abdomen was a solid block of pain. Wiping his mouth with the back of his hand, Alex swiped away sick before collapsing back against the wall of the tavern.

The reprieve was painfully short-lived. Once he had regained his breath, Alex forced himself to his feet and bodily dragged Drake to the edge of the main street. The man's head lolled through the muck, and Alex felt a strong surge of self-satisfaction as Drake's pale hair was stained the dirty brown of street scummer. Ignoring the stares of a group outside the Broken Cup, Alex beckoned the sleepy-eyed server from before over.

"There a guard here you trust for help?" She looked over the muddy man on the ground and nodded silently. "Ask him to go fetch Rodney Elk for me. Would you?" Alex fumbled for two silver coins. "Quickly."

CHAPTER 21

———

15th Day of the Harvest Moon

"What am I forgetting?" Caidy stopped pacing back and forth in her suite and turned to face Geoffrey, hands on her hips. She had officially hit a wall with the number of details to arrange for the Harvest Festival.

Patiently, he recited the list they had been working through for the past week. "Sort out the guard schedules and pay for the Festival."

"Yes. Thom told me that's all been worked out as of yesterday."

"Convince the merchant guilds to donate benches, stalls, and tables."

"I've got the signed contract somewhere around here..." Distracted, she began to rustle through papers on the desk. *How has so much piled up and it's not yet noon?*

"We'll say that's done, then. Deal with the shipment delays out of Torren."

She groaned, rolling her head on her neck. "Yes. That was my headache yesterday. Everything should be here on the eighteenth."

"Flyers and pamphlets?" Geoffrey gave up on standing and settled himself in one of the comfortable chairs near the window.

"Messengers were dispatched on the tenth. They'll go again on the seventeenth. Everyone knows anyway. It's pretty much just for visitors." She felt like she was saying the same words over and over, the details all bleeding together into one giant mess.

"All the stalls and vendors have been sorted out?"

"They're not all happy about it, but yes. Everyone wants the prime locations in Honey. But assignments are done and have been distributed." She found the contract she was looking for, confirmed it was signed, and then set it aside.

Geoffrey nodded, folding up the list. "Then really all that's left is meeting with the Player company doing the annual performance."

"Remind me what the problem is again?" She resumed pacing, listening carefully.

"The leader of the company, a woman named Thalia, petitioned to see you. It didn't say why."

I'm fairly sure I asked you to find out, but of course you didn't bother, she thought, annoyed. "Alright, then that's what I'll deal with today. What do you have planned?" She stepped into her closet, staring blankly at the rows of clothes as she tried to figure out what to wear.

"Playing Imperial chess with the new Ambassador," Geoffrey raised his voice slightly from the other room. "My father says she's fierce competition."

"Sounds like a very productive day," Caidy called back, trying to swallow her sarcasm.

Geoffrey sounded a little defensive, which gave her the impression the sarcasm had come through regardless. "I also need to discuss some of the current Imperial edicts around imports and exports on behalf of the Valance vineyards. We could improve our profits threefold if I can convince her to give us an exemption."

She poked her head around the door. "That *is* good. We could use the extra tax income."

He grinned at her. "Not if I can convince *you* to give us an exemption as well, my dove."

The name made her cringe, and she stepped back into the closet so he wouldn't see. There was no point arguing about it. They'd both just end up frustrated and unsatisfied. She'd deal with that problem later.

She stared at the clothes for a few moments longer before giving up and grabbing for a dress that hopefully wouldn't be too hot. Examining herself in the mirror, she felt a surge of satisfaction. Margot had braided her hair back that morning, and it had yet to break free.

Stepping back into the main room, she saw Geoffrey hovering by the door, looking very torn about whether he should stay or go. Suppressing the natural urge to roll her eyes, she fixed a smile on her face. "You should go to pre-pare for meeting the Ambassador. I'd imagine you have to go into the city."

"Well, yes," he replied, still looking uncertain. "I thought we might ride down together, love."

Gods. "I still have about an hour's worth of work to do before I can leave. You should go! I'll see you tonight." She stepped up and kissed him perfunctorily on the cheek and then squeezed his hands. "Have fun, alright? Good luck negotiating."

He brightened. "Very well. I'll see you for dinner, then. Good luck, dove."

Once he left, she let herself slump back against the door for just a moment. *I hate that nickname,* she thought listlessly. And yet, she would be hearing it for the rest of her life. *Wonderful.*

She spent a few more minutes bustling around her rooms, trying to tidy papers, before settling in front of the mirror to make herself presentable. Experimenting with painting her own face the way Margot did, Caidy quickly realized there was an art to it, and rinsed off the lip color she'd tried before leaving her rooms.

In the hall, Merric stood, chatting with another guard. When she emerged, he straightened automatically. She paused considering the most diplomatic way to ask her question.

Before she could figure it out, Merric spoke. "My Lady, Deputy Ohlm has informed me that Lord Geoffrey just rode out of the castle." The other guard, a woman with short hair, saluted with her hand over her heart.

For the first time that morning, Caidy broke into a genuine smile. "You read my mind, Merric. Thank you. How long will it take for us to be ready to depart?"

"Your horse is warmed up and in the courtyard, my Lady." Merric kept his face smooth, but she detected a glitter of a smile in his eyes.

The ride down to the city was brisk. With only her guards, Caidy rode quickly. Not much traffic marred the road in the middle of the day, so their journey was unimpeded.

The city itself was bustling. Decorations were going up everywhere—streamers and banners, colorful murals and posters. The streets were being swept clean, and Temple Acolytes circulated, urging the poor and homeless to bed down in the temples rather than outside. A sign outside a large inn near one of the main gates proclaimed deals for visitors while a young man advertised a tavern crawl for the evening before the Harvest Ball.

The Harvest Festival wasn't simply a tradition. It was the biggest event in Iera every year. Thousands traveled to Iera to retell the love story of Iya, the Goddess of flame and summer, and Erius, the God of justice and autumn. The Festival celebrated their story, how Erius had tamed Iya's fire and how her joy brought cool weather and bountiful harvests each year. In Rosemoor, nothing was more important than the harvest. They were the breadbasket of the Empire.

The first day of the Festival would culminate in the burning of the Great Effigy, symbolizing the way the summer heat scorched the earth clean and fresh and how Erius' rains brought forth life from the soil.

She had been working on her speech for the past week. It was Caidy's first year leading the Festival preparations. Usually that was in her mother's purview, but on her birthday earlier this year, her mother had said Caidy was finally old enough to head the celebration. It was an honor, and a point of personal pride. The Harvest Festival had been her favorite holiday as long as she could remember.

Before the Festival could start, she needed to sort out whatever dispute the Players were having. Every year, the Players reenacted Iya's and Erius' love story in one of the biggest performances of the year, and there was fierce competition between troupes to have the privilege. This year, Cami's Stare had been selected by the Entertainer's Guild. The troupe had just returned from performing in Canastel, the capital city of Colmar, to rave reviews.

Cami's Stare was working out of a performance house in Honey District, so Caidy and her guards clattered over cobblestones to the entertainment quarter. Here, it felt as though the Festival had already begun, though formal celebrations wouldn't begin for six days.

Street performers twirled, danced, and sparkled; folk gathered in crowds, laughing and cheering. It was busier than usual, and she dismounted to thread more easily through the crowd. Merric followed her, handing off their reins to another guardsman to manage.

She visited a street vendor's stall to purchase some honeycomb tea. When the woman recognized her, she tried to refuse payment, but Caidy politely ignored her offer, passing across the coins with a generous tip. "Gods bless ye, milady," the woman said, tears sparkling in her eyes.

"And you," she replied with a soft smile. "Do your children always help with the cart?" Caidy gestured to the six children scampering about.

"We get busy during the Festival, milady, so I hire some of the street urchins. They're good lads and lasses, and they love being so close to the entertainers."

"I can imagine! I would have loved a front row seat to a performance like that."

She made her way through the crowd to the acting troupe, pausing on nearly every street to exchange a friendly word. Most nobles, she knew, detested mingling with what they considered the common folk; Geoffrey hated when she did this, but Caidy loved meeting with people, hearing their stories, and easing their burdens. Especially now, when she could admit to herself hearing how excited everyone was for the Harvest Festival made the long hours she had put in worth it.

When they finally made it to the entertainment house, they were greeted by a very skinny boy with a shock of red hair, who seemed to bounce rather than walk. He brought them inside and then went to fetch the troupe leader, Thalia.

Caidy settled herself in a wooden chair beside a table. The building had clearly spent at least some of its life as a tavern. A long bar stretched along one wall, and chairs and tables were crowded inside. She thought she recalled that some limited shows were still held here, but it was mostly a lodging house for traveling performers.

Thalia was a small and round woman with a kind face and no-nonsense eyes. She marched in, her eyes sweeping the room and taking in every detail.

"Milady, thank you for coming to our humble quarters." She had the musical voice of a seasoned Player, someone who could draw you into her story with just a few words. "Please forgive the mess. Players are not the tidiest bunch."

"Neither am I," Caidy replied easily. "I'm sorry I couldn't come sooner. I've been tied up in arrangements for the Festival."

"Yes, milady, that's why I asked to see you." Thalia had long, curling hair the color of honey she wore piled on top of her head in a slightly lopsided manner. "My performers are concerned."

"Oh?" Caidy leaned forward. "By what?"

"Well, as you may know, milady, many of my performers come from farming families. Not altogether uncommon in Rosemoor, of course, but those of us who are lucky enough to make a living as a Player often send funds back to our homes to help ease the burden."

"Of course, that makes sense."

Thalia twirled a loose strand of hair about her finger, clearly a little uncomfortable. "Well, milady, recently we've gotten some strange letters from home. Imperial assessors, visiting farms and asking questions. Not unheard of, of course, but unusual. And then there was this." She drew out a formal letter that had been tucked into her belt and laid it on the table.

Leaning forward, Caidy read quickly. It was from the Entertainer's Guild, and warned that the Empire would begin collecting a small percentage of all the proceeds from any performance, starting the twentieth.

As she finished skimming the letter, Thalia spoke again, her tone careful. "I'm not questioning the right of the Empire to make these demands, milady, but you must understand that this is not sustainable. I've been on both sides of the stage. I started my career as a Player, and now I'm blessed by Cami to lead her Stare. I can tell you firsthand, milady, that it is not a life of wealth. We live hand to mouth, and any tips we scrape together, we send home to help our families." She paused, clearly considering what to say next.

"I appreciate the difficulty this poses," Caidy replied cautiously. "But I'm afraid I'm not sure what I can do to help. I do not levy Imperial taxes."

"Of course not, milady. But my troupe… we're unique this year." When Caidy frowned, she clarified. "Every year, you and your family attend the performance at the Harvest Festival. It is our honor to give you that performance this year. When we received your notice, asking for any issues to be brought to your attention, I decided to write to you."

Thalia folded her hands on the table in front of her. "I don't ask you to do anything, milady. But I would not be doing my duty, to my Players or to the rest of the Entertainer's Guild, if I did not bring this to your attention. We have been to Mezrani City. I've seen the wonders firsthand. I'm sure…" She paused, considering. "I'm sure the tax assessors haven't any idea how this tithe will affect us. But now you do, and perhaps you could say something."

"I can certainly bring it to the attention of the Imperial Ambassador," Caidy agreed. "But I cannot promise anything more than that. It is ultimately in their purview. If they choose to continue collecting the tax, perhaps we can examine other options, but again, I want to caution that I don't know what will come of this."

Thalia looked at her, and Caidy had the distinct feeling she was being sized up. "The rumors are true, milady. You have a truly kind and generous heart. All I ask is that you bring it to the Ambassador."

"Mistress Thalia, the best part of my life is being able to help people like you, who otherwise may not be heard by the nobles of our world." Caidy reached forward impulsively, covering the older woman's hand with her own. "I cannot promise change, but I can promise to be your voice."

The performer bowed her head. "Thank you, my Lady."

CHAPTER 22

———

16th Day of the Harvest Moon

Alex stood at attention back in Hendrick's cluttered office. The former Bandit Lord had his feet up on the corner of his desk, his eyes focused on his very long report, which trailed to the floor. Jakob perched on the windowsill, nibbling a thick slice of bread and reading over Hendrick's shoulder. Danila lounged beside Alex in a chair, drumming her fingers on the arm.

He watched Hendrick's bushy brows snap together almost audibly. "You want to charge him with treason, the murder of Evaline Alamay, smuggling, threats to life and property, intimidation, and attempted murder of city officials? Anything you want to add while you're at it? Counterfeiting the Emperor's coin? A plot to assassinate the Lord of Rosemoor?"

Pursing his lips, Alex said nothing. He knew he had thrown the book at the Freelark, and he didn't regret it. His side still ached. His report was a suggestion, which Hendrick was free to disregard, and Danila had agreed with him on the ride back to Iera.

"I don't see where the justification for this comes from. I don't care what our intelligence reports say, you don't have proof of anything other than the man landed a solid kidney punch on you. We can't just lock citizens up for supporting the Freelarks, Laurent. It undermines your entire job, your reputation. *Our* reputation."

"Respectfully," Danila began, in a tone a generous man would have called disrespectful, "We can. The Freelarks are a danger to Rosemoor and the Empire. They have made the first strike time and time again. A Dandelion, tangled in a plot to harm the beloved Roussel family during the treasured Harvest Festival? Our subjects will support you, praise you even, for throwing scum like him in the darkest hole you can find."

Alex actually heard Hendrick's teeth grind together as he rounded on Danila, and he contemplated ducking for cover. "*Respectfully*, Commissar, this is my decision, and I will make it regardless of your opinion."

He glared at her, pausing for a moment to let the words sink in before continuing. "How we treat this man sets a precedent for the entire province. I don't have the evidence here to charge him with more than simple assault since, by his own admission, Laurent here started the fight. What do you have tying him to Evaline or this alleged attack? The word of a Freelark also accused of smuggling? It's not actually illegal to be a Freelark, even a Dandelion."

"Yet," Alex heard Danila murmur.

Hendrick raised an eyebrow at her. "Until I hear differently through an Imperial Edict, Freelarks are lawful members of society. They feed the hungry and house the homeless. Some certainly commit crimes, as do many other people. As did I, in a past life. We charge for the crime, not for the affiliation. My job is not to increase Imperial popularity in Rosemoor or to deny its subjects rights guaranteed by the Imperial Authority. My job is to protect all members of the Empire.

"Now." He raised a hand as Danila leapt from her chair, taking a breath to speak. "If I get hard proof that the Freelarks are involved in something illicit, I'll drag them to the Magistrate's Court myself. But I will not let innocent people be targeted by political ambition."

Danila's eyes narrowed and she pressed her lips together into a thin white line. Alex watched her left hand tighten into a fist and then relax almost immediately. The silence that echoed between the Imperial Commissar and the Blade Commander was suffocating.

"You couldn't get him to talk, Laurent?" Hendrick rounded on Alex again, and he jerked in surprise.

"No. In my judgment, the best course of action was to return him to Iera and speak with you about moving forward. I have the right to detain him indefinitely following the edicts issued in the wake of the Mezrani Riots."

The former bandit nodded curtly. "At least you're not an idiot. Yes, we can detain him. But unless we get more evidence, this whole damn trip was a waste of my resources and your time. We would have been better off pursuing leads— and Freelarks, for that matter—here. Commissar, Jakob, give us the room."

It was an abrupt shift in tone. Jakob raised both his eyebrows at Alex significantly as he left, and Danila's mouth tightened almost imperceptibly. Despite her reaction, and the anger he knew would have sprung hot to the surface of her thoughts, she swept after Jakob, clattering down the narrow wooden staircase.

When they were alone, Hendrick tossed the report on top of the endless stack on his desk, and cracked his knuckles. "Sit down, boy." He pointed a thumb at a chair in front of him. Alex sat.

"Tell me what you left out of the report."

"What do you mean?" Alex raised both eyebrows innocently. "My report contains all facts relevant to the investigation."

"I'm sure. I want your speculation and observations. You're smart, Laurent, and your last tour was in Danen. That means you know how to spin. I don't want the truth you want the Citadel to have and file. I want to know what happened and what you saw. Give it to me straight, so I can make the right call."

Alex considered carefully. Hendrick was correct that his report was very exacting. Ingrid, the Warden he had supported in Danen, had always told him to only put what he could prove in the report, and let someone else make the final decision. In the corrupt cartels of Danen, it was the only way to save your own skin. Here, Alex knew things were done differently, but having witnessed the power struggle between Hendrick and Danila firsthand, he wasn't sure who would execute his recommendations.

Taking a deep breath, Alex trusted his gut. He told Hendrick everything—his speculation that Evaline was tied to Freelark smuggling and possibly the Iera attack, his opinion of Glynn's culpability, and the details of the conversation he had overheard in the tavern when he had detained Drake. He mentioned the matching tattoos both Evaline and Drake had sported, and the different number of seeds inked into their wrists as well as the unadulterated hatred he had felt radiate from Drake since he had been caught.

Hendrick listened quietly, rubbing his mustache as Alex spoke. When Alex finished, the Bandit Lord said, "And what of our lovely Commissar?"

Surprised, Alex paused. "I'm sorry?"

"She went after you herself. What's her angle? How is she in the field?"

"She was helpful," Alex replied honestly. "She's very smart and good with connections. But," he paused, searching for words. "It's limited. She represents a viewpoint—the Imperial viewpoint, to be specific. She sees the Freelarks as a threat to her power and the larger Imperial Authority. She wanted this case to connect back to the alleged attack. Since the report was written, I'd bet she's getting a lot of pressure to prove it—and to throw some Freelarks in jail. Two birds, one stone, as it were. I saw it at the Citadel too. Perception matters to the Mezrani. Danila thinks if we scapegoat the Freelarks, even if they're innocent, it'll solve two problems at once."

"What do you think?" Hendrick's voice was calm and measured, but his eyes bored into Alex.

Alex massaged his temples. "I think there are dangerous Freelarks. But I also think the more we make the Freelarks the enemy, the more sympathy they get. The average person hears Freelark and thinks of Hearth Halls, feeding the hungry and providing a warm bed. If we start rounding them up, we become the enemy."

Leaning back, Hendrick linked his fingers behind his head. "I agree with you, Laurent. Knowing all of that, what would you do to this Freelark we've detained?"

"Find out what he knows." Alex jumped and spun around as a woman spoke from behind him.

"Udo's curse, Starling, where in the Hells did you come from?" Swearing, and willing his heart to stop beating in his throat, he looked at the Blade who had trained him.

Starling Quinn was reckless and impulsive. She had never met a bad idea she didn't like and had dragged him into—and then out of—more than one life-threatening situation. Her spray of long, black hair was tied back, highlighting a sharp chin and dark eyes that never missed a beat.

Those eyes were fixed on him now as a cocky smirk played by her lips. "Got word you'd made a royal mess of things and had sullied my good name as your training officer." She gave a dismissive wave of her hand and strode to the center of the room.

"You sully your own name, Quinn." Hendrick's tone was cool. "You're here to do a job. We don't need Shadows running around making a mess of things. There's rule of law here, and I don't intend to let you destroy it."

Alex watched her eyes widen. She thought it made her look innocent. About a quarter of the time it worked, but the rest…

"I'm sure I don't know what you're talking about," she replied.

The Lord Commissioner stood and leaned over the desk. "Then let me be very, very clear. Your *kind* are at the center of every coup and behind the stab of every assassin's knife. We don't do things like that here, and I don't like you within a dozen miles of Rosemoor, let alone making yourself comfortable in her capital. You were brought here to do one thing— bring down the Freelark threat. Once we've done that, you're gone. Is that clear enough for you?"

Interesting, Alex thought as he kept his eyes on his old trainer. He'd worked with her for over a year—long enough to know her rhythms and the way she handled situations. He could read the line of tension between her shoulder blades as well as the tightness in her neck and jaw. She seemed more annoyed than angry, as though someone had shoved by her on the street.

Her eyes danced, and he sensed her pivoting into the verbal sparring match. "Some strong irony, that. Rawley Hendrick, *Bandit Lord.* That's what they called you. Isn't it? When you brutalized families and destroyed lives?" The emphasis she placed on his old title was unpleasant, like pressing on a bruise. "We all have a past, and people like you and me, well, we should know better than to judge others by what they've done."

The silence hung in the air for a moment, Hendrick's eyes icy with fury. Alex caught Starling's eye and felt his stomach turn over when he saw the spark of victory in them. She'd scented blood. She always went for the kill. He wanted to sink through the floor and pretend he wasn't there anymore.

Instead, a temporary bout of insanity overcame him and he felt himself stepping forward, between the two titans. "You asked me what I'd do." Alex focused his gaze on Hendrick, willing the man to look at him, to back away. He knew it would only get nastier if they kept sparring. Starling fought dirty.

"I don't know exactly what I'd do, but I think Drake knows what we *need* to know. He struck me as someone used to giving orders, not taking them. I'd bet a month's coin that if there's an attack coming, he's deeply involved in it." He paused to gulp air and felt relief wash from head to toe as Hendrick shifted his attention away from the Shadow.

He plowed on. "That's why she's here. Right? Sent by the Citadel? We don't have time to sweat the prisoner. If there's an attack, we need to stop it now. And, like her or not, Quinn's the best interrogator the Blades have."

"Didn't know you cared, Laurent," Starling teased, her tone light and easy. He turned so he could see them both and was startled to see the genuine twinkle of humor on her face. He'd always found it uncomfortable how quickly and unpredictably her emotions could shift.

Hendrick, too, seemed to have pivoted, but Alex could detect anger rumbling just beneath the calm. "Is what he knows worth driving people to the Freelarks if it gets out we're torturing one of them?"

"I'd risk it to stop an attack on Iera," Alex replied without hesitation.

"Damn straight, Laurent." Starling clapped him on the shoulder. "Glad you held on to some of that training."

"Despite my best efforts," Alex muttered.

Nodding approvingly, Hendrick directed his attention to Starling. "Festival's in five days, Quinn. Can you make it happen?"

She folded her arms across her chest. "Easy. If there's anything to be known, I'll get it."

"Alright then." Hendrick looked back at Alex. "The first step will be convincing the Roussels we have a problem. I've known Mattias for years and he's not going to want to take any action at all."

"Why?" Alex frowned. "If we think there will be an attack, why wouldn't he listen?"

"No proof, Laurent. It's suspicious. Hells, we know in our guts there's something going on. But we can't prove it. Mattias is hard enough to convince when I can tell him exactly what's going to happen. With this? We'll be lucky if he doesn't walk out of the room."

The description matched everything he knew about Mattias. Caidy had often faced the same problem with her father. "So what do we do?"

"You know the princess, Lady Caidelene. Think she would take our side?"

In truth, Alex didn't know. He had once known Caidy better than he'd known himself. And once, he would have said no, she wouldn't listen. She had inherited her father's headstrong nature and possessed the confident belief that she was untouchable. It came from ignorance, not arrogance. Her steps were trailed by bodyguards and her trips carefully protected. She had never been given any reason to believe anything bad could ever happen to her.

"Honestly?" He looked between the two older Blades as both watched him intently. "I wish I could say I did. But I don't."

Starling frowned. "Isn't that the girl? She trusts you. You can use it, exploit it. Make her believe you. I *know* you know how."

As she spoke, Alex felt a very righteous indignation course through his veins. "I don't manipulate my friends, Starling," he snapped at her. "We'll build our case, bring it to the whole family. Whatever they decide, we'll make it work."

"And you can live with that?" She sounded startled.

Glancing back at Hendrick, he could have sworn he saw a flicker of approval in the man's icy eyes. "I don't have a choice."

CHAPTER 23

18th Day of the Harvest Moon

Caidy rubbed her tired eyes and tossed the heavy tome aside. The old book of village tales landed with a dusty *thunk*, and she massaged the back of her neck, trying to stave off a headache. The last few weeks had been flat-out work, trying to get everything aligned perfectly for the Harvest Festival.

She had spent her limited spare moments pouring over dusty pages, trying to track down the village tale she *knew* she'd read once. It was about strange visions and a peasant woman who could communicate with the Gods through her dreams. But none of that seemed to matter because she couldn't *find* the damned story.

Slumped back in her chair, Caidy pressed fingertips to her eyelids, reveling in the darkness. She felt drained, physically and emotionally. *Who knew planning a Festival was this complicated?* No wonder her mother was fussy and short-tempered. If Caidy had to explain to one more vendor that they couldn't change their stall location, she would scream.

A knock at the door startled her out of her thoughts. Opening her eyes and blinking at the sudden light, she sat up. "Yes?"

Merric poked his head around the door frame. "A messenger just arrived. The Blades are on their way to the castle to discuss some security precautions for the Festival."

It took her a moment to sort through the words and then her scattered thoughts. "I thought…I thought the Rose Guard was coordinating security measures with the City."

"Yes, my Lady." Merric stepped inside and closed the door behind him. "I believe the Blades would like to give a threat briefing to you and your parents."

She frowned, standing and straightening her skirts. "Do you know what this is about?"

Her guardsman's eyes were unreadable. "I think it's important you're present, my Lady."

"Alright, if you say so. Where are we meeting?"

"The eastern study, my Lady. Overlooking the gardens."

Nodding and offering a word of thanks, Caidy briefly ran fingers through her hair, trying to smooth the curls, but then gave up and strode into the hallway.

The eastern study wasn't far from her rooms, and she took an old passage she and Alex had once discovered. It had probably been a shortcut for servants back when court was much larger and much busier. It wasn't precisely in disuse—the doors on either end swung open cleanly, fresh with oil—but dust clung to the walls, iron sconces, and stacked boxes.

At the end of the hall she paused, letting her thoughts settle. *Two more days*, she reminded herself. *Then all I'll have to do is enjoy the Festival.*

When the tapestry in front of him was pushed aside, Alex felt a surge of self-satisfaction. He'd known she would come this way. It was the quickest way between her room and the study, which was precisely why he'd chosen that location for the meeting.

His satisfaction couldn't stop the jolt his heart gave when he saw her emerge. Her hair was long and loose today, curling over her shoulders and down her back with small pieces pinned behind her ears to frame those large gray eyes. He leaned against the wall opposite the tapestry and nodded at Merric as the guard stepped out behind Caidy.

"My Lady," he began, coolly confident despite the fact his heart was in his throat.

She jumped when she caught sight of him. "Alex! What in the Hells? How did you get here?"

Shock melted to surprise and then anger across her soft features. Itching to hug her tightly, he folded his arms across his chest instead. "The castle? Through the front gate. I didn't feel like scaling a wall today."

"What a shame, you might have fallen and broken something," she snapped back, her cheeks aflame with emotion.

The barb bounced off painlessly. He knew her. She lashed out when she was embarrassed, startled or frustrated. "Next time," he promised with a smirk. "Just for you."

He could almost hear her teeth grinding together. *Gods, how is she this beautiful when she's angry?* He loved the way Caidy felt everything with her whole self, emotions painted across her face.

"What do you want, Warden?" She matched the cold in his tone with her own. "I'm busy."

"I know. I happen to be going to the same meeting," he replied, resisting the urge to keep bantering. *Don't wind her up. You need her to agree with you.* "I'm sorry if I surprised you. I wanted to catch you before you got to the study."

Now anger faded to confusion. Her dark eyebrows knitted together. "Why? What are you planning?"

His heart, so recently in his throat, dropped through his stomach. She always knew when he had an ulterior motive; it was one of his favorite things about her. It had always been easy for him to slip things by most people, but Caidy was usually onto him from the beginning. Apparently, she hadn't lost the skill.

The best play was probably honesty. "I need to talk to you about the Harvest Festival."

"And for some reason you felt the need to ambush me to do it?" Now she mimicked him, folding her own arms and glaring. "I've been here for weeks, working. Nothing was stopping you from visiting."

He opened his palms in a gesture of apology. "Caidy, please listen to me. I've been away from Iera. I only returned a few days ago." He paused, anticipating her cutting in. When she only continued to glower, he swallowed and continued, "I've been in Pheant, investigating a murder."

Her eyes widened in surprise, and he could almost hear the thousand questions on her lips. "I'm very sorry to hear that, but what does that have to do with me? Or the Festival?"

Sighing heavily, Alex stepped toward her. "Give me five minutes, alright?" When she didn't move, merely watched him, he took that as an invitation and dove into the story.

Despite her best efforts, Caidy found herself only half listening. She used the time as a refuge to control her breathing and calm the waves of emotions that threatened to overwhelm her. When he began talking about Freelarks and plots, she held up a hand.

"I'm sorry, you expect me to believe that you've uncovered a massive conspiracy to destroy the Harvest Festival? Are you out of your mind? One dead girl, while very sad, does not mean there is a coordinated plot to tarnish one of the most cherished holidays in Rosemoor."

"You're not listening," he snapped back at her, and she nearly took a step back from the intensity in his voice. Alex didn't snap at anyone. "Please, Caidy," he placated.

"I *am* listening," she countered. "I just don't buy it. So, you caught a Freelark trying to bribe…what, another Freelark? And you expect me to believe that the only daughter of the most powerful merchant in Rosemoor is tangled up in all this? Anyone else you want to throw in while you're at it? The Imperial Authority, perhaps, or the Mage Council of Karath, meddling in our affairs?"

Alex ran his fingers through his hair until it stood up at odd angles. She itched to straighten it and folded her hands together instead. "I know something bad is going to happen, Caidy. Our interrogator has gotten the Freelark in custody to admit he was planning an attack on Caldir's temple…"

Shaking her head, she gave up on the conversation. Brushing past him and toward the study, she called over her shoulder. "I'm not listening to this more than once. You may as well take it up with everyone, but I can tell you right now what the answer will be. I'm not canceling the Harvest Festival because you can't do your damn job."

Weak, she berated herself as she marched away. She could never seem to come up with clever quips in the moment. They always came to her later, when she was nearly asleep. Caidy rubbed the back of her neck absently. She just wanted the Festival to be successful and then to be over until next year. It was so, so close.

Inside the study, she recognized the other Blades she'd met at a smattering of meetings—the Lord Commissioner, a tall and bulky man with a bushy silver mustache; the Archivalist, with clever eyes and a habit of bouncing his knee; and their Political Commissar, a Mezrani woman who sat very still. Her father stood by the window near the Lord Commissioner, his back to the room, while her mother was settled on a low couch near the Mezrani woman.

On the other side of the room, a woman Caidy didn't know leaned against the wall with her arms folded, a pose that reminded her strongly of Alex. She was small and slight, with hair and eyes that were shockingly dark against pale skin. When the woman saw her looking, she smiled, and something about it sent a shiver down Caidy's spine.

She stepped aside to make room, and Alex entered the room beside her. His jaw was tight. Caidy saw him catch the eye of the Lord Commissioner and shake his head almost imperceptibly. *Sorry to ruin that part of your plan,* she thought viciously, frustrated at being used.

Mattias turned from the window to face the small audience. The lines around his mouth and eyes had deepened, the way Caidy knew they did when he was facing a difficult decision. "Let's have it, Hendrick," her father said, looking to the Lord Commissioner. "You've got a lot of important people in this room. What couldn't wait?"

Alex spent most of Hendrick's briefing mentally kicking himself. They needed Caidy on their side. He *knew* she'd been instrumental in planning the Harvest Festival this year. Given their tenuous-at-best evidence, if she disagreed with the need to cancel the Festival, Lord Roussel was apt to take her side.

She refused to look at him, though they stood near each other. When he'd walked in all the Blades had looked for some sort of signal. He'd seen the disbelief—or was it disgust?—in Starling's face as she put together what had happened. Hendrick didn't miss a beat, pivoting to try and convince the Lord of Rosemoor.

It was a losing battle. When Hendrick finished explaining the situation, he saw the frustration cross Mattias' face.

"You think there *might* be an attack on the temple? So you want to cancel the entire Festival?" He turned to his daughter, his wife, and then back to Hendrick. "You've been here long enough to know how important this is to Rosemoor."

"Yes, my Lord, I have. That's why you should heed my warning." Hendrick looked around the room and then settled on Caidy. Alex felt her shift uncomfortably under his stare. "I know months of work have gone in. I know the harvest is the very lifeblood of Rosemoor, and this tradition dates back to when Iya and Erius themselves walked among us. But it's not worth the lives of hundreds who could be threatened."

Mattias' frown deepened. "Which of you did the interrogation? Spoke with the prisoner?"

"I did," Starling straightened from where she had slouched against the wall, and Alex exchanged a nervous glance with Jakob. His old mentor wasn't famed for her diplomacy.

"What exactly did the Freelark say?" The Lord pivoted to face her.

She tossed her head proudly. "He told me there was going to be an attack on Caldir's temple."

"That makes no sense," Caidy burst out. Alex fought not to snap to her too quickly, trying to mimic Hendrick's calm motions.

"The Freelarks worship Caldir," she continued. "They wouldn't blaspheme their own God."

Starling turned her cold gaze on the princess, and Alex felt his own stomach turn. Nothing good ever happened when her eyes went flat like that. "Oh? And are you an expert in Freelarks, my *Lady*? Tell me, which scholar did you study under? How many years have you spent living among them?"

When Caidy didn't answer, the Shadow took a step toward her. "Learn to keep your opinions to yourself unless you know what you're talking about, princess."

Mattias drew himself up, but Hendrick's voice lashed out first. "That's enough, Quinn. Get out." He moved toward her, putting his bulk between the princess and the Shadow. "Now."

Starling cast another look around. Alex avoided her gaze, knowing she'd try to catch his eye. He'd been in this situation with her before, and this was one time he wouldn't have her back in a fight. He could feel her rapidly assessing the situation, trying to decide if she should push her luck. Abruptly, she stalked toward the door, shouldering past Alex on the way out of the room.

As the door swung shut behind her, the tension in the air nearly visibly relaxed. "I'm sorry, my Lord, my Lady," Hendrick said carefully. "Quinn is an excellent interrogator but doesn't play politics well—or really at all. She's used to spending her time in the company of assassins and traitors, not nobility."

Caidy, whose cheeks were still stained red with embarrassment and anger, spoke. "I don't trust her. She's the kind of person who would say anything to further her own agenda."

She turned to Hendrick, still steadily ignoring Alex. "You have ideas and theories, not facts. If there *is* going to be an attack—which I doubt—that's your problem to solve. I keep being told that the Rose Guard and the Blades are the best there is. Are you telling me you can't handle a disorganized band of rebels?"

Alex watched Hendrick decide to try one last time, his eyebrows meeting together the way they did when he was angry. "My Lady, with all due respect, we are the best there is. And we're telling you we can't guarantee your safety, or the safety of anyone else at that Festival."

He almost missed the glance that passed from father to daughter. Caidy had looked for his approval, and Mattias had granted it in the flick of a hand. He watched her roll her shoulders back, drawing herself up.

"Well then you have less than three days to figure it out. I recommend you stop wasting time here and get started."

CHAPTER 24

20th Day of the Harvest Moon

She couldn't shake the deep sense of foreboding, which had settled over the castle since her confrontation with the Blades. What should have been a glorious victory, an opportunity to relax before the Festival, was now tense and tinged with fear.

Caidy was sprawled on the floor of her studio, painting meditatively. The self-doubt that had encroached since Alex had cornered her in the hallway seeped through her fingers, her landscapes becoming dark, jagged, and moody. The world still moved outside, but she felt frozen, trapped in worry and doubt.

"My Lady?" Margot knocked on the door.

Pushing herself up into a seat, Caidy rubbed a hand absently across her nose and then cursed as she realized her fingers were stained with navy dye. "Yes?"

"Lord Geoffrey is here to see you, my Lady." Margot stepped forward and brought the corner of her apron to Caidy's nose, dabbing the smear away.

Sneezing as soon as her maid stepped back, she shook her head to clear it. "Of course he is. I'll meet him in the sitting room."

Margot withdrew, her lips pursed, and Caidy stood, surveying the mess she had made. Paints, charcoal, and pastels were strewn across the floor, and papers were scattered amid pillows and cups of water. Briefly, she contemplated trying to pick up but then resigned herself to the fact that her maid could do it more quickly—and do a better job.

When she stepped into the next room, Geoffrey turned to her with a bright smile. "Come now, my dove, you've been hidden away for the last day and a half. We should be out celebrating! Let me take you into Iera."

He was right. She'd been avoiding him. But then, she'd really been avoiding everyone, Caidy reasoned with herself. "I'm run down, and I'm worried," she confessed, settling herself on a couch and clutching a pillow.

Geoffrey sat next to her, wrapping an arm around her shoulders and drawing her close. "What's happened?"

She told him of the meeting with the Blades, of the nasty, vicious woman—Starling—who had called her a fool. He stayed quiet through it all, smoothing a hand over her hair in soothing motions until the finished.

"She could be executed for treating a noble that way!" he said indignantly when the story was done. "What did you say her name was? Sophia?"

"Maybe in Colmar, or maybe by the Emperor," she replied. "It's not worth it here. It doesn't matter."

"It does matter." Geoffrey placed two fingers under her chin, tilting her face to his. "You're going to rule Rosemoor one day, Caidy. It's the job of advisors to *advise*. Your decisions are the only ones that matter. Disrespecting you is the same as disrespecting the Province, even the Emperor himself!"

She couldn't stifle a snort. "I think that's a little extreme. Don't you?"

He looked at her seriously. "Absolutely not. I know you think of yourself as a woman of the people, Caidy, but you have to remember what station you hold. That *Blade* had no business challenging your authority. Nobody knows how hard you've worked on the Harvest Festival. And what? Now a few days before it's supposed to happen, the Blades want an easy way out of doing their jobs?"

She hadn't thought about it that way. Alex had never been one to shirk his duty or look for the easy way out, but she couldn't shake the timing. *Geoffrey's right*, she admitted to herself. *Maybe it is all just an excuse.*

"Thank you. That helps." She sat up and kissed him. Then she pushed to her feet, determined to shake off the dregs of doubt. "You said you wanted to go to the city?"

They had whiled away the afternoon together in one of the first truly pleasant times they'd had in a long time. Relaxing into a bath after her afternoon adventure in Iera, she sighed dramatically to herself. Yes, he still used pet names that made her skin crawl and he could get tangled up in his noble sensibilities. But he struck her as a good person—just flawed.

It was a pairing she'd struggled with for a long time. When Alex had left so abruptly, she had been heartbroken. Even after it was confirmed he'd been taken by the Blades, she had waited, convinced he would abandon it all and come back to her. But weeks and months had slipped into years, and eventually her parents began talking to her seriously about who would be her partner.

Geoffrey—and House Valance—had been her mother's idea. After the Roussels, the Valance family was the wealthiest and most powerful nobility in Rosemoor. Their fortune lay in the southern vineyards and rich trade with the Empire. And while relations were good, there was nothing quite like a marriage to bring comfort and prosperity to all.

So at the urging of her parents—and Geoffrey's older sister, Valarie, who promised they would grow to like one another—Caidy had accepted the courtship. In the first few months things were awkward. They didn't know one another, and she hadn't been ready to give her heart to someone else.

Despite her distance, Geoffrey had persevered.

We used to have good times, she reflected. Then, as often seemed to happen with relationships, they had grown irritated with one another.

However, days like today reminded her why she liked him in the first place. He had walked with her through Iera, bought her hot cinnamon rolls drizzled with sweet honey, and sat patiently with her through an illusionist performance. She knew he'd rather be riding, or fencing, or doing pretty much anything else—but he had stayed with her, had smiled and laughed, and had brightened her day.

Annoyed with herself, Caidy dunked her head under the steaming bath water, holding her breath for a long moment before resurfacing. "I need to get over myself," she said out loud, the words echoing in the empty room.

Somehow, saying it made it more real. She wrapped herself in a fluffy robe and padded back to her rooms, Merric falling into her shadow as she emerged from the baths. Near the door to her bedroom she paused, turning back to him.

"Do you think I made the right decision?" she asked carefully, watching her bodyguard's face.

"Which decision would you be referring to, my Lady?" Merric replied stiffly.

"Any of them. All of them." She shrugged. "Do you think I've made a terrible mistake somewhere along the way?"

Merric tilted his head slightly as he examined her. "My Lady, I think we all make mistakes. I couldn't say if you've made one of late, but I think it's not our mistakes that matter but what happens next."

Biting her lip, she tugged on a strand of curls, considering. "That sounds like something my father would say about leadership," she said finally.

The bodyguard inclined his head. "My Lord is very wise. It's a lesson I learned serving in the Provincial Guard. Sometimes, mistakes are truly terrible. But how we respond can really make the difference."

"Thank you, Merric." She wrapped her arms around him, hugging him. Begrudgingly, he patted her on the back.

"Have a good night, my Lady. Big day tomorrow."

Stepping through the door, she saw that Margot had already turned down her bed. Thankful for the maid's knack of anticipating her needs, she curled up under the covers, hoping to fall into a dreamless, restful sleep.

Caidy couldn't remember how long she had been running. The heavy iron door slammed shut behind her, urging her forward as it sent icy shards splintering from the stone, twinkling through the air and bouncing off her shoulders. One slice, deadly sharp, tore through fabric and opened a gash on her shoulder. The chilled air made her skin tingle with needles of pain.

All of the visions had come true, horrifying omens shadowing the everlasting summer which wrapped the world. Desperate Prophecies danced across the swirling eddies of time, harbingers of disaster. They had been forsaken long ago by the Gods, and what once had been commonplace had faded to myth and legend.

They inhabited a dying, abandoned world, mere flashes of meaningless existence in the eternal nothingness of the universe. As the shadows had grown longer, the constant, gentle breeze from the Winds of Magic had whipped into a frenzied tempest. She rushed into this storm, head bowed against the weight of fear and doubt shrouding the tunnel.

Small orbs of pale, icy blue cast flickering shadows into the recesses of stonework, illuminating the passageway with a haunting light. Her shoulder twinged and she ignored the pain. She had to reach the Eladyr.

She emerged into a massive stone cavern buried deeply beneath the glaciers above. Shards of fragmented light fighting through the layers of ice cast haunting images on the ancient walls. Skidding to a halt, she surveyed the scene in horror.

Four mages lay crumpled on the freezing stone. A hollow wind whistled through the cavern, and the walls glistened with ice. At the center of the room, in a deep recess, a gleam of purple flame danced. The room was shadowed. As Caidy stood frozen, eyes wide, the amethyst flame briefly flickered higher and then abruptly snuffed out.

Pain lanced through her chest and she collapsed to her knees, wrapping her arms tightly around her body. She shook uncontrollably, her fingers twitching and frame convulsing on the rough stone floor. Her heart felt as though it had shattered into thousands of pieces, each sliver a new, invisible wound. Dark spots blinked across her vision and terrified tears slipped down her cheeks. Everything was empty, meaningless. It felt as though a piece of her soul had vanished into the darkness with the flame.

The chamber was ominously, starkly silent. The wind had stopped, and the icicles no longer glittered. Caidy felt tears freeze to her eyelashes as her sobs faded to quiet gasps. It was the loudest sound in the room and echoed off the mirrored walls. The ice reflected her haunted, twisted visage as she struggled to push herself up and return to the surface. She felt a deep, aching fear settle within her body, a sense of foreboding weighing down her limbs. She was exhausted and slow, as though she was treading water and struggling for air. One thought burst through the sluggish mist with a shocking, sharp clarity—escape.

Staggering to her feet, she whirled toward the door and screamed as another wave of spasms gripped her body. She tumbled to the ground, rolling to the center of the room, to the very edge of the deep, flameless recess in the center. The cold seemed to drag her toward its dark, empty depths. She braced an arm against a sharp ridge on the floor, the pain grounding her in this plane. The uncontrolled twitching across her body slowed.

The eerie silence thickened. Carefully, Caidy lifted her fingers to her face and felt a shiver along her spine. Smears of deep crimson blood spattered the shining, icy floor. The room began to spin, and to her left, the nearest body lay. A look of pure despair—eyes stretched, mouth contorted, skin paled with the cold—gripped the body. She saw the stains of blood beneath the figure and watched a single droplet crystallize before it could drip from her own fingertip to the ground.

An inhuman howl tore through the room. The ice clinging to the walls shattered, freezing daggers tumbling to the floor.

Caidy threw herself back to the ground, covering her head with her arms as the ice pelted her body. An ear-splitting tremor shook the world. Daring to raise her eyes from the shelter of her bloodied arms, she helplessly watched the cavern convulse, great stalactites cracking and ancient stone tumbling toward the ground to crush her.

Caidy screamed as she sat up, gasping for air. She was frozen with fear and overwhelmed with pain. Her bedroom door was flung open and Merric charged in, a sword naked in his hand. Pivoting, he checked the corners of the room before rushing to her bedside. She curled up in a ball, shaking uncontrollably.

"My Lady? My Lady! Are you alright?" The bodyguard crouched next to her, shaking her shoulder.

She felt tears drip down her nose as she struggled to breathe. It had felt so *real*. "Bad dream, I think," she panted. *So real.*

"You're alright now, my Lady. Nothing bad's going to happen to you." She felt him sit back on his heels beside the bed.

The tortured images felt painted behind her eyelids—faces contorted in pain, the echoes of the inhuman howl still ringing in her ears. She felt like a child again, young and terrified of the raka. "Promise?"

"Rest, my Lady. I've got you."

CHAPTER 25

———

21st Day of the Harvest Moon

"And so, Erius drew Iya ever closer, and her flames enveloped them both as they spun in eternal harmony and everlasting passion." The narrator paused dramatically for effect, and a swell of lute music punctuated the silence. On the impromptu stage, two of the Players of Cami's Stare leaned together, locked in an embrace.

"The cooling rains of autumn soothed Iya's summer tempest, and the world flourished in peace." The narrator clashed two cymbals together, and the audience applauded on cue. Caidy rose to her feet, and the rest of her small party followed suit. Geoffrey straightened beside her, smoothing his tunic before clapping politely. Merric shifted his weight behind the pair, his hand resting loosely on the pommel of his sword. Lord Mattias applauded and smiled approvingly, and Lady Julianna's back was straight and proud.

The Player portraying Iya, a strong woman with wild black hair wearing glinting golden armor and a crimson cloak, bowed deeply, flipping her hair over her head so it brushed the ground. Her partner, a solidly tall man with short brown hair garbed in hunting apparel, gestured to the narrator before taking his own bow. The audience was insatiable, whistling and cheering as the pair bowed a second time.

"I thought last year's performance was better," Geoffrey muttered in Caidy's ear. "I don't see why you wanted to go again, dove. It's all rather predictable. Isn't it?"

Caidy pretended she had not heard him and stepped forward. She smiled widely when the two Players glanced at the elevated, cordoned-off area where she and her parents were seated in honor. The wild-haired woman smiled broadly in return, pumped her fist in the air, and let out a joyous cheer.

Two Temple Acolytes crossed to the center of the stage as the Players stepped back, applauding with the crowd. The left, an Acolyte of Erius, wore flowing white robes embroidered with the triangular circle symbol of his God and a gold medallion. The Acolyte of Iya wore a long tunic the color of autumn foliage, a tattoo of swirling flames climbing her bare arms. The two bowed to one another and then clapped twice, dismissing the crowd.

Merric shepherded Caidy and Geoffrey from the platform while another member of the Rose Guard offered a balancing hand to Lady Julianna. The royal family made their way through a neighboring alley and emerged into a street bordering Market and Guild Districts, a few blocks from the crowds and major festivities.

Caidy felt Geoffrey's hand at the small of her back, guiding her forward, and almost instinctively she stopped walking and turned toward her parents.

"Caidelene, why don't you and Geoffrey take a few hours to explore the Festival. Your mother and I need to attend a brief meeting in Guild District." Mattias' tone made it clear that, while phrased as a suggestion, he was giving his daughter an order.

"Of course, that sounds lovely." Caidy dipped a small curtsey to him.

Mattias was already turning away, toward his wife. "Don't be late to the Burning, Caidelene. And make sure—"

She said the words under her breath along with him, "That your speech is prepared." Geoffrey guided her away from her parents. Merric walked a few paces behind the couple with several guards.

"Where would you like to go, my dove?" Caidy swallowed a sarcastic quip and allowed herself to be nudged along, back toward Market District. "We could visit the Noble Feast, see what trinkets the merchants are peddling, find a quiet corner near a lute player..." He trailed off.

Caidy didn't notice Geoffrey had stopped speaking. She had seen an odd twitch of movement beside a crate and could have sworn someone ducked behind a line of drying laundry. Her eyes narrowed as she searched the area, completely distracted. She had been seeing raka on every corner since her strange dream the night before, and she shook herself a little. *You're safe.*

"Caidy?" Geoffrey sounded worried, and she realized she had physically shivered, in spite of the heat. Behind them, she felt Merric move a step closer. Plastering a smile across her face and looking up at Geoffrey, she tilted her head so her curls tumbled over one shoulder.

"I'm sorry. I'm sorry. I'm just nervous about my speech later," she lied. It had become very easy to not tell Geoffrey how she actually felt about things. It was as natural as walking. "What about Honey District?"

Before Geoffrey could speak, Merric cleared his throat, and they both turned to face him. "I'm not sure Honey is a good idea, my Lady," the guard commented diplomatically. "The celebrations there tend to be a little more raucous than those in Market."

Caidy waved a hand. "Don't be absurd, Merric. It's not like I want to go to Dock or stay out late. Honey is perfectly safe. It's the middle of the day."

Merric ground his teeth together but said nothing, falling back a step to his original position. Geoffrey watched Caidy for a moment and then replied, "That sounds exciting. I don't think I've ever spent any of the Harvest Festival in Honey. It's always seemed a little...lowbrow."

Ignoring the casual ignorance in his tone, Caidy started walking purposefully across the western edge of Market District where it hugged City Hill. The streets had been swept clean of manure and debris for the Festival, and everything was bright and vibrant. Streamers fluttered between tree branches, colorful lanterns were perched on window sills and flowerbeds, and strands of music danced on the breeze. Determined to be cheerful and to shake off the remnants of her nightmares, Caidy squared her shoulders and held her chin high as they wove through the crowds toward the entertainment district.

The spirit and energy infusing the air of Honey District was effervescent. It felt as though the group had crossed a magical barrier into a place where time stood still and joy permeated every breeze. Gaudy crowds pressed together, flower petals drifted through the air, and the delicious scent of roasting meat and frying dough wafted toward them.

She paused in wonder, forgetting her nerves entirely as she watched a street performer perched like a falcon on top of a pile of boxes. The woman, her hair dyed an impossible shade of red, had complex amber tattoos covering much of her bare skin. Her eyes, piercing and bright blue, twinkled as she easily tossed flaming torches into the air, juggling what seemed like an ever-increasing number. The fire created streaks of light across Caidy's vision, dancing impossibly quickly. When the woman caught the final torch and bowed, flourishing the fire she held dramatically, Caidy applauded and screamed her approval with the rest of the crowd.

Beside her, Geoffrey cleared his throat. "Do you want to find somewhere to sit, dove? It's a bit cramped on the street with all these people."

An excited hush gripped the audience, and she flapped a placating hand toward Geoffrey. The performer handed her torches to the crowd and then reached down behind the boxes and pulled out a long wooden skewer wrapped with a piece of cloth. Sweeping the skewer in front of her like a sword, she ignited the end in a puff of purple smoke. Shaking back her hair, the performer took a swig from a flask at her hip and then winked into the crowd, tipped her head back, and fed the flame down her throat.

The jostling noise and frivolity of Honey seemed to fade away as the entire group watched her, holding their breath. Caidy thought she saw the tattoos on the woman's throat move, undulating and curling like living flames, but it could have been a trick of the light. The moment stretched, tension building, and then the woman opened her mouth and roared flame into the sky.

Delighted gasps, shrieks, and laughter jolted the crowd. The woman bowed once more, and the pounding rhythm of the Festival slowly returned to Caidy's chest. She turned to Geoffrey, eyes shining, "Wasn't that the most incredible thing?"

Geoffrey started and turned toward her. He had been cleaning his jeweled dagger with a handkerchief. "I certainly think you are." He smiled toward her.

Caidy heard Merric snort softly, but before she could round on him, a flicker of motion again caught her eye. It was barely there, the twitch of a cloak or perhaps a catch in a stride, but there was definitely *something*. She searched the crowd but saw only excited eyes and sweaty foreheads.

"Come, dove, I'm famished. Let's find some food." He offered his arm again, and Caidy reluctantly slid her hand through the crook in his elbow, still examining the crowd. He started tugging her back to Market District, but Caidy dug in her heels.

"There's plenty to eat here," she offered gently. "If I remember correctly Annabeth's stall is in Honey this year."

With the heavy sigh of a Player, Geoffrey pivoted back toward the entertainment district and started to clear a path through the crowd. "Your wish is my command."

Biting back several retorts, which were varying degrees of sharp and harsh, she fell into step beside him. They passed the performer, now seated on a box and sipping from a water-skin. The woman glanced up and caught Caidy's eye as she passed. Caidy flipped a coin in her direction, and the fire dancer snatched it from the air impossibly quickly.

"You don't have to give them charity, you know. Any performer worth their salt is Guilded, and the Guilds don't let their own go hungry." Geoffrey's voice was slightly too loud.

"It wasn't charity but a compliment on a beautiful performance," Caidy replied, her tone much softer.

Geoffrey smiled down at her. "You're too goodhearted, dove. You want to save them all, and I love that about you. But it will make it awfully difficult to run a kingdom, you know."

The crowd seemed to press closer, and she felt the familiar flare of anger and indignant pride in her heart. Caidy chewed the inside of her cheek and took several deep breaths. She felt the heat, which had risen to her face cool. "My kindness," she said slowly, "does not make me weak."

"Nothing to worry about, dove. You'll always have my help." Geoffrey patted her hand. "Ah, you were right after all! Here's Annabeth."

CHAPTER 26

———

21st Day of the Harvest Moon
Several hours later, after many cups of chilled honeycomb tea and a delicious assortment of pastries, Caidy, Geoffrey, and their retinue made their way up the winding road to the summit of City Hill. The crowds were mostly at their backs, but Festival-goers were starting to make their way to City Plaza, overlooking Feather Lake. Soon, the final summer sun would set, and Caidy would light Iya's Great Effigy, burning away the last thrash of summer's heat.

One of her earliest memories was the first time her mother had allowed her to light the Effigy. She'd been five summers old, barely tall enough to reach her father's hip. He had lifted her on his shoulders and supported the bottom of the great ceremonial torch. It was so large that her hands hadn't been able to wrap all the way around the heavy bronze object, and she had nearly singed off her father's eyebrows. She remembered looking out at the sea of people, melting into the waves of Feather Lake and the spectacularly bloody reflection of the setting sun. She'd shrieked with glee when she dipped the torch too close to the straw effigy, engulfing the sunset in flames and billowing, colorful smoke.

Not all her memories were happy. During her seventeenth summer—*right before Alex left*, she thought bitterly—her mother had insisted that Caidy give the speech normally reserved for Mattias. Her stomach still fluttered nervously at the thought. Thousands gathered for the lighting of the Effigy every year. A wry smile crept across her lips as she remembered Alex dragging her to the Festival over her vigorous protests and then helping her write her speech mere moments before she took the stage.

Now, it was a comfortable tradition. She had grown more accustomed to the public eye and had gained an appreciation for the way her actions were viewed. Gone were the midnight adventures through the countryside, the eating competitions in the City, the blackberry wine and bawdy jokes, replaced with discipline, composure, and diplomatic laughter. *The sacrifices*, she reflected, *we make for duty.*

This year, her speech had been written for weeks. But, since Alex had returned, she'd been fretting over the words. She didn't know if he was at the Festival, let alone if he would be in the audience on City Hill. Blades seemed to be always traveling, busy with some mystery or other. But on Udo's coin-flip that he was going to hear it, she wanted this year's speech to be meaningful, not just filled with tired, pithy niceties from the preceding years.

As they reached City Plaza, Geoffrey broke away to go chat with some of the other nobles, muttering that he would meet her later. She felt a great, invisible weight lift from her chest as he strode away from her, throwing out his arms and wrapping another young man in a bear hug. Something tickled the back of her throat and she coughed.

Upon seeing her daughter, Lady Julianna broke away from her conversation with Mayor Kluk and drifted over to Caidy. She fussed with her daughter's curls for a moment, her lips pinched together. "I trust you had a good day?"

"It was lovely, Mother." Caidy smiled, and Julianna patted her shoulder.

"I'm so glad. Your robes are inside the Mayor's offices, just that way. Margot is waiting to get you dressed, with Acolytes of Iya and Erius to bless the gown, of course." Julianna smiled and waved at someone over Caidy's head before returning the full weight of her attention to her daughter. "Are you ready?"

"Of course," she replied, not missing a beat. "I look forward to it."

"Good! Off you go, get changed. And see if Margot can fix whatever the wind has done with your hair." Julianna looked her daughter up and down once more and then flitted to her husband's side, joining in his conversation with a laugh.

Merric held the door to the Town Hall open for Caidy and positioned himself comfortably outside. It was always an odd thing, being inside an empty building that so often bustled with life. Papers were still piled on desks, and chairs scattered haphazardly in makeshift meeting spaces. Lanterns flickered every few yards, casting a slightly haunting sight over the normally bright room.

Margot waited with the Acolytes for Caidy in the mayor's office—where, just a few weeks ago, she had argued with Kluk. The ceremonial robes, a rustic amber over white skirts, were scattered across the desk. The two Acolytes quickly blessed Caidy, raising a candle to the back of both her hands and then dousing the heat with a sprinkle of water. When they left, Margot made quick work of the rose gown Caidy had worn and laced her into the amber dress. It was a beautiful thing, but terribly heavy. The embroidery on the hem of the skirt used golden thread, and her wrists were adorned with heavy bangles.

"My hair," Caidy started apologetically, but Margot chuckled.

"Not to worry, my Lady. I learned a long time ago to always carry smoothing cream in my bag."

Caidy laughed genuinely for the first time in several hours. "My mother was concerned."

"I can imagine, my Lady." Margot twisted her fingers, coated in some sort of serum, through the curls. "Not to worry. The shadows will help, too."

After several more minutes of work, Margot had untangled most of the knots, and braided the mess back into a knot at the nape of Caidy's neck. "Are you ready for the crown, my Lady?"

Caidy rubbed her eyes. "Give me a moment? It's so heavy, I don't want to put it on until I must."

"I don't blame you." Margot paused with a mischievous twinkle in her eye. "I'll give you a few moments to compose yourself. I don't know how you talk in front of all those people."

The maid left the room quickly, and Caidy heard the door to the Plaza open, letting in a rush of sound before snapping shut once more.

She leaned against the desk, facing a gaudy tapestry on the wall opposite the door. Her head pounded lightly from the heat and sound, but her fingertips fizzed with excited energy. She rolled her head on her shoulders, rubbing the back of her neck.

"You're beautiful." A tortured whisper echoed across the small room, and Caidy jumped. She whirled, her heart in her throat, the familiar voice bringing a flush to her collarbone.

A man leaned against the door frame, arms folded and ankles crossed, silhouetted against the hallway lanterns. The brazier in the room danced light across his face, and his eyes seemed to snap like crackling pine boughs. "Alex," she breathed. His guarded eyes flicked to hers, catching her gaze, and then away again to a point over her shoulder. "You're here."

He straightened and stepped forward into the light. He wore the Blade uniform she was familiar with, black and gray, with a navy cloak and that silver, circular pin. "I'm on duty." His words sounded choked and unfamiliar, his tone cool and controlled with no trace of the emotion she had heard when he first spoke.

"I didn't realize protection was part of your assignment." An unbidden wave of crushing disappointment washed over her, and it took all her willpower to keep her spine from wilting. He wasn't here for her. He was here for his work.

Alex folded his arms again and met her searching gaze. It was discordant, complex emotions playing out behind his eyelashes. Caidy watched a spark of fear shimmer against a wall of tight control and then felt her stomach turn as he stepped toward her again. Something in his eyes was hungry, a deep yearning that made her feel very small and her knees feel weak. He held her gaze for a moment, the silence stretching between them, and she felt her heartbeat in her throat.

"You need to finish getting ready, my Lady." His voice was slightly lower, rougher, than it had been. He lifted the heavy golden coronet, set with amber and emerald, from the desk. "Allow me."

He crossed the remaining space between them in a step, and she tilted her head up toward his face. The scar on his cheek stood starkly in the uneven light, and his hair fell untidily across his forehead. Her fingers itched to brush it back, and she balled her hands into fists, digging her nails into her palms. She could see the familiar, faint laughter lines framing his eyes and the shadow of hair on his jaw. He smelled of comfort, of the juniper trees and hot honeycomb tea. His face was nostalgic and exotic all at once, a faded memory overwritten by new experiences.

His deep green eyes caught hers again and he looked at her through veiled lashes, examining her face carefully. She nearly jumped a second time when he settled the crown on her head and felt a line of fire when his fingertip tucked a stray curl behind her ear. Blood rushed to her cheeks, and she was positive her heart was beating so fast he must be able to hear it. Her earlier anger with him forgotten, she itched to throw her arms around his neck, to feel him wrap her in a tight, unending embrace. Her breath caught in her throat as his head tilted slightly, still looking at her as though he was memorizing her face. The deep, dragging yearning beneath the veneer of his gaze taunted her closer.

As suddenly as he had appeared in the doorway, Alex stepped away. From a distance, he tilted his head further and then nodded. "That's perfect. Now you're ready." His tone was cool again, disinterested.

"Thank you." Her voice caught in her throat. Then, emboldened by a force greater than herself, she continued, "Why are you here, Alex?"

At the door, he paused, a hint of rigidity tracing the strong line of his shoulders. "To keep you safe." The words were barely a ghost in the air. "I'm here to protect you." And he was gone.

Caidy let out a rush of breath and leaned back against the desk once more, her whole body shaking. She pressed her hands to her cheeks, trying to cool the blood that stained her face with a blush, and took several deep breaths. Her heart still beat in her throat, and her stomach was filled with butterflies. Her ear tingled where his finger had brushed it.

When her head stopped spinning and she had regained her composure, she pressed the backs of her hands to her cheeks and took a deep breath. *Pull it together,* she ordered herself, stubbornly refusing to let her conversation with Alex distract her from the Harvest Festival. *You're angry with him. Don't lose your focus.*

Carefully holding her skirts in one hand, she made her way out of the building. Merric waited outside, his face perfectly smooth and unreadable. "Are you ready, my Lady?"

She frowned at him. "I thought you were supposed to keep people away from me."

"My job is to keep you safe, my Lady. That can mean a lot of different things at different times." The guardsman's eyes were unapologetic.

Sighing dramatically, she stuck her nose in the air in mock outrage and flounced away toward the stage. Merric and the squadron of Rose Guard who had accompanied her throughout the day fell in step behind her as she approached the makeshift platform.

Behind the wooden stairs she paused once more, feeling distinctly unsettled. Seeing Alex again was definitely *not* what her nerves had needed right before her speech. She couldn't shake the feeling that he was somewhere nearby, watching her every motion.

"My Lady?" Merric prompted her. "Are you ready?"

She looked up at him, then past him to the sparkling waters of Feather Lake at the base of the cliffside. The sky was a clear, perfect blue without a hint of a cloud. She could hear the excited roar of the crowd behind her, energizing the air around them.

Fixing a smile on her face—and pointedly ignoring the nerves building in her belly—she nodded. "No time like the present."

One foot after the other, she reminded herself, climbing the stairs. *Look across the crowd, not at them.* The sea of people stretched ahead of her, packed into the square and spilling out through the streets. As she reached the center of the stage, beside the ceremonial torch in its sturdy bronze setting, the sound swelled to a fever pitch and then died away. She took one more deep, steadying breath and then began to speak.

"Every year, summer draws to a close. Iya's flames die down to embers, and Erius wraps us in his soothing autumnal winds. Our crops, so lovingly tended over the Moons, have borne fruit to sustain us another year." Caidy looked out at the colorful mass of people beneath her feet. The Effigy stood by the edge of the cliff, and the crowd stretched as far as she could see. The setting sun cast long shadows over the city.

"To me, it is an inexorable reminder that, as we grow, our responsibilities change. Our relationships shift. We become beholden to something far greater than ourselves. We must either rise to that challenge or allow it to overcome us, to crush us as time marches on. For many summers I have been afraid of that responsibility, as I know many of you are now. I have walked among you. I have heard your stories. And those stories, the complicated, meaningful lives each and every one of you leads, are my responsibility."

She paused and then reached and lifted the heavy bronze ceremonial torch from its setting. "Just as Erius tempers Iya's hottest passions, I have learned and I have grown into the person I am today because of each of you. I am honored to ask Erius to bless our harvest, to soothe us from the summer flames, and to help us grow into the next year. By the grace of the Gods."

"By the grace of the Gods," the crowd murmured in one voice that billowed with the smoke of countless lanterns. Caidy tilted the torch toward the Effigy, anticipation building in her heart. The first flare was the best moment.

Something slammed into her, hard, knocking her to the side as she prepared to touch fire to straw. The torch flew from her hand, flames igniting the Effigy, even as she tried to break her fall.

A thunderous boom of magical energy ripped through the air and a roaring inferno burst forth, the air itself on fire. She felt herself yanked backward and then tossed like a leaf through the air, off the raised platform and onto the hard stone of the ground. Her head slammed backward, the coronet tumbling off and over the edge of the cliffside, and her vision went black.

CHAPTER 27

———

21st Day of the Harvest Moon
Holding his breath against the acrid fumes, Alex shielded
Caidy with his own body, nestling them both against the
back of the platform and blocking the worst of the magical explosion.

Almost too late. He'd seen the oily, slick magical gleam on
the straw of the Effigy just before Caidy had lifted the torch.
His body had started moving before his mind had caught
up, shouldering through the Rose Guard and jumping onto
the platform, desperately trying to keep her from igniting
the Effigy.

If it had taken him even a second longer, they both would
have been incinerated.

Slightly stunned, he blinked furiously, trying to return to
his senses. The shocked silence that had followed the explosion was shattered by screams of terror as the fire rippled
across the audience, licking at trees and incinerating clothes.

Forcing himself to his knees, he felt cold fear grip him as
he saw Caidy, limp and splayed on the ground with blood
trickling from a gash on her head. Gritting his teeth, he lifted

her with both arms, staggering to his feet, determined to get her to safety.

Everything was chaos. There was no smoke, just hot, ravenous fire. A half-remembered thought twinged in the back of Alex's mind, but a wave of heat washed over him and he doubled over. He started making his way around the platform, searching for a path through the panicking crowd to safety. Caidy's head lolled uselessly on his shoulder, blood staining his tunic, and his stomach churned.

Out of nowhere, Merric Adley, Caidy's bodyguard, appeared. He pulled Alex close with one arm, cupping his free hand around his mouth and yelling, "The Judgment Stair! We've got it cordoned off!"

Alex nodded and started shouldering his way to the northern edge of City Hill as flames rained down on them. A molten chunk of burning debris landed on one of Caidy's arms as it hung limply. Quickly and methodically, the bodyguard used his own cloak to stifle the flame, leaving her skin underneath blackened.

Intense heat, no smoke, a very small part of Alex's mind noted, even as he kept moving. Merric kept his body between them and the crowd, his sword unsheathed. The bodyguard yelled at the crowd, directing them back from the flames and toward the main promenade. The top of the Judgment Stair, an old wooden signpost, came into view through the sea of bodies, and he pressed on.

The heat seemed to be everywhere, pushing them to the ground like a giant, invisible hand. He heard the snap of flames and the sickening stench of burning hair and flesh. Reaching the top of the stair, he saw a member of the Rose Guard holding back the crowd, directing panicked civilians back toward the plaza.

As the tide of people threatened to shove the guard down the stairs, Merric forced his way to the front, bellowing, "Get back! The path down to Market is clear! There's naught but death this way! Iya damn you, get back!" He brought the pommel of his sword down hard on the shoulder of a hulking man at the front of the crowd. The man fell to his knees with a crunch of bone and a scream of pain. Alex, reaching the guardsmen, turned back to face the panicked mob.

The Effigy burned, but so too did the crowd. Bodies littered the plaza near the platform, and four juniper trees were incinerated. Three more were aflame closer to the buildings, and the mass of people slowly pushed its way back toward Market. A squad of guards carrying water buckets, as well as some intrepid citizens, formed a line to hold the fire back as three mages with glittering fingers traced warding symbols in the air. It looked like the buildings would survive the blaze. A few thatched roofs were smoking, but the flames seemed to be concentrated on the crowd.

It was odd, the way the fire seemed to cling to the people, devouring clothes and skin with an insatiable appetite, but failing to catch on the larger buildings around the square. The inferno licked the crowd pushing down the hill, spreading devastation closer to the densely populated Market District.

Together, Merric and the other guardsman started steering the crowd back. Alex edged toward them and shouted over the dull roar of fire and fear, "I'll take her to Raven House!" The bodyguard nodded once and then turned his full attention to the crowd as Alex faced the stair.

On a good day, Judgment Stair was an ambitious journey. Alex's exhaustion and the threat of the guards being overwhelmed by the sheer press of people made it a deathtrap. The stairs wound precariously and steeply, at points carved into the stone protruding from City Hill. Adjusting his grip on Caidy and whispering a prayer to whatever God might be listening, Alex started down.

He placed his feet carefully in the center of steps. Twice in the first hundred stairs he nearly slipped, only barely managing to balance in time. When they disappeared below the summit of the hill, the pandemonium of the crowd faded to a soft echo. Alex felt his breath sharp beneath his ribs, and his arms burned with Caidy's weight. *One foot after the other.*

He reached a small landing and stopped, gently setting her on the wall of someone's house, built back into the rock. Using the edge of his tunic to wipe sweat out of his eyes, he quickly assessed her head wound. It didn't look too deep—no bone that he could see—but it was still bleeding profusely. The side of her face was coated with a slick sheen of blood, and her curls were matted with the stuff. The skin on her left arm was charred and darkened, oozing and shiny at the same time.

Alex ripped a strip off his tunic and tied it around her head, attempting to stop the flow of blood. When he tightened the knot, she moaned and opened her eyes, starting to push herself up. "Stop, stop, you'll fall," Alex placed a hand on her right shoulder, holding her in place. Caidy blinked up at him and rubbed her eye, her fingers coming away caked with blood. Was she paler than usual? Alex couldn't tell. His stomach did a backflip, and he took her hands in his.

"Caidy, I need you to listen to me. I need you to put your arms around my neck and hold on. Can you do that?" She nodded slowly and then raised her arms and wrapped them around him, not seeming to notice the burned skin. "Keep holding on, okay? We've got to keep going down." He scooped her up again, one arm under her legs as her wrists dug into his neck. "Good job, just like that."

His legs trembling, Alex started slowly down the stairs once more. He traced his free hand along the walls lining the Judgment Stair where houses had been built nearly on top of one another, carved back into the rock to make more room. The houses were almost all deserted since most people were at the Harvest Festival. He focused on taking each step one at a time, as Caidy pressed her face into his shoulder, her breathing labored. "Shhh," Alex murmured as he continued picking his way down, "You're okay."

He paused once more at another small flat area. The ten steps he had just climbed down were nearly vertical, more notches carved into the cliffside than anything else. He had maneuvered carefully, urging Caidy to hold on and gripping stone with his free hand until the stairs flattened to a more natural gradient.

They made it to the street, and Alex staggered up the steps to Raven House, his legs nearly numb with exhaustion. Using his free hand and shoulder he shoved the door open, stumbled inside, and nearly dropped Caidy onto the couch. He collapsed into the chair next to her, his legs and arms trembling.

"Alex is that—Three Hells!" Jakob took the stairs two at a time from the second floor.

"I'm fine. Do you have any bandages?" Alex's breath was coming in rough gasps, but he pointed at Caidy. Jakob nodded and dug in a cabinet, emerging with two rolls of linen and some sort of ointment. Untying the soaked rag Alex had knotted over her head, he cleaned the wound, poking the edges as she moaned.

"I'm sorry, my Lady, but you need stitches." Jakob rummaged in the cupboard once more, and while Alex watched, the Archivalist smeared the ointment on Caidy's forehead.

She stared at him, wide-eyed, and he narrated, "That'll numb the pain. You won't feel a thing, just a couple of stitches to stop the bleeding." Jakob threaded the needle with practiced ease, and quickly stitched the skin back together. "There you are, my Lady," he said kindly, patting her cheek clean with a damp cloth.

With Caidy curled up on the couch, groggy and disoriented, cradling the oozing burn on her arm, Jakob turned his attention to Alex. "What happened?"

Alex ran his fingers through his hair. "I'm not totally sure. When she touched the torch to the Effigy, everything went up in flames. It was everywhere, the fire, rippling through the crowd." Jakob's eyes went wide and his mouth fell open. Alex nodded in silent agreement with his shock. "It was a mob. Might still be. Not sure how long it took us to get down the stairs."

"You carried her down the Judgment Stair?"

"Didn't have much of a choice." His breath was starting to come more easily. "People were everywhere. I was lucky to get her out without getting trampled."

Jakob chewed on his lip nervously. "Freelarks you think?"

Alex shrugged. "Most likely."

"Was there smoke?" Jakob rubbed his chin as he sat back on his heels.

"I don't —" Alex paused. "No, I don't think so. Not from the fire, anyway." Something again whispered in the back of his mind. He frowned.

"And it raced through the crowd, you said? It sounds like magefire, Alex."

Magefire. The jelly turned to gas when it ignited and clung to anything it touched. The audience would have spread the dangerous substance quickly, and the fire had engulfed it all.

For whatever reason, magefire never smoked, and its burns were horrific, tending to fester and scar terribly. He shouldn't have missed it.

"Are you okay?" Jakob placed a hand on his shoulder.

He rubbed his eyes. They itched with exhaustion. His arms and legs felt heavy. "Yeah I am. Just...tired."

Jakob nodded. "Take a break, Alex. I'm going to head out and see if I can get a situation report from the Guard. Is someone coming for her?"

"I think so," he replied slowly. "I told her bodyguard where I was going."

"Merric's good. He'll come, or he'll send someone." Jakob fetched a waterskin and placed it in easy reach. "Drink that when you can. She should be okay. The wound is clean and it should stop bleeding now. Keep half an eye on her. If she gets paler, that's bad."

"Yeah, I remember my training," he said drowsily. His legs and arms felt heavy.

"I'll be back as soon as I can. Hendrick and Starling are both out. I'm going to try and find them too." Jakob raised a hand and then snapped the door shut.

CHAPTER 28

———

21st Day of the Harvest Moon

Alex dozed fitfully, his mind unfocused and swamped in exhaustion. He drifted through memories, mixing reality with history. The last time he'd been so bone tired was when he had finished his training in Tanunt.

Along the Coral Coast, in the very southern reaches of the Empire, there was a curious phenomenon. Over thousands of years, the ocean waves had worn labyrinthine caverns through the soft sandstone beneath the desert dunes. As the tides rose and fell with the stars, the ocean roared through the caverns and then drained back out to sea. The Mezrani fishermen had rigged a pulley system—catching large hauls of the saltwater fish as the water rushed out of the caverns by trapping the fish in nets dropped at high tide.

One of Alex's final assessments for his Blade training had involved descending into the caverns to the Watcher's Eye, a vortex where several cavern systems connected and created a swirling whirlpool as the high tide rushed back to sea. Alex had lashed himself to the sandstone stalactites and held on for what felt like hours as the water roared and buffeted him into the rock. He had emerged breathless, bruised, and shaking with exhaustion.

Someone thumped urgently on the door, startling him awake. Groaning, Alex forced himself up and then hissed in pain as he realized he had raw, burnt skin on his right shoulder. He swore colorfully and then steeled himself to take the ten or so steps between himself and the door.

His legs felt as though they had been encased in molten metal, and his shoulders burned. He had no idea how much time had passed. It all seemed like a hazy nightmare. With a groan, he staggered to the door and opened it. Relief washed over him when he saw Merric's sweat-stained face, and a man with sharp features, brown hair, and the habit of a mage.

"She's here." The bodyguard beckoned his companion inside, and the mage went straight to Caidy's side, muttering over the burn on her arm and prodding the wound on her forehead gently. Merric leaned against the doorjamb, looking exhausted. His maroon tunic was stained with sweat, dirt, and a dark substance Alex hoped wasn't blood. The guard had tucked his leather gloves into his belt. His hair was caked with sweat, and his boots were dirty. His sword, once more sheathed, looked battered and worn.

"How long did it take you to get here? Has it calmed down?" Alex asked tentatively.

Merric looked as though the doorframe was the only thing keeping him from collapsing onto the floor. "It's been a few hours. We were nearly overwhelmed at the top of the Hill. Things have calmed down a little. It looks like they've got the fire mostly contained and the buildings should be fine, but the jelly hit the crowd and spread before we could stop the panic.

"We've got at least three dozen dead, likely four or five times that number when all is said and done. It had to be magefire, smokeless like that. Magefire burns take forever to heal, so that'll strain the temples. Fritha's Maidens are already out trying to gather the wounded, but there's still a panicked mass in Market District. It's a disaster." He rubbed one hand across his eyes, and Alex saw a blistering, pink burn on the back of Merric's hand.

"She'll be fine," the mage called from the floor beside Caidy. "Who treated her?"

"Jakob, our Archivalist," Alex replied, turning toward the mage. He looked very familiar, and after a moment Alex placed the face. "Nolan, right? The Court Mage?"

"That's what they call me." Nolan straightened. "We'll need a stretcher to get her out of here. She's in no shape to walk or ride."

"Nonsense," Caidy squeaked from the couch, struggling to sit up. Nolan gently placed a hand on her shoulder, holding her in place. "I'm fine!"

"My Lady, with all due respect—" Nolan began, hovering over her.

"*Lie down.*" Merric's voice was sharp and exasperated, and Caidy stopped trying to stand. "Nolan, could you go fetch the guard contingent and ask them to bring in the stretcher? We need to get her back to the castle before Lord Roussel has me executed for losing his daughter."

Nolan nodded and straightened his crooked habit before leaving. When the door closed behind him, Alex offered Merric his waterskin, and the guard drank from it gratefully.

Minutes ticked by. Merric went over to Caidy and knelt beside her, examining her injuries carefully. Alex, feeling uncomfortable and unsteady, settled himself on the stairs.

A few moments later, several sets of boots tramped up the steps, and Merric beckoned what seemed like half the Rose Guard into the small room.

Nolan supervised three soldiers as they moved Caidy to a makeshift stretcher and tied her securely, and Alex hid a reflexive smile as Caidy loudly insisted she was fine and could walk by herself. Merric politely ignored his charge, and directed the guards back out the door. When the guard passed Alex, he pushed himself to his feet and nodded formally, returning to a shroud of professionalism. The door swung shut behind the crowd, and he started prowling back and forth across the room, ignoring the deep, dull ache in his legs.

It was deeply frustrating to feel as though he had come so close to stopping the attack but had failed. Merric was right. There was just too much ground to cover. The Amaranth Khmal—the formal, Imperial name for the Blades—was a small intelligence organization. They relied on local contacts and networks that had existed for decades to do most of the actual intelligence work. His ability to do his job was so reliant on good relationships, and he had been in Rosemoor for such a short period of time. Getting any intelligence at all was an uphill battle to ingratiate himself to informants.

In Danen, at his previous post with the Amaranth Khmal, there had been a different set of problems. The Blades in Danen worked more as a mercenary group than anything else. The lawless plains were infamous for their corruption, and they operated accordingly. In order to gather information, they had often worked for the highest bidder in exchange for useful intelligence.

It was a cruel world but relatively easy to navigate. Danen's thieves and criminals, he had quickly discovered, were some of the most honorable people to deal with. If they went back on their word, they were quickly out of money, jobs, and friends. Many criminals couldn't be trusted much past their promises, but that was human nature. He had quickly adjusted to the bribery and favors that ran civilized society in Danen. It was a world he understood how to manipulate.

Here in Rosemoor, however, he found himself floundering. The province was teeming with information—most of it useless and all of it rippling just below the surface. Everything and nothing seemed connected at the same time. In isolation, it made sense, but the moment he tried to see the bigger picture, to examine the larger stratagems and games the nobles played with one another, something would shift and the chessboard would become clouded once more.

The problem, at its heart, was that he had no idea what the truth was. It had been too long since he had lived in Rosemoor, and he had not yet redeveloped his sense of reality. Everything was disorienting simply because he did not yet have the ability to tell fact from fiction, perspective from truth. It was a painful lesson, doubly so because of the head count it now carried. Dozens were dead because he had missed something. Alex balled his hands into fists, digging his nails into his palms as he paced back and forth.

He stopped marching and threw himself into a chair, drumming his fingernails incessantly on the wooden arm as thoughts chased circles around in his head. By the time Jakob returned with Hendrick and Starling, he was still deep in thought. The door creaked open again and Alex snapped upright, his legs protesting. The two older Blades stomped inside, followed by Jakob. The scent of burning flesh and hot air wafted through the door with the group, and Alex squared his shoulders, ready to be sent back to the Citadel for remedial training—or to be expelled from the Warden Corps altogether.

Hendrick was streaked with soot and sweat, and a bandage was wrapped around his upper arm. The former Bandit Lord had his hair tied back, and the scars on his forearms stood out, harsh and white. To Alex's surprise, however, his gaze was not furious, but soft, almost kind.

"Where's Lady Caidelene?" Hendrick coughed deeply, and Alex quickly offered him a fresh waterskin.

"The Rose Guard took her back to the castle not too long ago. The new court mage said she would be fine." Alex paused while Hendrick drank and then continued defensively, "I handed her off to the Rose Captain, Merric. I knew him personally before —"

Starling, her own hair braided tightly back and soot smudging sharp cheekbones, made a disdainful noise. "Oh, sure. Why not. Just hand the princess off to the first person in a guard's uniform you —"

Hendrick waved a hand as he cut her off. "I know Adley. He's a good man. You did the right thing. Taking care of the girl is his job, not yours."

It was an offhanded comment, but Alex knew it was a quiet reprimand, which was somehow much worse than the lash of Starling's fury. He swallowed hard and examined the ground by Hendrick's feet, digging his thumbnail into his palm as penance. He couldn't bring himself to look up at either of them.

Cracking his knuckles loudly, Hendrick continued, "I want you to understand something, Laurent. We've got thirty-seven dead so far. That's on you." His eyes were shards of ice, cold and unfriendly. "I want you to think about that and remember it. But, Laurent, whoever did this hasn't been caught, and it's our job to bring them before Erius' courts. Am I clear?"

Alex felt sick and dizzy, as though the world spun around him. His ears pounded with the heavy silence, and he swallowed hard. "I understand."

"Good!" Hendrick opened his mouth to continue, but the door opened again and Danila stormed in. It was dark outside, and the Imperial Commissar stood for a moment, silhouetted on the threshold, before she stepped inside and slammed the front door.

"How in the Hells did this happen?" Danila's voice whipped across the room. "Do you have any idea what you've done? I thought the Blades were the best of the best, capable of anything. *You* have certainly sold yourself that way." She rounded on Hendrick, who had half turned to look at her. "You let some ragged band of beggars threaten the stability of a city!"

Jakob threw a sideways glance at him, and Alex caught his eye before watching the battle unfolding before them. Hendrick turned fully toward the Mezrani woman, placing himself at the center of the argument. "If you genuinely believe the Freelarks are, how did you put it, a *ragged band of beggars*, you are sorely misinformed, Commissar." His voice rumbled. "Jakob, what are our most recent numbers?"

The Archivalist cleared his throat nervously. "There are dozens of Freelark Dandelions—er, radicals—within Rosemoor alone, and thousands of sympathizers. The Freelarks aren't just anarchists. They defend the poor and the abandoned. They are worshippers of Niwe and Caldir. They advocate for equality and justice, and they protect travelers in the wilderness. They have credibility within our society, and their organization is older even than the Mezrani Empire. Commissar," he added as an afterthought.

Danila opened her mouth to respond and Alex sensed Starling about to say something rash, but Hendrick silenced them both with a raised hand. "We are the best, Commissar. But we are only as capable as the information we have. You can point fingers all you want, and I'm sure you will. But," he continued, ignoring an outraged squeak from the Commissar and a frustrated hiss from the Shadow. "I'd like to hear how you would have stopped this from happening. You had the same information we did. More, probably, in all your missives."

"That isn't my problem," Danila shot back, striding forward so she was nose to nose with Hendrick. "My problem is that scores of dead civilians lie on the streets of Iera, and that's not my fault."

"The responsibility lies with both of us, Commissar." Hendrick's eyebrows snapped together nearly audibly. "We are charged with protecting this kingdom—these people—and we have failed. And so *we* will fix it. You aren't going to just throw us in front of whatever Imperial punishment is about to rain down from Tanunt. You're going to help us." He seemed to grow taller.

Danila's eyes smoldered. "There are dead children, Lord Commissioner. Someone has to pay for that."

"And they will, as soon as we've had more than an hour to catch our breath." Hendrick's voice was calm and level. "This will not go unpunished, Commissar. I promise you that."

Danila stood very still for a moment and then stepped back abruptly. "I need to send a report to the capital. Your thoughts?" Her tone was flat; Alex could see exhaustion painted across her face.

Hendrick rubbed his mustache. "Do your job, Commissar, and we'll do ours. The slop that's about to hit us from the

Authority will only pull our attention away from security. I don't think I need to explain to you that the Freelarks will, in all likelihood, try to strike again soon. Do you want us working to stop future attacks or taking punitive lashes because of something that's in the past?"

She appeared to consider the statement for a moment before nodding slowly. "I'll handle the Authority. I expect daily updates until we get the Freelark situation under control." Alex glanced at Jakob, who couldn't keep the surprise out of his face.

"Of course, Commissar." Hendrick extended a hand, which Danila took delicately and shook before turning her heel and leaving.

"What just happened?" Jakob asked, the moment they heard Danila climb down the front steps.

Starling snorted. "She's embarrassed. The Freelarks bloodied the Empire's nose today. They need someone to blame."

Jakob whistled through his teeth. "Does this mean we like her now?"

"This means she may be more reasonable than we thought," Hendrick replied. Alex looked up at him, and Hendrick raised both eyebrows again. "You're not off the hook, Laurent. But you're my problem, not hers. Understand?"

A wave of unexpected relief gripped Alex, and he nodded emphatically. "I do. Thank you."

"Don't thank me, Laurent. Until we hear differently, we have to behave as though the Ball tomorrow is still happening. Get us through the rest of this damned Festival without another attack."

CHAPTER 29

———

22nd Day of the Harvest Moon

"It's not a debate," Caidy said flatly, glaring at Geoffrey. She absently rubbed the still-fresh stitches the Archivalist had put in her forehead and then winced as she bumped the burn on her wrist. "Bartholomew has been slaving in the kitchens for weeks, the flowers have been blessed, and the guests are all here. We aren't canceling the Ball."

"Don't you think it's a little selfish?" Geoffrey's voice had taken on a whining tone that made Caidy want to throw something at him. "People are in mourning." His hands twisted nervously as he watched her.

"I am well aware of the tragedy." Her stitches itched painfully. "But we need a return to normalcy, and the Ball does that."

"Caidy—"

"No." She cut him off before he could start arguing again. "It's my decision. If we send everyone home, all we are doing is teaching every dissident in Rosemoor that we can be easily manipulated with cruelty and violence. I will not have it." The dull ache that had been pounding in her ears all morning sharpened. "Go get ready. I'll see you this evening."

"I'm happy to stay and help," Geoffrey replied after a moment of silence. It sounded kind, but she suspected he would remind her that she owed him a favor in the near future. She knew the appearance that they were unified, that this was his choice too, was important to Geoffrey. To his *reputation*. *Valance men and their stupid pride*, she thought angrily.

"Just go, please." Caidy knew her tone was clipped, that he thought her rude, but she didn't care. It was all she could do to not collapse into a chair. Her pride held her by the window, her back to Geoffrey, until she heard his footsteps echo down the stone hallway.

She was exhausted. When they had returned to the castle the previous evening, it had been hours before she had been able to sleep. Her parents had interrogated her. Her father had rounded on Merric for allowing her to be hurt. Her mother had fussed and hovered until Nolan had performed a more thorough examination of her injuries. Then, when Margot had tucked her into bed, Caidy had cried. The fear she had ignored and beaten down until she was alone flooded her body, paralyzing her limbs and racking her chest with sobs.

She had finally fallen into an exhausted stupor, though the pure terror of the moment she had been knocked to the ground—perilously close to the sheer cliff, she knew—still gripped her. Her dreams tumbled her through the air over and over, slipping her between wakefulness and sleep. Over and over her stomach soared to her throat and then slammed into the ground. Over and over she heard that awful crunch of bone. Everything smelled like burnt, dying flesh and hair, acrid and hot. The poisoned air filled her lungs as she struggled to breathe.

Struggling clear of the nightmares at last, she had risen with the sun, surprising Margot by emerging before her breakfast was ready. Everything hurt, and muscles she didn't realize she had were stiff and sore. Her head throbbed, and the world seemed to be slowly spinning around her. Nolan had stopped by with a small bottle that he promised would help the world stop moving, and, indeed, soon after swallowing it she had begun to feel more like herself.

She had briskly made up her mind. The Ball would *not* be canceled. *We will not hide in our castle, frightened of our own shadows, showing the Freelarks that all it takes is one attack to send us fleeing. The people need to see me stand, laugh, and dance, to see that it will take more than a cowardly attack to force Rosemoor to her knees.*

Unfortunately, opposition was around every corner. She had spent her morning arguing, first with her parents and then with Geoffrey, about the state of the Harvest Ball that evening. What she had thought was a simple idea—keep moving forward, show strength in the face of a threat to the kingdom—was strongly opposed. Her parents claimed that many nobles were afraid of another attack. Merric lectured her about the precarious security situation, and Geoffrey vehemently disagreed with her at every turn, making her grind her teeth with his apparently arbitrary obstinance.

Deep in her heart, she knew she had made the right decision when she ordered the head steward to finalize arrangements for the Ball, though how she knew she was not sure. A sense of calm and ease gripped her aching joints now that she knew what was going to happen, and the wheels of protocol had been set in motion. That feeling was one she had become more accustomed to as she had grown up and started making choices that mattered, seeing the consequences.

When she had turned thirteen, she had refused to invite the daughter of the Imperial Ambassador to her birthday celebrations. Her mother had argued for hours until her father had shooed Julianna out of the room and sat down beside Caidy. He had tucked an unruly curl behind her ear, cleaned a smudge of dirt off her nose with a handkerchief, and asked her why.

She had grumbled that she didn't want to, and Mattias had shook his head. "That's not good enough, Caidelene. If you don't want her to come, that's your choice. You're old enough to start making your own decisions, but you must have a reason. People like us, we don't have the luxury of not having a reason. Our reasons define who we are, and how we lead."

Those words echoed in Caidy's mind every time she was unsure of her next step. It was a haunting refrain, but it grounded her and reminded her of the kind of leader she wanted to be—the kind of leader she planned to be.

Footsteps approached, and Margot hovered behind her. "My Lady? I have your dress if you're ready."

Caidy rolled her shoulders and drummed the knuckles of her uninjured hand on the stone sill of the window before turning to face her maid. She plastered a smile on her face and squared her small frame. "That would be lovely. Thank you for your help, Margot."

It took less time than usual to get ready. She insisted on wearing her injuries as a badge of honor. The maid laced her into the gown and swept her hair back, but the usual affair of painting her face with various hues was ignored. *It's important to be a symbol of strength,* she told herself.

The moment Caidy walked into the Harvest Ball, she knew she had made the right decision not to bow to the

Freelark terror. Of course, there was tension in the air. Nobles sat in small groups, talking nervously and glancing around. Triple the number of guards were on duty, and some prominent names and faces were absent, including the patriarch of the Riverlord Trading Cartel, Sylvester Alamay. Despite the tension, the music that floated through the room was cheerful. The smell of roasted chicken and candied yams wrapped everything in a warm, comforting embrace, and several peals of laughter punctured the nervous atmosphere.

While they dined, the atmosphere continued to ease. Bartholomew had outdone himself, cooking dozens of dishes to appeal to every palate. Caidy ate two helpings of thick acorn noodles tossed with rhubarb, radish, and saffron, and drank three flagons of honey peach cider. Geoffrey helped himself to several biscuits slathered with honey, soft cheese, and fried eggs, and some sort of charbroiled game meat. The room filled with the contented sounds to food and good cheer, and slowly, the tension in the air melted into the night.

Geoffrey began a heated discussion with Mattias, and the two men argued over her head as she ignored the debate. They were talking about Imperial taxes—Geoffrey was making a complex case for increasing the Imperial share of agricultural revenues—a topic she found insufferably boring on her best days. Making occasional noncommittal noises when one of the two men made a particularly emphatic point, she leaned forward and scanned the room, doing her best to ignore the deep ache that permeated her body.

Three of the four major noble houses of Rosemoor—other than the Roussels—were represented: Valance, Ambroy, Ernault. House Laurent was conspicuously absent, and she suspected they knew Alex had returned to court. Caidy saw many of her peers, young noblemen and women she had grown up with, chatting and drinking with one another. They were close—if she squinted, she could count the freckles smattered across Theresa Ernault's pert nose—but unreachable, more like Players or statues than real humans.

When she had begun to spend more and more of her time on matters of state, the petty games of court had started to hold less interest for her. She could guess that tomorrow's gossip would be about the daring cut of Theresa's magenta gown, yet it seemed so unimportant compared to everything else happening.

Farther away, at a lower table, she caught sight of Alex. He had his head inclined toward the woman seated next to him, listening intently and smiling. Caidy felt her stomach churn uncomfortably and took a swig of elderflower wine. The liquor seared the back of her throat and she swallowed a cough. With a start, she recognized Farah, the Mezrani ambassador, as Alex's dining partner. The young Imperial seemed captivated by some joke he was telling, tossing dark, shimmering curls back with laughter.

As Caidy surveyed the table they were seated at, she observed Hugo Ambroy and his wife Charlotte listening with polite faces to the ambassador, tension and distaste outlined in the rigid lines of their spines. Couples at neighboring tables glanced over their shoulders toward her and leaned in close to carry on quiet conversations out of earshot. *The Mezrani have never been popular in Rosemoor*, Caidy thought with some satisfaction.

Farah seemed unconcerned with the stares and whispers that eddied around her. Caidy admired the proud way she held her head and the easy, fluid hand motions that animated her words. She liked the way Farah leaned toward Alex and whispered in his ear much less, and the way he smiled brightly in return made the acorn noodles feel heavy in the pit of her stomach.

When the nobles finished eating, servants began to move tables and chairs out of the great hall. Several performers carrying a variety of instruments—a lute, a dulcimer, two horns, and a flute—began to set up and tune on one side of the room. Geoffrey nudged her elbow. "Are you ready to dance, sweetling?"

Caidy watched Alex slip his arm around the Tanu woman's waist and turned rather suddenly back to face Geoffrey, who watched her expectantly. It was the tradition, after all. "I would love that."

He offered his arm, and she slipped a hand around it. He was dressed in a burnt orange tunic and cerulean silken shirt. The colors didn't precisely match those in the magnificent gown Caidy wore, but she put it out of her mind. *Nothing to be done about that now.*

He led her around the dais where they had been eating and down onto the clear dance floor. The nobles were now in small groups around the periphery of the room, talking and munching on sugared desserts. It was tradition that a member of the ruling family start the dance, and as the pair approached the musicians, they started playing the jaunty introduction to the traditional Autumn Sparrow folk dance.

Geoffrey was a comfortable dance partner, she admitted to herself. He led her easily around the dance floor, one hand resting lightly on her waist. The Sparrow dance was lively and fun, lots of swirling skirts and light dips. The footwork wasn't particularly difficult either, and Caidy flung herself into the dance with an enthusiasm that appeared to briefly surprise her partner.

She spun around Geoffrey, trailing her fingers across his broad chest and smiling brightly as he caught her. As they moved across the dance floor, she kept her steps close to his, their feet almost touching with barely a breath of air between them. When they reached the final pattern of the folk dance, he dipped her deeply and she leaned into it, arching her back over his arm and trailing her arms dramatically over her head to sweep the floor. A few nobles had watched them dance, and some of her peers let out whoops before being shushed by their more conservative parents.

More pairs joined them for the next few dances, and by the time the musicians began the sixth dance, a lively jig, more were dancing than not. She spun and danced among them, moving from partner to partner as the jig continued, careful to protect her injured wrist. She sashayed past Theresa and noticed with a twinge of satisfaction that the other woman's steps were out of rhythm. The dance spun them away from one another as it wound down, and she placed her palm flat against that of Miles Ernault, revolving in a slow circle.

As the dance ended, Caidy faced Miles, Theresa's younger brother, and curtsied deeply. She and Miles had always gotten along well, despite how thoroughly Theresa detested her. Miles was two years younger than she, but very quiet and thoughtful for his age with little patience for the games of court Theresa enjoyed and a disinterest in his older sister's envy. He was bespectacled and always looked vaguely lost, as though he had forgotten his destination halfway through the journey.

"Miles, a pleasure," Caidy caught her breath between words, her cheeks flushed. "I thought you were studying at the Mirror Falls monastery?"

The young nobleman offered his arm and led her to the side of the room, near a platter of cookies made from spun maple sugar. "I am, but right now the monks are on retreat and it's dreadfully boring. I returned to Iera for a few weeks rather than go home. Besides, it's nice to see many of the old guard." He paused, raising an eyebrow. "And my sister is always a delight to be around."

She stifled a smile at his wry tone. "There is some comfort in the consistency of things," she agreed, fanning herself with one hand. It was starting to get quite hot in the large hall, and she could feel a bead of sweat drip down her spine. *Where was Nolan when she needed that wind spell again?*

Helping herself to one of the maple sugar cookies, she offered one to Miles, who accepted happily. Turning back toward the dancers, she surveyed the room. Alex and Farah were nowhere to be seen, and hot nausea tumbled in her stomach. Shaking herself slightly, she nibbled the cookie and did her best to brush off the unpleasant jealous sensation that tickled her heart.

"It's so hot," Miles remarked as he finished the dessert. "Do you want to go for a walk?"

Jerking her attention back to him, she nodded vigorously. "Yes please." He offered his arm again, and they walked through a side door out into the gardens.

CHAPTER 30

22nd Day of the Harvest Moon

According to Jakob, the final count was ninety-eight dead, many of magefire burns. The burns were notoriously hard to treat, tending to infect, fester, and scar terribly. Two hundred and forty-three additional people were injured, and Fritha's Maidens of Mercy had turned several local establishments into triage centers for the wounded.

During their morning preparations, Jakob noted coolly that it was the most deadly Freelark attack Rosemoor had seen in over a decade. "But," he added, with a decidedly wry tone, "twice as many people were killed in the Danen coup a few years back, so it could definitely be worse."

In spite of the attack, messengers had flooded the city, assuring nobles and commoners alike that the harvest festivities would continue, in honor of the dead and in defiance of the anarchists. Alex, whose legs jolted with pain every time he shifted his weight, and whose shoulder was decidedly tender, was ready to make up a thousand excuses not to attend the Ball. Then Danila arrived.

The Mezrani, normally so composed, had dark bruises of exhaustion under her eyes and was wearing the same scorched harvest garb she had worn the day before. She brought the scent of acrid fire and death with her into Raven House; it clung to her clothes and hair like a diseased perfume.

Despite her disheveled appearance, she easily parried all of Alex's excuses, making it clear that he had no other option than to attend the Ball and telling him flatly, "Given the current security situation and *your* role in protecting the Roussels, would you risk leaving them defenseless?" In a final, weak attempt, he told her he had no guest to bring with him. Her only response was a dark smile.

And that was how he had wound up escorting Farah al-Kalim, the new Imperial Ambassador to Rosemoor, to the Harvest Ball. The Commissar framed the pairing as an opportunity for him to bring the Ambassador up to speed on the affairs of Rosemoor—but he had a sneaking suspicion that Danila knew about his history with Farah in the capital.

During his time training, he had quite literally run into her. She was the second youngest daughter of one of the powerful Tanu noble families, completing her formal schooling in diplomacy. One evening after a particularly challenging mental exercise, Alex had gone for a walk through the waterfront district to clear his head. He had collided with her at a sharp corner and sent both of them tumbling into a bed of succulents.

Luckily, the damage had not been permanent to either them or the plants, and she had handled it with grace. They had struck up a conversation as he helped pick cacti spines from the back of her leg, and a brief romance soon followed. Farah was very beautiful, with long shining hair, smoky skin, and captivating eyes. But she was also much more interested in her work than anything else and several summers his senior. They had parted amicably enough, but Rosemoor was the last corner of the Empire he had expected her to appear in.

"I thought you were trying for a more exotic assignment," he remarked conversationally as dinner was served. During their journey up to the castle they had briefly discussed the attack, but Farah had made clear that tonight was about saving face and appearing strong and infallible after the attack. *Mezrani pride*, he reflected, *is an incredible thing.*

The rest of their table was alternating between politely ignoring Farah's presence and sneaking glances at her behind wine glasses. Farah greeted every surreptitious look with a bright, friendly smile, and leaned closer to him to respond.

"I was, but my father made a political misstep," she lowered her voice conspiratorially. "He married my younger brother to a woman one of the princes was secretly bedding. My family is currently trying to bribe their way back into Imperial good graces, and my chances at traveling somewhere interesting are looking increasingly slim."

Alex noticed with interest that her eyelashes made complicated shadows on her cheekbones as she looked up at him. Her lips were painted a muted shade of red, like the end of a sunset, and her eyes were outlined with some sort of dark kohl, making them appear even larger and brighter than normal. "I'm sorry to hear that."

Farah waved a hand lightly. "No matter! I've only just gotten to Rosemoor this moon. You can imagine how pleasantly surprised I was when Danila mentioned you had also been assigned here. I'd love a private tour." She rested a hand on his arm.

She had always possessed an intoxicating sensuality that made his head swim. Farah was never crude or crass, but with her flirtatious touches, easy laughter, and that silky hair, she drew him in. *It's what makes her a good diplomat*, Alex reflected. Farah was eminently likable.

"I'll see what I can arrange. Unfortunately, I'm rather busy at the moment," he replied, widening his eyes innocently.

"Of course you are, with your mysterious Warden business." She pouted prettily, her cheeks flushed. "What have you done since leaving the capital?"

"I've traveled the Empire in search of the perfect succulent," Alex lied easily, winking at her. "I thought I came close in Colmar, but it was just a farmer's tale."

"Are you a budding gardener now?" Farah's voice was full of quiet laughter.

"Oh you know me, I've always had quite the interest in horticulture." He smiled at her and swiped his fingers unconsciously through his hair.

They passed dinner in a gentle flirtation with glasses of wine, ignoring the nervous conversations of the nobles seated at their table. Two of them he vaguely recognized from years ago, members of House Myreall. The major, influential Houses of Rosemoor were all seated closer to the dais, and the minor Houses and visiting Imperial Delegation were toward the entrance to the great hall. It was a subtle snub on the part of Lady Julianna, who he knew would have personally overseen the seating charts. The whole room seemed slightly muted as people whispered in undertones about the recent disaster.

Caidy, however, was radiant. He did his best not to look at her too often—it made his heart beat uncomfortably in his chest—but she was the picture of a battle-scarred heroine. The stitches on her forehead stood out, stark and unhidden, and when she moved her hands, he saw the snowy white of a fresh bandage wrapped around her forearm. *Of course she wouldn't hide them,* he thought tenderly. *It would be a sign of weakness, and she wants to appear strong.*

When a slightly awkward pause stretched at the table, he cast about for a new subject. Settling on an odd pendant he'd noticed Farah wearing earlier, shaped something like an inverted crossbow, he asked, "What's that for?"

Farah touched the necklace reflexively and then laughed. "You really haven't changed a smidge, Alex!" She wrinkled her nose at him. "It's the Shadow Crown, Naia's symbol."

When he looked at her blankly, she rolled her eyes and continued, "The Goddess of secrets and rulers? The patron of Tanunt? Gods Alex, isn't your job to know things about people?"

He shrugged, raising his hands in defeat. "The Gods were never really my area, you know that."

"Still," she paused. "You can't have forgotten everything about Mezrani City. Naia's symbol is everywhere back home."

Alex caught her eye with what he sincerely hoped was roguish charm. "I've remembered what was important." He gave her a cocky half-smile, and she laughed again.

He was doing a very good job ignoring the burning snake-nest of guilt and nerves that had taken up residence in his stomach since the attack yesterday. Farah made it easier too, he admitted to himself. She was delightfully distracting, leaning in close to him and running her fingertips over his shirtsleeve. Everyone and everything else seemed slightly muted, her face and laugh in sharp focus. Alex fed her samples of different dishes, watching the way her eyes widened with the new flavors, and joined the Mezrani in ignoring the rude stares from their dinner partners. It didn't really matter what they thought, anyway.

As dinner wound down, he finished his fifth glass of wine and rubbed his eyes. He rarely drank this much, and elderberry wine was strong. *Maybe not my best idea*, he admitted ruefully, carefully ignoring his guilty conscience. Farah had kept up with him glass for glass, teasing and encouraging the friendly competition. Now, she seemed even more giggly and forward than she had before, one of her hands firmly resting on his arm. Dishes were cleared by roving servants, and they stood with the rest of their group and drifted to the side of the room.

Alex noted with satisfaction how many guards were in the room. At least one guardsman covered each exit, and several drifted near the important nobles, out of earshot, yet close enough for an emergency. They had no indications that the Freelarks would try something else, though he knew from experience that trusting anarchists to follow logical expectations was folly. It was pleasing to see that security was not as lax as it had been when he arrived a few weeks previously. The nervous energy lingered, but nobles were beginning to relax into smaller groups.

Along the walls, servants had filled long buffet tables with a variety of desserts: steaming fruit tarts with cool frozen cream, honey biscuits and piles of fresh berries, at least eight different varieties of pie, fried apple dough dusted with sugar, and maple crunch cookies all within easy reach. Alex filled a plate to share with Farah and then offered her a piece of fried dough. She watched him with large eyes and let him feed her, powdered sugar clinging to her nose.

"That's delicious!" she exclaimed in surprise.

"Bart, the cook, is incredible," Alex agreed amicably. "And I love dessert."

"Who doesn't?" Farah smiled up at him, tilting her head back. He watched the way the torchlight flickered off her warm skin and danced in the dark waves of her hair.

A sudden hush gripped the room as a group of musicians in the corner started playing a folk dance. Glancing up, Alex watched for a moment as Caidy and Geoffrey danced, their feet moving quickly to the rhythm of the music. Her dress, a beautiful cream and orange conflagration, swirled around her ankles as she moved. She was graceful, her movements fluid and full of dreams. He could see intensity in the gaze she leveled toward her partner, a familiar determination. It made the snakes in his stomach move uncomfortably the longer he watched.

Geoffrey's movements were crisp and clean. He was a good match for Caidy in that respect. They had danced together before, that much was evident in the confidence he exuded and the easy way they moved from pattern to pattern. Alex frowned. He had never particularly liked the other man.

The noble was the second eldest child of the Valance family. His younger brother was serving in the Imperial Army, and his older sister, Valarie, spent most of her time on the Valance Estates, overseeing their vineyards. He had always struck Alex as very quintessentially noble, full of entitlement and sweeping proclamations. He distinctly remembered once watching Geoffrey patronizingly explain to a merchant's daughter that she did not properly understand how Imperial taxes affected her family's business.

"You're not listening even a little. Are you?" Farah's voice pulled his attention back to her. She had a lovely voice, full of mischief and dancing good humor.

"I'm sorry, milady," he swept her a ridiculously deep bow. "However can I make it up to you?"

"Dance with me for this next song," she ordered, eyes twinkling.

"Your wish is my command." He offered her his arm.

Farah was a spirited dance partner, twisting around him in complicated steps he had no idea how to follow. He spent most of the dance trying to keep up with her apparently endless stamina and energy as she twirled and sashayed. She trailed her fingers across his chest on a slow turn, her nose inches from his, before whipping away in a flurry of golden skirts. His legs ached with every step, protesting after yesterday's unexpected exercise.

As the music concluded, Alex bowed to Farah, breathing hard. To his dismay, she appeared fresh and ready for more. When she raised an eyebrow at him, he shook his head immediately. "I haven't danced in years," he gasped between heavy breaths. "I don't know that I could do that again without collapsing."

Mirth sparkled in her eyes again. "Don't they teach you flexibility at the Citadel? Dancing seems like a natural place to start," she teased.

"Milady, it's been four years. Dancing's a nobleman's skill, not really that of a Blade." He returned to the side of the great hall and she followed on his heels.

"Would you rather go for a walk, then? I'm sure we could find some way to pass the time." As she spoke, Farah intertwined her fingers with his, squeezing his hand gently.

Alex felt his heart in his throat again. He knew it was a dumb decision, probably the worst one he could make at that moment. He was here to support the guard detail, not to canoodle in the bushes. But he was pleasantly lightheaded from the wine, and Farah was very beautiful when she stuck out her lower lip in a slight pout. A small part of his mind protested that he was ignoring the problem and running away from his guilt. He ignored it with ease.

"It would be my honor to escort you," he replied evenly, controlling his tone as best he could. The snake nest in his stomach turned over, and he focused on the way the torch-light flickered off Farah's dark hair.

With another mischievous smile, she raised her hand for him to kiss. "Then lead on, my brave shadow-chaser."

CHAPTER 31

———

22nd Day of the Harvest Moon

They giggled through the gardens. Everything seemed a little too bright and slurred to Alex. He could feel blood pounding in his ears, and his head spun. The gardens, once so familiar, all seemed to tangle together as they swirled through the rose bushes and juniper trees, trading hidden laughs and quiet moments.

He had liked Farah from the moment they met. She was feisty and spirited with a wicked sense of humor and a love for exploring new places. She had shown him the famous Mezrani Spice Market and the Tanu Fish Docks, feeding him the best curry in the city and introducing him to famous fishmongers. She seemed to know people everywhere she went and naturally drew him into conversations.

Her family was quite influential. He knew that her uncle sat on the powerful Noble Council, advising the Emperor directly. Despite her noble blood, Farah came alive when she spoke with commoners in a way few nobles ever did. She was fascinated by details and had a mind for random facts, remembering the names of merchant's children and asking about the cost of importing ylang-ylang from the Distant Lands.

He had no idea how long they spent in the gardens, but eventually the pair stumbled into a copse of willows by the stables. Farah nearly tripped and fell against him. He wrapped his arms tightly around her and watched her open her mouth to speak.

A whisper echoed around them.

Suddenly, the hazy world sharpened and he placed three fingers on her lips in a reflexive signal to be quiet. His mind worked slowly, like a sluggish muscle, struggling to place the sound his ears had caught. Hushed voices rippled through the trees again and he leaned close to Farah. "Stay here," he whispered before disentangling himself from her arms and ducking through the trees.

He wasn't sure what had caught his attention, but one of the first lessons of his training had been to trust your instincts. The whispers could be young lovers hidden in the gardens, the way he and Farah were. But it was very early in the evening for that. Something about the way the voices whispered—urgently, secretly—nudged him forward. He slunk around the stables, clinging to the shadows. The instincts that had been beaten into him over and over kicked in, and he edged around a corner, peering into the darkness.

Torchlight flickered against the stone walls of Caldir's Temple, floating smears of light against the night. Three figures were silhouetted against the flames. One carried some sort of heavy pack, and a second was examining the lock on one of the side doors to the temple. The third stood back, hissing orders.

The whispers floated to Alex on the cool autumn breeze, "Work faster, Dandelion!"

There was a hushed whoop of success, and the door swung open. The three figures entered the temple quickly, closing the door with a snap. Without pausing to think, Alex crept forward. His legs ached as he moved quickly, but he ignored it. The muscle pain would pass.

He put his ear to the door and listened closely. There were no sounds inside, probably a smaller room adjoining the main chamber. After another moment of silence, he eased the door open a hair and then just wide enough to slip inside.

It was some sort of storeroom stuffed full of ceremonial paraphernalia. The door at the other side was ajar, and he heard louder voices within the temple. "Hand me the packet. No, no, not there!"

Peering around the open door, Alex moved like the wind into the temple, hugging a pillar on the side of the room. The Freelarks had placed their torches in sconces on the walls to free their hands and were now illuminated in the flickering light.

A woman dressed in earthen hues was tucking something into a crevice on the massive statue of Caldir behind the altar of the temple. Two men stood behind her, one with a long, scraggly beard and wild hair with the other wearing black robes and a belt sporting many pouches. As Alex watched, he saw a sparkle of pine-green magic and he swore under his breath. *Why did it always have to be mages?*

"Bramblerose, put the last one closer to the base." The mage commanded. The woman, Bramblerose, took the packet the wild-haired man offered her and knelt again.

"I know what I'm doing, Darkleaf," the woman hissed, annoyance turning her words to staccato.

Not good. Eyes narrowed in concentration, Alex considered his odds. Three of them—one a mage. The guards were too far to hear commotion, and they were worried about another attack on the Ball, not the temple. *Who attacks a temple?* he wondered before pushing the thought aside.

The torches could be a help—although they could just as easily a hindrance. Knocking a flame onto the wooden benches would cause chaos, and more than likely one of the Freelarks would escape in the smoke. He had no weapons other than fists, feet, and wit. He was fast—but fast enough to outmaneuver two fighters and a mage? *Probably not.*

He kicked himself for not sending Farah to get a contingent of Rose Guard. More times than he could count in Danen he'd started fights to delay until the guard or Blades could arrive in force, though he'd always known help was coming. He'd made it a point to avoid situations exactly like this one, alone and outnumbered.

Something in the air shifted, and Alex sensed that whatever they were doing was going to happen soon. *What could be in the small packets?* Maybe magefire again, sure, or something else more nefarious. Either way, he knew he had to act fast while he still had the element of surprise on his side.

He crept forward, edging closer to the trio. The woman and Wild Man were close together, kneeling near the altar, while the mage stood a few paces further back. The mage was the biggest threat because Alex didn't have anything with him that could restrain magical power. *He'll have to go first. Strike quickly, overpower one before the other two realize what's happened.*

Flattening his back against the pillar and saying a quick prayer to Udo, Alex edged around, waited until the mage looked back toward the altar, and then leapt through the air.

His sap was back in his rooms with the rest of his weapons, so he went with a hard punch to the jaw. The mage—Darkleaf—yelled, stumbling backward. Using the momentum from the jump, Alex forced him backward, slamming the mage into the wall where he crumpled to the floor.

Pivoting into a crouched, fighter's stance, Alex faced the other two Freelarks. The woman was still near the altar, fumbling with something, while the Wild Man bared his teeth in a snarl. "Last time I checked, Caldir didn't take too kindly to sacrilege," he quipped, circling slowly as the larger man moved closer to him. "He is the God of revenge, after all."

With an angry shout, the Wild Man lowered his head and charged at Alex like a bull. Alex stepped nimbly to the side, letting the man barrel past as the woman jumped to her feet and turned, a sharp knife flickering in the torchlight.

"You know nothing of Caldir, city-dweller," the woman spoke in a low voice, stalking toward him and tossing the blade from hand to hand.

With a *fwomp*, Alex found himself skidding to the ground, jaw slamming hard against the stone floor as the Wild Man plowed into his back. Seeing stars, he rolled to his side, instinctively curling into the fetal position to protect his core. He heard a whistle and barely rolled away again as the woman's knife sliced through the air, a hair from his cheek.

Forcing himself up, Alex spat blood to the ground as he circled, keeping both Freelarks in his vision. The torches seemed more like smears of light as he shook his head once, trying to bring the world back into focus.

The woman moved in first this time, diving with the knife toward his heart. Crossing his wrists, he caught the hilt of her blade on his forearms and then wrapped a hand around her wrist, yanking her close and using her own momentum to throw her to the ground. Stepping aside, he turned and ducked as the Wild Man threw a punch. Then he shouted in pain when the larger man followed it up with a kick to his gut.

Dancing backward, searching for air and for a moment to breathe, Alex evaded another punch. *Knife's the biggest threat. That'll kill the fastest.* The woman had picked herself up but was favoring her right side, the wrist he'd grabbed, and the hip she'd landed on. Gritting his teeth, Alex moved to the left, fending off blows from the larger man as he moved to the woman's bad side.

When he was close enough, he charged. She didn't have time to move out of the way, but he also miscalculated. As he slammed into her bad hip, eliciting a swear of pain, he felt the knife come up in her other hand, slashing across his chest. He twisted, forcing his arm between the blade and their bodies and feeling the bite of the blade as they tumbled to the ground.

Against the stone he pinned her and trapped her legs in his own as he dug nails into her wrist, forcing the blade from her fingers. He saw her eyes flick up and instinctively leaned to the side. A kick moved past his head as the Wild Man caught the side of the woman's head.

Alex heard a nasty crack as the woman collided with the floor and twisted away while his bloody fingers scrabbled for the blade. His palm slick, he nearly dropped the weapon twice as he dodged more blows.

He could feel himself tiring. The fight was going on too long. Even though there was only a single Freelark left, he was battered and bleeding, lightheaded and seeing spots. The other man was larger and stronger, and Alex knew his reflexes were sluggish from pain and exhaustion as adrenaline slowly seeped from his muscles.

The Wild Man snarled, crouching as the two men circled each other. "You should not have come here, sand slave," he growled.

Spitting blood to the ground again, Alex bared his own teeth. "What are you going to do, insult me to death?"

The man feinted to the left, but Alex, watching the coil of muscles, stepped into it, driving an elbow into the man's side. "Don't you Freelarks *worship* Caldir? Think he'd be happy about the blood that's been spilt here?"

"I think he'd be pleased we defended his freedom." The man charged forward, wrapping his arms around Alex's waist and driving them both to the floor once more. The knife clattered out of his bloody hand, and Alex twisted, forcing a knee between his chest and the other man as he searched for a way out.

The Freelark, sensing victory, pressed a thick forearm to Alex's throat, cutting off his windpipe. Already dizzy, his vision went black at the edges and smeared. He felt his nails scrabble uselessly on the man's wrist, searching desperately for air that didn't come. Light nearly gone, he desperately drove a knee up, thrusting it as hard as he could between the larger man's legs.

His chokehold slackened as the man cursed in pain, and Alex wrapped a leg around the man's torso, twisting so he wound up on top. Without waiting, he yanked the man's head up by his oily, wiry hair, and slammed his head into the ground twice until he felt his quarry still.

Breathing hard, Alex stayed on the ground, lying on top of the man. His heart was pounding, his head ached, and dark spots danced across his vision. Blood was seeping from the wounds across his chest and arm, staining the shirt of the man beneath him. The flickering light cast long, moving shadows on the walls and made him dizzy. With great difficulty he sat up, and the room spun so quickly he nearly threw up.

"Gods-curst tree-scummers!" Alex swore. Forcing himself to his feet, he turned and spat blood onto the flagstones beside the man. His heart fluttered too fast in his chest, and he braced his hands on his knees as he willed the temple to stop moving. *The pressing heat of the fire was back, the crowd choking him, and he slipped and tumbled down the stairs with Caidy in his arms, smashing into the ground below.*

A gasp echoed from the side of the room and, disoriented, Alex snapped back to the present, his hand flying to the place he normally kept his dagger—tonight, abandoned at Raven House—stealing himself for another fight.

To his shock, Caidy was standing near the door he had entered through, a dreamlike hallucination. He blinked several times, wondering if she was really there. "Alex?" She sounded confused. He straightened and she took a step toward him, holding her hands up, palms open. "Alex, it's me." The quaver in her voice was grounding.

Anger flooded him. "What in the Hells are you doing here?" Forcing himself to his feet, he crossed the room in long strides, reaching out to her. Adrenaline and fear coursed through his body. It wasn't safe. *She wasn't safe.* She couldn't be here.

As he reached her, he saw her brow furrow in confusion and then her eyes widen in fear. "Alex!" She just had time to cry out his name, pure terror in her voice, when a shock of green magic tossed him aside, a leaf in a storm, and struck her in the chest.

CHAPTER 32

———

24th Day of the Harvest Moon
She swam through darkness. Caidy realized she was dreaming
with a jolt as the world oozed, slipping and sliding through
her fingers. She spun, hair and gown swirling about, drifting
through water.

"*I don't know what you want.*" *Her voice sounded far away,*
a whisper though she was sure she had screamed it into the void.

A presence pressed her down, drowning her in the inky
blackness until, once again, she found herself in a dark stone
cavern, a deep recess in the center of the chamber. A flame
flickered against the rock, snapping. This time, however, four
robed figures stood around it. Though ice clung to the walls
and a wintery wind rippled through her frame, the sense of
overwhelming terror was gone.

Slowly, she stepped forward. "*Can you hear me?*"

Nobody moved. When she approached the first figure, she
saw a young man, his eyes focused and eyebrows knitted in
concentration. "*Hello?*" *He didn't move. With a jolt, she real-*
ized it was the same young man whose body had been con-
torted in agony on the ground, dead.

The Eladyr is dying.

The words echoed through her mind. She did not know what an Eladyr was, or how one could die. She frowned. "What do you want?" she asked, again.

Silence greeted her. It was an unnerving silence, and she could hear nothing but the crackle and snap of the flame. Slowly, she stepped forward until she was perched on the edge of the recess, the flame a mere arm's length away.

Strange, she thought. It's cold.

For a moment, the heat from the Harvest Festival washed over her once again and she fell to her knees, doubling over as tremors of fear shook her body. Roaring flames, columns of smoke, the screams of hundreds of people tore through her psyche, threatening to yank her back to the darkness.

The cold, rough stone seeped through her knees and chilled her core. The cold was grounding as Caidy clawed her way out of the nightmarish inferno and back to the frozen cavern. Transfixed, she watched the flame undulate before her, flickering complex patterns of purple and silver against the dark rock.

This flame is so different from those towering monsters, she thought. How could that be?

She slowly reached forward, fingers inching toward the flickering light. When she touched the flame, she jolted, energy shocking her body. Stumbling backward, she gasped in wonder. A ball of purple flame danced across her palm, threading through her fingers and twining about her wrist.

Remember it, a voice whispered in her mind. **Do not let it vanish.**

"I don't understand—" When she spoke, an invisible force grabbed the back of her gown and yanked, sending her tumbling, falling, back into the darkness. With a final snap, the purple flame vanished.

"Caidy!" Her name sounded muffled, as though through a haze. She struggled to answer, to move a hand or open her eyes.

"Get back *now*. Let me work. Where are the damn Maidens?" A scuffle and then someone knelt near her. "My Lady, can you hear me?"

She fought to surface from the darkness, but it drew her closer. The voices continued speaking, though she could no longer make out what was being said. She felt a deep sense of unease settling in her bones. Panic seeped into her spirit as the voices grew more frantic.

Time slipped by—moments and hours blending together, for the differences no longer mattered. She floated, hovering between light and dark, consciousness and blissful nothingness. People came and went. She heard voices as though from a great distance, muffled and muted. She was bumped and jostled, but it all felt very far away.

She struggled to hold on to the strange vision. The flame, a dark room. The skin on her hand tingled, tracing the pattern of the purple fire threading between her fingers and around her wrist. The name…what was it? She couldn't remember, though she knew it was important.

A great light sparkled through the darkness, drenching her eyes. She instinctively curled into a ball, bringing her knees into her chest and wrapping her arms around them tightly as the light bore her back to the moment.

"Lady Caidelene, can you hear me?" The voice was unfamiliar, female and soft. Cool hands rested on her own. "I need you to wake up now."

Caidy struggled to open her eyes, and the bright light was blinding. "Water," she croaked, trying to shield her eyes from the whiteness.

Someone lifted her head as another held a cup to her lips. "Drink, my Lady," the soft female voice said again, soothing. She swallowed obediently, tasting the cold, mint-flavored water. Slowly, she relaxed her arms, letting her knees fall to one side against something solid.

"That's it, good job." The cool hand stroked her cheek. "My Lady, we're going to help you sit up. Alright? I need you to lean forward."

Arms wrapped around her, and Caidy let herself be pulled up. The light was beginning to fade now, leaving nothing at all behind. She swallowed hard, longing for more water. Obediently, she leaned forward, shifting her weight over her legs so she didn't slump back once again.

"—happening? I demand to be let in!" A booming voice reverberated. She heard someone placating and then loud arguments, which drowned each other out. Wildly, she turned, searching for something, anything to grab and hold on to.

"My Lady, I'm here." Merric's familiar, gentle baritone washed over her and she reached toward it. Her hands found his, and she felt him move around to sit against her side, wrapping an arm around her shoulders. "I'm here. I've got you. It's alright."

"What is this?" The woman who had drawn her out of her dreams now spoke from a distance, steel in her words. "I said no visitors. She's been to the Hells and back."

"I don't take orders from you," Caidy heard her father snap back. She instinctively hid her face against Merric's shoulder, and he murmured soft words against her hair.

"Fritha has fought to drag her back from the Nightmare Realms. She shields your daughter even now," the woman replied as cold as the icy stones Caidy had knelt upon. "Unless you want her returning to the raka, you will *stay back*."

"Merric, what's happening?" She clutched at him, her fingers scraping down hard leather.

"You're safe, my Lady. I promise you that." His voice was low and hoarse, sharpened with a hint of what sounded like terror masked by calm. "You're safe."

"Aye, my Lady." The woman had returned. "Fritha has you in her grasp. We'll protect you."

Fritha. The Maiden of Mercy. "Why did I need her help?" She struggled to find the right words. "What happened?"

The pause was too long. Caidy pushed herself up, Merric's arm dropping from around her shoulders, though he remained close beside her. The gray had settled firmly about her now, as though she was caught in a deep fog. "What happened?" she repeated, fighting to keep a tremor out of her voice.

"My Lady, my name is Aimee." She felt the woman settle to the ground in front of her. "I am one of Fritha's Maidens; I have been in her service my whole life. I grew up in the Temple."

Caidy felt herself frown as something familiar sparked in her mind. "I've heard of you. You're the Head of the Order in Iera. I think we've met."

"Aye, my Lady. You have an excellent memory." She heard the smile through the priestess' words. "We've met a few times. I admire your leadership and your composure."

"Thank you," Caidy replied slowly, still confused. "I don't understand what that has to do with me." Through the gray mist, she saw a shadow shift and a shaft of light slice through.

"My Lady, can you tell me what you remember of the Harvest Ball?"

Caidy furrowed her brow in concentration. "I wanted the Ball to go on. I knew it was important. If we didn't, the

Freelarks would see that we were scared, that they had won by striking fear into the hearts of us and our people. Geoffrey didn't want to. Nobody wanted to. But I did, and I argued, and I won. So we had the Ball.

"It was wonderful, at least I think. All the nobles came, the merchant families and even many of the commoners from the city. The food was incredible. There was dancing and laughter and fun." She felt the cool hand return to her forehead, and the shaft of light grew stronger, glowing with power.

"Did you stay at the Ball?" The woman prompted gently.

"No, I don't think so. I think…Miles. Miles and I went for a walk in the gardens. I'd seen some nobles, some friends, making fools of themselves and I wanted some air, so he went for a walk with me. We wound up near Caldir's temple, I think."

"And then?" Merric spoke from beside her, the edge of fear gone from his voice, replaced by something else she couldn't quite name.

"Then—we tried one of the doors, I think, and it was unlocked." For some reason she felt dread beginning to twist in the pit of her stomach. She wrapped her arms around her midriff tightly. "We snuck inside, but then I heard something strange. Fighting."

"Do you remember anything else, my Lady?"

She did, but more than anything in the world she wished that she didn't. She remembered the pure fury on Alex's face when he had seen her, the mixture of shock, fear, and anger, which had cowed her. She had seen another side of him then, a side she didn't recognize. In the years she had known him, she couldn't even remember seeing rage contort his features the way it had in that moment.

It was the last thing she remembered.

Haltingly, she finished the story. "I saw Alex, and some other people. I don't know how many. Maybe two?" She knew her voice was barely above a whisper, but she couldn't force herself to speak any louder. "He was angry I was there. And then..." Caidy broke off. "I don't know. I just remember him being so, so angry."

She could feel tears welling up in her eyes and she rubbed them furiously. The light faded, leaving her surrounded by cold gray. "What happened? Please tell me."

Merric spoke first. "The Warden reported that he had confronted three Freelarks who had broken into the temple. According to his report, they were trying to deface Caldir's statue. He overpowered and restrained them, and sustained some injuries while doing so. When you arrived he had just finished the fight."

When he fell silent and nobody else spoke, Caidy shifted. "And then?"

"My Lady...somehow one of the Freelarks had worked free from the restraints. Or perhaps had not been restrained yet. We don't know. But that saboteur had some connection to the Winds and struck you down with a magical force."

Something stirred in the back of her mind: flagstones, Alex's shout. He had been close enough to touch, but something had whipped between them and thrust her back.

"And then?" It took all her willpower to keep a quaver out of her voice.

"Then the Warden restrained the third Freelark, the mage. He called for help and the Rose Guard...we arrived as soon as we could, my Lady. I saw you —" He broke off, and she felt him swallow hard.

"Merric, whatever it is, it's alright," Caidy promised. "You've always kept me safe."

She felt a heavy sigh. "No, my Lady, it isn't all right, and I didn't. The Guard failed you. I failed you. I came running and I saw you on the ground. I thought you were dead. You were so cold and pale." He stopped speaking, but she didn't push him to continue, letting him gather his control. She had never witnessed Merric so close to losing his nerve before.

"Nolan came, and we sent for the Maidens. He did something—I don't know what. You seemed a little more alive then, some color came back to your cheeks. But you were unconscious. Gods, my Lady, you were unconscious for so long."

"How long?" Caidy twisted her fingers together, turning her head toward where she felt his warmth.

"It's been a day and a half, my Lady," Aimee said gently. "Fritha has been with you. You were caught in the Nightmare Realms, somewhere between life and death, but she fought and brought you back to us."

Rubbing her eyes and leaning forward, Caidy felt the stiffness in her joints as she tried to move her legs. It was all a muted, dove gray now, as though her head had been wrapped in a scarf. But, as her fingers traced her eyelids, lashes, and brows, she knew that wasn't true.

"Why can't I see anything?" she asked quietly, cold fear washing over her once more.

The silence told her everything. Merric shifted slightly away and then leaned back toward her, wrapping an arm tightly around her once again. The priestess placed two cool fingertips under Caidy's chin, lifting it up. She smelled like lilac and the rushing water over smooth river stones. Neither one of them spoke.

Summoning her courage, Caidy swallowed hard. "Is it permanent?"

She felt Aimee shift away from her as the fingers left her chin. "My Lady, when Fritha must wrestle one from the edge of the Rakatash's Hells, well, it is not an easy battle. Our revered texts suggest that when she performed true miracles, such as this one, those who came back were not entirely whole."

"You're saying I'm...you're saying I can't see." She found she couldn't bring herself to say *blind*.

"I'm saying you made a great sacrifice to return to us, my Lady." Aimee sounded as though she was choosing her words very carefully.

"How can it be a sacrifice if I didn't have any choice?" Caidy felt her control crumble. Tears spilled out of her useless eyes, leaving rivers coursing down her cheeks and dripping into her lap. "I didn't have a choice," she whispered, sobbing. She turned her head toward Merric, burying her face in his shoulder once more as he held her close.

"I'm so sorry, my Lady," he whispered. "I'm so, so sorry."

CHAPTER 33

———

24th Day of the Harvest Moon

"Why did I pick a job that gets me punched on such a regular basis?" Alex complained to nobody in particular. He groaned as he rolled over onto his good side, tenderly avoiding his abused kidneys, and then swearing as he leaned on his burnt shoulder. "I need a new line of work."

After several more long minutes of moping and feeling sorry for himself, he forced himself up. It had been an endless day and a half. After the mage had lashed out at Caidy and she had collapsed, the Rose Guard had arrived in force. Merric had scooped his charge up and spirited her away elsewhere in the castle—probably to mages and healers. He didn't know what had happened to her, and a small part of him didn't particularly want to know.

The Rose Guard had dragged the Freelarks to cells in the dark cellars of the castle while Danila had shown up with a carriage to bring Alex back down to the city. A *carriage*, for Udo's sake! What was he, a cripple? But he'd admitted to himself after settling inside, it was definitely better than dragging himself down the hill and through the streets.

At Raven House, Hendrick, Starling, and Jakob had all been waiting. Danila had sent a messenger to them from the castle, and instead of being allowed to down a beer—or three—and sleep off the worst of the pain, Alex had given a briefing. Then he'd been eviscerated for his troubles.

He'd known it wasn't going to split his way when he saw Starling's face. Hendrick was as unreadable as usual, and Jakob looked worried, but his old mentor's eyes smoldered with a deep, angry fire.

"So let me be clear," she had spoken softly, but the words reverberated around the room. "While you were *on duty*, you got drunk, went out into the gardens to canoodle with the Imperial Ambassador and happened to stumble into Freelark sabotage, wherein you were promptly overrun, the heir to the Rosemoorian throne was injured, and you failed to properly restrain a mage? Is that about the size of it, Laurent?"

He had snapped back at her, and in the cold light of morning, regretted it fiercely. Yes, his body hurt, his pride was bashed to pieces, and he'd deserved every inch of it. It seemed as though every choice he'd made was the wrong one.

Alex covered his face with his hands, leaning forward and bracing his elbows on his knees. Gods, he wanted nothing more than to run. Briefly, he contemplated it, packing up his meager belongings, saddling his patient mount, and riding hard for the Karath border. He could make it in less than a week if he pushed himself, through the Somber Mountains in another three days. Then, he could go anywhere: the icy expanse of northern Karath, the magical wasteland the tribes of Asaka called home, even wind back down south to the Unending Desert.

Then, as quickly as he'd plotted it all out, he discarded the notion. He wouldn't—couldn't—leave Caidy. Her name made his stomach churn, the nausea from pain and guilt a potent combination. He didn't know if she was alive or not, and that was sheer terror.

Pushing the thought aside, Alex rose and forced himself through some stretches in a desperate attempt to loosen his muscles. "Hag's teeth," he swore under his breath, as he tried to touch his toes and failed miserably.

He dressed quickly, strapping on blades and layering a cloak over his shoulders. Erius had brought autumn forth with a vengeance, cold winds blowing the last dregs of Iya's summer heat away. Winding quickly through the fish market and doing his best to ignore the stench, he made his way toward Raven House.

In the light of day, the city was scarred. He passed two shops, which had been hastily converted into healer's wards, the shield of Fritha marked in charcoal on the door. Magefire jelly caused nasty, oozing burns that took weeks to heal, and its acrid fumes drew a painful, hacking cough forward that never truly seemed to settle.

There were a few skeletons of buildings, and many more with streaks of soot and ash—damaged but not destroyed. The streets were emptier than usual, especially for Market District in the morning. He didn't see any merchants setting up stalls or wagons trundling through. It felt like there were City Guards on every corner, though he knew that couldn't possibly be right. There weren't enough of them.

Outside Raven House, he paused. For the first time in a long time, he didn't quite know what to do, how to act. Though he'd said nothing, Alex suspected Hendrick was even more angry than Starling had been, and somehow that was worse. He steeled his nerves and then climbed the steps, ignoring the sharp ache in his legs.

Inside, Jakob was settled near the fire with a pile of reports and a steaming bowl of stew. He glanced up when Alex entered and nodded at him. "Morning, Laurent."

"At least you didn't say good," Alex replied, deciding to go for humor.

Jakob eyed him and then shrugged with a small smile. "Good, bad—who's to say?"

Alex paused and then stuffed his hands in his pockets, feeling awkward and uncomfortable for the first time in the Blade headquarters. "Hendrick upstairs?" he asked, looking at the worn wood of the floor.

"Nope." His head snapped up at Jakob's answer. "Up at the castle with Quinn, dealing with the Freelarks."

"Thanks," he replied with a nod. The archivalist returned to his papers, and Alex left the building. He wound his way through the city and slowly climbed the hill up to the castle, his legs protesting every step. *Just one more form of punishment*, he thought ruefully.

The castle too was strangely quiet, free from the normal hustle and bustle of everyday business. More guards were on the walls, Alex noted, unsurprised, and several more pairs patrolled the ground. He had to pass through two sets of them to gain entry into the courtyard, one of whom still eyed him suspiciously.

He wound around through the vegetable patch to the cellars underneath the kitchen, where four more guards were posted. The cellar had been converted into a makeshift dungeon during the Cleansing several decades prior, and he knew it was rarely used. When he was younger, he used to explore them with Caidy, and nobody ever found them.

Pushing the pain of that thought away, he ducked through the low door and into the firelit cellar. Two of the three

Freelarks were behind metal bars: the mage—Darkleaf—and the Wild Man. When Alex approached, he noticed the heavy band, inscribed with sparkling script, locked around Darkleaf's throat. *Mage collar*, he thought, though he'd never actually seen one. The Glittering Hand had created them. The magic written on the metal somehow severed the wearer's connection with the Winds, neutralizing their magical abilities as long as they wore it.

Darkleaf stood near the bars, watching Alex carefully. The peace in the mage's eyes was unnerving. He stepped away, turning to the Wild Man. When he drew to the cell, the man leapt up and spat at him with a string of curses thrown toward Alex.

A door on the other side of the room opened, and Hendrick peered out. "Laurent, get in here. You're late."

Not angry, Alex decided from the Lord Commissioner's tone. *Disappointed.* He wished Hendrick was angry. That would be easier to deal with.

On the other side of the door, Starling Quinn was at work. Black hair tied tightly back, eyes as empty as midnight, she circled the third Freelark, Bramblerose. The Blade Shadow wore a gray shirt, open at the collar, with her sleeves rolled up. Blood, sweat, and muck spattered her pale forearms as she stepped toward the prisoner.

Bramblerose, her wrists tied above her head with thin, strong rope, struggled to twist away. Starling ignored the motion, drawing a glowing piece of metal from the fire and holding it by the woman's nose. "You like playing with fire?" Starling's voice was calm and conversational as she examined the glowing light.

Alex joined Hendrick, leaning against the wall near the door, as he watched his old mentor get to work. He hated this part. He'd nearly failed his interrogation classes at the Citadel because he couldn't stomach torturing another person. That, he supposed, was the purpose of the Blade Shadows.

"She's very good," Hendrick commented, watching the scene before them calmly.

A shriek pierced the air, and Alex felt himself wince, turning away from the scene. "She's the best there is. It's lucky she was sent over from Colmar."

"Aye, that's a way to see it." The former bandit looked over at him. "Had a chance to calm down some, Laurent?"

Alex felt shame grip him anew and decided he was very glad the room was relatively dark. "Starling was right yesterday. I made a royal mess of things."

"That's true enough," Hendrick agreed, turning back to the whimpering Freelark as Starling stepped back, watching her quarry.

"I'm sorry," Alex said softly.

The pause stretched punctuated by miserable, pitiful moaning, and then Hendrick sighed before turning back to him and smoothing his mustache. "Laurent, did you stop the Freelarks from defacing the temple?"

Taken aback, Alex searched for the trap he was about to walk into. "Um, I interrupted them. The temple is unharmed."

Hendrick grunted. "And did anyone die in the process?"

"I…" He started and then stopped, realizing he didn't actually know the answer to that question. The Freelark let out another shriek as Starling raised the brand again. "I don't know if Caidy—Lady Caidelene—is all right."

"She's alive," Hendrick confirmed, and Alex felt cool relief wash over him. *Thank Fritha.* "So you stopped the attack, and nobody died. In fact, we've now got three prisoners to interrogate." He turned to face Alex head on. "Were you a bit of an idiot? I'm not going to argue on that point. Maybe next time remember yourself before you throw caution to the winds with the Imperial Ambassador."

Feeling heat on his cheeks, Alex looked at the ground. "We met when I was in Mezrani City."

"Don't care," Hendrick interrupted. "Don't want to know. Feel guilty, sure. But let's not waste time being sorry. Let's move on and figure out our next move. Got it, Laurent?"

Alex nodded. "Understood."

"Good. Update, Quinn?"

Starling turned and joined them. Alex noticed flecks of blood—some fresh, some a little older—splattered across the pale skin of her face. Those sharp, dark eyes were empty and cold when she looked at him, and the gaze made him want to cringe.

"I think she may be ready to have a conversation." She turned back to the Freelark prisoner, dangling from the ceiling. "What do you think, tree-scum? Ready to talk? Or would you rather spend some more quality time with me?"

Bramblerose blinked at them through sweaty hair and dripping blood. The skin around one of her amber eyes was dark and swollen, the white shot with red. Alex could see fresh burns fading into her skin, Starling's latest mark.

"What do you want, sand slaves?" She spat the words toward them. It by far wasn't the worst name Alex had ever been called, but it was interesting. He knew many in Rosemoor hated the Mezrani, but few would dare voice it. Then again, what did the woman have to lose?

Hendrick stepped forward, his arms folded. "Was that the entire plan? Attack the temple? Bring down the wrath of the Gods upon you and yours? Stupid, even for Freelarks."

Bramblerose bared bloody teeth at him. "You know nothing of the Gods, city-dweller. I am one of Caldir's warriors, a spirit of revenge from the God himself!"

"Caldir wanted you to destroy his own temple? Do you listen to yourself?" Starling rolled her eyes at Hendrick.

"The Fury of the Earth was never meant to be trapped behind these thick stone walls," the Freelark spat. "I set his spirit free."

"Actually, all you did was cause quite a commotion and get yourself locked up." Hendrick sounded bored. "In fact, it only took one of us to overpower all three of you. Some divine warriors you are."

"You sand-servants wouldn't understand." Something menacing flickered in the woman's injured eyes.

"I've had enough of this," Starling said abruptly, stepping forward. "I'm done talking. Give me a few more hours with her, and I'll get you what you need."

While Hendrick stepped back, Alex found himself stepping forward into the light. He couldn't say what drove him, but he drew closer until the battered woman's eyes locked on his.

"You'll never be free from stone walls again," he told the Freelark, his eyes cold. "You'll wither and die here, a flower without sunlight until there's naught left but dust."

"The tide is rising, Blade," Bramblerose murmured, her voice little more than a whisper. "The world is fighting back against its oppressors. Soon, we will all be free."

"Well, you most certainly won't be. We're planning on sticking you in the deepest, darkest hole we can find and losing the key." He smiled coldly at her, showing his teeth. "I don't like people who threaten the stability of Rosemoor."

Bramblerose tossed her head back in a harsh cackle. "Burn a dandelion and eight more will grow in its place, boot-licker. There are too many of us for you to stop us all."

She kept laughing, even as Alex stepped away and Starling once again began to work.

CHAPTER 34

———

24th Day of the Harvest Moon

Alex paused at the end of the hallway when he realized his palms were sweaty. Embarrassed, he rubbed his hands on his thighs, trying to soothe the tingle of nerves. Puffing out a hard breath of air and rolling his shoulders, he rounded the corner, trying for a confident stride. With an internal grimace, he realized belatedly that perhaps confidence should not be what he projected at the moment.

A female Rose Guardswoman, a Deputy Lieutenant by the insignia on her shoulder, drew to attention outside the door. When Alex approached, she eyed him up and down, eyes cool. She wore her hair cropped close to her head, an unusual style for this far north.

She saluted, her hand over her heart, and then stood again at ease. "Warden." She nodded at him. "May I help you?"

"Is Lady Caidelene available?"

The Deputy looked carefully at him. "Lieutenant Adley is in with her. She's not been receiving visitors, on orders from the Maidens. She's supposed to be resting."

Alex looked at the floor, suddenly feeling every emotion he had pent up over the past few days. His throat and eyes burned with tears, and his entire body ached. And all he wanted was to see his best friend, to hug her and know that, despite it all, she was alright.

But not today. Forcing his eyes back up to the guardswoman, he tried to speak, cleared his throat, and tried again. "I understand. I'll come back later."

Something in her eyes softened at his words. "Wait a minute. Let me check with him." She knocked gently and then poked her head around the door, exchanging quick, terse words. He didn't bother to strain to hear the conversation. He could imagine it playing out. *I'd be surprised if Merric forgave me, let alone himself,* he thought. The bodyguard, normally so inseparable from Caidy's side, was no doubt taking her injury hard—and personally.

Merric left the room. Alex's hunch had been right. The guardsman's eyes were hollow, deep shadows of exhaustion surrounding them. The scruff on his chin was patchy and uneven; his clothes looked like they'd been slept in.

He felt Merric looking him up and down, too. He probably looked as bad, if not worse. The fight had left him with bruises, cuts, and stiff limbs. Meeting Merric's gaze, he recognized the guilt deep within them. The bodyguard jerked his chin at the room. "Go on, then. Ohlm'll be on the door if you need anything. I'm going to get some air."

"It wasn't your fault," Alex blurted out before his mind could catch up with his mouth, and then he resisted the urge to melt into the floor.

Merric seemed to look through him, his eyes boring deep into his own guilty conscience. After a long pause, the older man said quietly, "It's not about fault, Warden. It's about learning from it. That guilt I've got in my gut, that you've got in yours, that's a lesson."

The words struck home. It was a familiar sentiment, Alex realized, something his instructors had echoed in training. When you were on a battlefield, mistakes cost lives. You couldn't afford to make the same one twice. This certainly wasn't the first mistake he'd made, but it hit home in a new way.

Meeting the bodyguard's eyes, he nodded and clapped Merric on the shoulder. "We'll do better."

"Aye, that we will, Warden." Merric returned the gesture and then stepped aside. Taking a breath, Alex stepped inside the room.

She was leaning against the window, looking out. Sunlight dappled her pale skin. The burn on her arm and cut on her forehead were stark against it. When the door opened, she turned toward him, her eyes searching.

"Hello?" Her voice quavered, calm but with a hint of fear. Alex felt his heart in his throat as he looked at her, memorizing every detail of her face and body once more.

Carefully, he padded across the room, settling himself on the window seat next to her. As he moved, he noticed her eyes didn't follow him.

Gods, please no. Unbidden, he felt hot tears blurring his vision. Blinking furiously, he gently put two fingers on her chin, tilting her face toward his own.

It broke his heart all over again, to see those bright, dancing gray eyes vacant. *She's blind,* he realized, the cold shame, guilt, and anger mixing together and washing down his spine. He searched her face desperately, looking for a hint of recognition, for anything. Her eyes slid past his own, staring at the wall behind him, not a sparkle of recognition to be found.

He put both hands on her face now, his palms on her smooth cheeks, as he began to sob. "Caidy," he whispered, his voice rough and low with emotion.

When he said her name, he watched her control vanish. Crystalline tears sparkled on her eyelashes and slipped down her cheeks, dampening his hands. He drew her to him, holding her as tightly as he could, burying his face in her soft, sweet hair. His own tears fell in tandem with hers as their bodies shook together, overcome.

"I'm sorry," he found himself murmuring over and over, his arms wrapped about her slender frame even as she shook and sobbed against him. "Forgive me."

He smelled like horses and rain and copper. It felt so painfully familiar, the way his arms cradled her, drawing her head to his shoulder, taking her weight against him. She felt the deep rumble in his chest as he made quiet soothing sounds, one hand stroking her hair gently.

The haze that had surrounded her since she had woken up in this strange, gray, world suddenly lifted. With painful clarity it all settled in. She was blind. She would never again see the people she loved or the land she cherished. In an instant, it had all been snatched away.

She cried until there were no more tears, and he sat with her, solidly and comfortably *there*. He shook against her as he held her, and she was shocked to realize he was crying too. In the years she had known him—had loved him—he had been the steady one. The rock that weathered all her storms.

Finally, Caidy felt her sobs reduced to hiccups and sniffs. She reached up slowly, feeling along Alex's shoulder, damp with her tears, to his jawline, and tracing her fingertips across his cheeks. She found the scar on his cheekbone she'd first noticed when he returned to Rosemoor, a sharp line under her fingers. A puffy bruise under his eye—she felt his sharp intake of breath as she touched—and a fresh scrape on his jaw. A portrait of pain and suffering, sacrifice and duty began to meld beneath her fingertips, painting a picture in her mind's eye against the gray.

"Caidy," he spoke softly again, murmuring her name as her fingers touched his lips.

"Alex," She whispered his name, and he pulled her closer once more. "Alex."

"I'm here." He spoke into her hair, his own voice raw and broken. "I've got you."

"I need you to tell me what happened," she said quietly when her own tears had halted once more. "I need to know why you're sorry."

There was a pause and then a heavy sigh. "Are you sure you want to know?"

"I don't want to know. I need to know." Caidy turned, resettling herself against him so she could feel the sunlight on her face once more. "Please, Alex. Tell me what happened."

She felt him shift behind her, a heavy sigh followed by acquiescence. "Alright. I was walking in the gardens after dancing to get some air and some quiet. Then, I heard something strange, a whisper almost, that seemed like it didn't belong." She noticed he didn't mention the way Farah had clung to his arm, or the significant looks they'd exchanged, and then immediately felt very small and petty for thinking of it at all.

"There were three Freelarks—a woman, Bramblerose; Darkleaf, the mage; and a third who spat on me when I tried to ask his name. The Wild Man, I guess—he looks like he's been living in the woods. I watched them break into the temple, and then I decided to follow them." He stopped talking. The pause lasted so long she nearly thought he'd lost of train of thought. But then he continued, his tone much softer.

"I should have gone for help. Grabbed a guard, found Nolan or Merric…anything. It was foolish to go after them, but my curiosity got the better of me. And, well, I think part of me wanted a fight."

"Why?" she prompted him, curious for more. He was acting so differently from normal, so open and honest, she wanted to press, to find out why he had pulled all this away from her in the first place.

"I think… I think I wanted to prove myself. I messed it all up, Caidy. I couldn't stop the attack on the Festival. I couldn't keep you from being hurt. I couldn't even catch the people behind it all. I saw them, and I thought it was my chance to redeem myself, to earn back your trust and to make it right." His voice broke near the end, raw.

"You have nothing to make right," Caidy replied firmly, more sure of that than anything else in her life. She sat up and turned to face him again, feeling the warmth of his face mere inches from her own. "Absolutely nothing. You warned us. You warned me. We—I—ignored you. Holding the Festival was *my* choice. The Ball, too. Don't you dare take that on yourself."

The silence stretched for a moment, and then she felt the back of his hand brush gently against her cheek before pulling away. "Thank you."

She settled back against him once more, and he cleared his throat. "So I went in, and I picked a fight. Three on one—stupid, I know. But I was feeling lucky, and honestly, I got lucky. I surprised them and managed to turn the tables.

It hurt—Gods, it still hurts. I haven't been that badly beaten since I was in a pirate brawl in Swansea."

She sat up very suddenly, nearly knocking them both off the window seat. "You did what? Pirates? *You?*" She was incredulous. *The adventures we had as children—he's lived them!* She heard him chuckle, another lost memory, before continuing.

"Yeah, I guess I haven't told you about what's happened since I left. Have I? I even met the Pirate Queen, you know."

"No, what!" Everything else melted away, as a powerful, dark-haired woman carrying a curved saber appeared in Caidy's mind's eye. "Is she as beautiful as they say?"

"To be honest, I don't really remember how beautiful she was. I just remember being completely and utterly terrified of her. I once saw Esmerelda Valencia knock a burly pirate twice her height and weight to the ground with a single punch." She heard the smile in the memory.

Relaxing once more, Caidy searched for one of his hands and then intertwined their fingers. "You'll have to tell me the whole story someday."

"Soon, I promise." She felt him absently stoking her hair, untangling the silky curls. The silence lengthened until she spoke once more.

"So? What happened then?"

"That's when I saw you," he replied. "My heart jumped into my throat I was so scared. All I wanted was for you to go, to be back at the Ball, safe and happy. But you were there, in the dark underbelly of the world, with me.

"I saw you, and the world stopped. I wanted you to leave, told you to. But, just like always—"

"I didn't listen." Saying the words aloud was shameful. *I never listen*, she admitted to herself. *And at what cost?*

"Well, yes," he agreed with her. "And it all happened so fast. I should have checked the mage first, but I didn't. I just wanted to get you away. And that was my weakness. Darkleaf saw it and attacked you, and through you, me. I don't know what he did. I think Nolan is still trying to sort it out. All I knew was that there was a flash of magic, and then you were crumpled on the ground. I thought you were dead."

As Alex finished his story, Caidy searched for the right thing to say. She had no idea how she felt. There weren't words for the number of feelings fighting for her attention. Frustration and anger, guilt and sorrow—nothing that she could do a single thing to change. She could feel the guilt radiating from Alex in heavy waves and spoke almost without thinking about it. "Thank you for saving my life."

"I feel like I destroyed it," he whispered into her hair, so quietly she nearly didn't hear him.

Pushing herself up once more, she braced a hand on the window for stability and pivoted so she sat facing him. Reaching forward, she found his chest, then his collar, and finally his face. She placed her palms on his cheeks, trying to will her forgiveness, her love, through her hands and into him. And, most of all, trying to force the truth of her words upon him.

"I owe you my life, Alex, a thousand times over. My life isn't over. It's just beginning. We're going to find the Gods-forsaken *animals* that did this to me, to my kingdom, and we will bring them for judgment before Erius. I swear it before you and the Gods, right now. This is not the end. It's the start of the next chapter."

ACKNOWLEDGMENTS

———

This book, like any big project, would not be possible without a literal army of people. First, my endless thanks to the people who believed in me from the beginning, who encouraged me to go after a childhood dream, and who read every word of every draft (you know who you are).

My endless gratitude goes to my friends who offered words of wisdom, inspired scenes, and let me talk about the triumphs and struggles of writing and publishing *ad nauseum:* Ali, Daniel, Michael (x2), Eleanor (x2), Megan, Caitlin. You are the moral support that dragged me over the finish line.

To Robin, Ned, and Peti—thank you for always reminding me what true perseverance and strength looks like, being my constant cheerleaders, and encouraging me to go after my dreams.

Tin, there aren't enough words to express my thanks for all your help and guidance throughout this process. From letting me borrow liberally from your D&D world (hello, Freelarks) to helping me problem solve when my characters had boxed themselves into a corner, my world (both fictional and literal) is so much brighter for your help with it. Also, thanks for letting me make weird sounds when I'm stressed.

Each and every one of my former students were critical to this process because each of you reminded me the importance of chasing what is important and never letting circumstances get you down. Thank you for your honesty and bravery, your creativity and genuine curiosity. I am so proud of each and every one of you.

To my editors and help at New Degree Press—you have made my words infinitely better. Special thanks to S.D. Howard and Kristy Carter, for your endless guidance, and for the brutal honesty when things just weren't working. To Brian, Amanda, Eric, Linda, Haley, Jamie, and Lyn, thank you for your organization, your support, and for giving me the opportunity to make this dream a reality.

Without my beta readers, this entire process would not have been possible. I am endlessly grateful for all your help, and your willingness to take a chance on me. To Alyssa, Drew, Lucas, Krysta, Henry, Hali, Amy, Matt, Robert R., Rachel, Melissa M., Jonah, Trish, Shelby, Sydney, Keenan, Katie, Ned, Kelsey, Eleanor L., Clare, Zach T., Courtney, Jonathan, Gerard, Jess, Steph, Anna, Szerb, Meghan, Jaimie, Zach K., Naomi, Sheona, Xiaoling, Ericka, Corey, Ginabeth, Maya, Mary Kate, Briana, Michael Y,. Carly, Tyler, Michael T., Emma, Nora, Robert R., Joe, Renee, Martha, Eric, Holly, Hira, Kyle, Lan, Amanda M., Eleanor R., Michael M., Ron, Stephen, Rose, Ashley, Peti, Ali, Tin, Anne, Russ, Amélie, Reijana, Vicki, Noel, Jacob, Megan, Kasey, Daniel, Jasmine, Edward, Branwen, Isabella, Christina, Sarah, Tristan, Laura, Michael W., Melissa M., Ann, Leah, John, Amanda K., Alice, Caitlin, Connie, Robin, Meilin, Robert O., Kendrick, Elizabeth, Ellie, Anna, Kristen, Suzie, Ken, and Heather (in no particular order): THANK YOU. You've heard me say it over and over, but I'm not going to stop. You made this possible.

And finally, to you, dear reader. Whether we know one another or not, you have now joined an incredible journey I am undertaking. Thank you for exploring a new world with me, for getting to know Alex and Caidy, and for taking this first step on our grand adventure together. I am so excited to keep discovering new parts of the world with you.

May your mind stay curious, your shot true, and your heart brave.

Bridget Smith
December 2020

CPSIA information can be obtained
at www.ICGtesting.com
Printed in the USA
BVHW080718231220
595998BV00004B/15

9 781636 765174